A Scientist
in the
City

JAMES TREFIL

A Scientist

in the

City

Illustrations by Judith Peatross

DOUBLEDAY
New York
London
Toronto
Sydney
Auckland

PUBLISHED BY DOUBLEDAY
a division of Bantam Doubleday Dell Publishing Group, Inc.
1540 Broadway, New York, New York 10036

DOUBLEDAY and the portrayal of an anchor with a dolphin are
trademarks of Doubleday, a division of Bantam Doubleday Dell
Publishing Group, Inc.

Library of Congress Cataloging-in-Publication Data

Trefil, James S., 1938–
A scientist in the city/James Trefil. —1st ed.
p. cm.
Includes index.
1. City and town life. 2. Technology—Social aspects.
I. Title.
HT153.T74 1994
307.76—dc20 93-24961
CIP

ISBN 0-385-24797-4
Copyright © 1994 by James Trefil
Illustrations copyright © 1994 by Judith Peatross
All Rights Reserved
Printed in the United States of America
January 1994

First Edition
1 2 3 4 5 6 7 8 9 10

To Dominique and Flora,
who will soon travel
to distant cities

and to Tomáš,
who will not

Contents

Introduction

It was a special day. I had taken my daughters to the observation deck on the Sears Tower in Chicago, the world's tallest building. From our vantage point we could see the curve of Lake Michigan as it came down from Wisconsin, defined the edge of the great metropolis at our feet, and then passed the refineries and steel mills of Indiana and Michigan to the east. It was a splendid view, and as I pointed out the highlights of the city, I realized that the day was special in many ways. Not only was I having a good time with my children, but I was doing something that most human beings in recorded history could not have done: I was standing on a man-made structure almost 1500 feet above the ground.

What problems had needed solving for me to be able to stand on that observation deck? I asked myself. City planners had to wrestle with zoning regulations, bankers had to raise money, builders had to pull together all the necessary contractors. But before anyone could even have considered a building like the Sears Tower, a far more fundamental question had to be addressed: Were there materials strong enough to hold up the enormous weight of such a building? The development of cheap steel in the nineteenth century, I knew, had been the key break-through that made my trip to the observation tower possible. As I stood there, I thought about the unbroken chain of science and technology—from those Victorian blast furnaces to the modern steel I beams holding me suspended in the air. I began to won-der what else in the city depended in a similar way on our basic understanding of science and nature, what other such stories the city had to tell me.

In a sense, this book is the result of those questions. I know that any city is multifaceted, that it can be seen in many ways—economic, social, governmental, and so on. My goal in writing this book is to provide yet another way to see the city—to ex-amine it through the eyes of science and technology. (Through-out the book, I will use terms like "city" and "urban" in a loose sense to refer to entire metropolitan areas. When I want to talk about a specific part of the urban environment—central city, suburb, exurb, etc.—I will use those terms explicitly.)

I hold to the scientist's standard conceit that important changes—fundamental changes—in the way cities function de-pend on the development of new insights into the functioning of nature and on the technologies that follow from them. Cities wouldn't exist, for example, if someone long ago hadn't figured out that you can plant crops and domesticate animals to supply food. In the same way, the steam engine, the automobile, and the computer have shaped our cities in ways that transcend the dictates of custom, established economic hierarchies, and inter-national borders. Social constraints may have profound effects on cities in the short term, but in the long run the changes that matter most are driven by science and technology.

Let me cite just one example to back up my claim. There is a reason why the most opulent Renaissance or baroque palaces were only a few stories high, why the tallest spire on a Gothic cathedral reached only a few hundred feet into the air. There is a reason why quite ordinary apartment blocks and office buildings, constructed on modest budgets, are much taller today. The rea-son has to do with the kinds of materials that make up each kind of building and, ultimately, with the ways individual atoms lock together to give those materials their strength.

The desire to put up a tall building may depend on social and economic factors, but the *ability* to do so depends on the science and technology available to the builders. The kinds of cities we build depend on our understanding of the natural world—what we call science—and on our ability to turn that understanding to our own ends—what we call technology.

If I were writing this book in 1794 instead of 1994, there would be many social and economic issues affecting the size and shape of the cities of the day—the growth of mercantilism, the opening of America to Europeans, the rise of capitalism, and so on. Yet it's clear that the single most important agent of change in that world was the steam engine. It powered the factories, drove the railroads, and provided the means for the eventual electrification of entire continents. There was poverty in 1794 and there is poverty today, but the cities have changed almost beyond belief. It is on this sort of deep change that I want to concentrate.

There are advantages—bonuses, if you will—to looking at cities through the eyes of science. If you can see the history of the technological threads that have been woven together to make cities what they are, then you already have come a long way toward seeing where they are going. At the very least, you can identify new or continuing threads of technologies that will strongly influence the cities of the future. But although I would argue that the general form that cities take is shaped by our scientific understanding, I would not go so far as to say that technology, in and of itself, determines how cities will develop. Instead, technology sets the limits on what cities can be, defines the general directions in which they will grow. In the language of the engineer, technology defines the "envelope" inside of which cities can develop.

I will argue that we have reached a crucial stage in the development of cities because, for the first time in history, we are approaching an era in which there really are no more technological limits on the kinds of cities we build. We can build anything we want—provided, of course, we know what that is.

I want you to see modern cities, then, as products of a series of discoveries about the physical universe. In particular, I will look at three of these discoveries, each of which has irreversibly altered the kinds of cities we live in, and will continue to shape the cities of the future.

THE ABILITY TO MANIPULATE ATOMS

You can't build a city without materials, and you can't make new materials unless you learn how to put atoms together in new and useful ways. In the nineteenth century, the availability of cheap structural steel altered the kinds of structures we could build. Without it, there would be no high-rise buildings or skyscrapers, no bridges or subways.

THE ABILITY TO UNLOCK STORED ENERGY

Until the late eighteenth century, virtually all energy used by human beings came from muscles—our own or animals'. The development of the steam engine allowed us to tap into the solar energy stored in coal and use it to drive both industry and railroads, and the electrical generator made it possible to produce the energy in one place and use it somewhere else. The result of these two developments was an enormous growth in both the population and the size of cities. The internal combustion engine, allowing us to tap solar energy stored in petroleum, accelerated this growth. Today, every large city runs almost entirely on fossil fuels.

THE ABILITY TO STORE AND TRANSMIT INFORMATION ELECTRICALLY

The telegraph and the telephone changed forever the way we communicate with each other. The leisurely exchange via spoken or written word has been replaced by the flood of electronic information that flows through our cities every minute of the day. The variety of devices that exploit this discovery—commercial radio and TV, the fax machine, and computer networks, to name a few—has grown rapidly in the past few decades and shows no signs of slowing down. (I don't include the scientific advances associated with public health in this list because, although they have been important in shaping the modern city and need to be implemented in many of the world's population centers right now, they represent a solved problem that will not make the city of the future different from what it is today.)

. . . .

I should caution you that the cities you will encounter in this book are probably not going to be like any particular city you've ever known. They will be composed of magnificent buildings, they will be dynamic places where materials, energy, and information interact constantly. We will come to understand how these things work and how they all fit together.

But the people for whom these buildings are built, those for whom the transportation systems are created, those for whom the information is prepared, will be largely invisible. This isn't because I fail to realize the importance of people or the fundamental way in which human behavior affects the shape of cities, but because *as a scientist* I don't have any special insights into why human beings do what they do. I am fascinated by the way people behave, and I watch and gossip as much as anyone else. But I can pretend to no special knowledge in this area, and my insights are no more valid than yours (and perhaps less so). If you want to read about urgent urban issues that revolve primarily around social and economic behavior—the decay of central cities and racial politics, for example—you'll have to look elsewhere.

So I'll tell you mainly about what I know and leave the theorizing about human beings to my colleagues in the social sciences. When I have to say something about human behavior (when I try to predict what the city of the future will look like, for example), I will state my assumptions explicitly and, so far as is in my power, divorce them from the purely scientific and technological issues.

There is a school of thought, called technological determinism, that invests technological changes with a kind of inevitability: if something can be built, it will be; and when it is, the effect it will have on cities is inevitable. I want to make it clear that I am not a technological determinist.

You can't just draw a straight line from what is possible to what will be—predicting the future of cities just isn't that easy. To give just one example from the body of the book: When streetcar lines became widely available, Americans quickly built suburbs for the well-to-do, leaving the central cities for workers' slums. At the same time Europeans, using the exact same technology, developed their cities in exactly the opposite way. Workers' flats were put up at the ends of the trolley and train lines, and the well-to-do retained their luxury flats near the city center. Same technology, different outcome. Technological determinism suffers from what most physicists consider to be the cardinal sin: it doesn't explain the data.

Finally, we have to recognize that any discussion of cities in America inevitably becomes almost a religious debate. Each of us, by background and education, has a view of how people ought to live, and this carries with it a view of what a city is and what it ought to be. There is a strong antiurban strain in American thought. It is certainly evident in the views of Thomas Jefferson, who argued strongly that only the life of the rural yeoman was worthy of respect. You can see the same sentiment in the "wicked city" of the nineteenth-century dime novel, in the "small is beautiful" movement of the 1970s, and in the current distaste for "urban sprawl." Like it or not, everyone has an opinion about cities. The only way I know to deal with the possible unconscious bias in what follows is to tell you about my own background and let you decide for yourself what my own biases are.

I like big cities. I grew up in a blue-collar neighborhood in the Chicago area, and I still get a little thrill when my plane passes the lakefront on its way to O'Hare. I agree with Norman Mailer that "Chicago is the great American city"—a comment, incidentally, that puts another of my prejudices on the table. I've lived in three other of America's great metropolitan areas—Boston, San Francisco, and Washington, D.C. (my current home)—and am frequently in a fourth (New York). I understand the attractiveness of city life—being able to find new and unusual restaurants, being able to read a great newspaper with your morning coffee, having a choice of plays and concerts every evening. As my wife once remarked during a sabbatical we were spending in Chicago, "A city is a place where there's always something interesting to do on Tuesday night."

I like small towns. For the past 20 years, I have spent my summers in my wife's hometown of Red Lodge, Montana (population 1000, elevation 5500 feet). I have developed a real appreciation for the intense effort people in small towns put into maintaining the web of interpersonal relationships that make one "belong." I understand the attractiveness of small-town life—never having to present identification when you cash a check, never being able to walk down Main Street without chatting with half a dozen people, never having to lock the doors of your house or car.

I like the country. During the 1970s I bought an abandoned farm in the Blue Ridge foothills of Virginia, built a house on it with my own hands, raised bees and vegetables, and generally participated in the "back to the land" movement. I can appreciate the country life—the feeling of connectedness that comes from being close to nature, the sense of wholeness that comes from working with your hands.

Oddly enough, this rural experience has made me much less tolerant of urban critics than I might otherwise be. Whenever I hear (or read) someone going on and on about the wonders of living in tune with nature, I always wonder how many times he or she has nursed plumbing through a subzero night, how often he or she has tried to run a household for a week without electricity.

I like the suburbs. Since 1987, I have lived in a classic suburb of Washington. I like living on a quiet street lined with old trees, but with restaurants and theaters a 20-minute drive away. I like the fact that I can send my kids to a neighbor's house without worrying about their safety. I understand why the suburbs have become the homes of the majority of Americans, and suspect that they will serve that function for some time to come.

What I have learned from a lifetime spent sampling different modes of life is that there is no "right" setting for a home, no "best" way to organize society. There are both plusses and minuses to urban life, and I think I can evaluate them realistically.

THE OUTLINE

To start our tour of cities, I'll talk about the city as a natural ecosystem and discuss what this means in terms of limits to urban growth. After this introduction, I'll turn to the three scientific threads listed above, talking about physical structures, energy and transportation, and communications. The aim will be to identify the key scientific discoveries that made the modern city possible and to trace the history of how those discoveries have played themselves out.

Once we understand how cities came to be what they are, we'll turn to the question of what they will become. In the spirit of defining envelopes, I will examine five possible urban futures, ranging from a compact city in which everyone lives in huge new skyscrapers, to a "city" in which people live in dispersed homes and interact through the new technology of virtual reality, to a new human city in space. Finally, to bring things full circle, I will close with a discussion of how cities, like all natural systems, end their lives and die.

In putting together a book like this, the wise author seeks out and receives help from a wide variety of experts. With the usual warning that any errors that remain in the text are mine alone, I would like to thank Steven Diner, Iris Knell, Harold Morowitz, Jeffrey Newmeyer, Paul and Judith Peatross, Victoria Runsdorf, Egon Verheyen, and Vern Waples for reading the manuscript and offering their perspectives.

JAMES TREFIL
Fairfax, Va.
June 1993

PART ONE

The City
of Today

1

The Birth of Cities

And I John saw the holy city, new Jerusalem, coming down from God out of heaven . . . and the city was pure gold, like unto clear glass. . . . And the city had no need of the sun, neither of the moon, to shine in it; for the glory of God did lighten it . . .

—Revelation 21:1–23

What is a city?

There are many answers you can give to this question, most of them equally "right." Cities are large collections of people, they are hubs of commerce and industry, they form the nodes of national and international transportation networks. Each of these points of view adds something to our understanding of our great urban areas.

What I want to do in this book is suggest another point of view —another way to look at cities—that can add another dimension to this understanding. This other point of view is that of the natural scientist, who sees the various parts of cities as examples of the laws of nature in operation, and the whole as a system that can be described in much the same way as other systems in nature. When we're done, we'll have a much better understanding of how our cities got to be the way they are and how they're likely to develop in the future.

Through the ages, people have thought about cities in many ways. When the author of the Book of Revelation wanted to symbolize a new world, for example, he wrote of a "new Jerusalem," a city of gold. When Victorian dime novelists wanted to describe cities as dangerous and evil places, they spoke of the "wicked city." As a scientist, I find that only one vision of the city really gets my hackles up—the notion that a city is somehow "unnatural," a blemish on the face of nature.

The argument goes like this: Cities remove human beings from their natural place in the world. They are a manifestation of the urge to conquer nature rather than to live in harmony with it. Therefore, we should abandon both our cities and our technologies and return to an earlier, happier state of existence, one that presumably would include many fewer human beings than now inhabit our planet. This line of thought is perhaps best expressed in the slogan of people who call themselves deep ecologists: "Back to the Pleistocene!"

There is an important hidden assumption behind this attitude, one that needs to be brought out and examined if only because it is so widely held today. This is the assumption that nature, left to itself, will find a state of equilibrium (a "balance of nature") and that the correct role for humanity is to find a way to fit into that balance. If you think this way, you are likely to feel that all of human history since the Industrial (if not the Agricultural) Revolution represents a wrong turning—a blind alley, something like the failed Soviet experiment in central planning. Cities, and particularly the explosive postwar growth of suburbs ("urban sprawl"), are agencies that destroy the balance of nature, and hence are evil presences on the planet.

What bothers me about this point of view is that it implies that human beings, in some deep sense, are not part of nature. "Nature," to many environmental thinkers, is what happens when there are no people around. As soon as we show up and start building towns and cities, "nature" stops and something infinitely less worthwhile starts.

It seems to me that we should begin our discussion of cities by recognizing that they aren't unnatural, any more than beaver dams or anthills are unnatural. Beavers, ants, and human beings are all products of evolution, part of the web of life that exists on our planet. As part of their survival strategy, they alter their environments and build shelters. There is nothing "unnatural" about this.

The city, in fact, can be thought of as a natural system on at least three different levels, each of which can give us insight into what a city is. At the most obvious level, although we don't normally think in these terms, a city is an ecosystem, much as a salt marsh or a forest is. A city operates in pretty much the same way as any other ecosystem, with its own peculiar collection of flora and fauna. This way of looking at cities has recently received the ultimate academic accolade—the creation of a subfield of science, called urban ecology, devoted to understanding it.

At a somewhat deeper level, a natural ecosystem like a forest is a powerful metaphor to aid in understanding how cities work. Both systems grow and evolve, and both require a larger environment to supply them with materials and to act as a receptacle for waste. Both require energy from outside sources to keep them functioning, and both have a life cycle—birth, maturity, and death.

Finally, our cities are like every other natural system in that, at bottom, they operate according to a few well-defined laws of nature—laws that are knowable and, indeed, largely known. There is, for example, a limit to how high a tree can grow, which is set by the kinds of forces that exist between atoms in wood. There is also a limit to how high a wood (or stone or steel) building can be built—a limit that is set by those same interatomic forces. We will examine many of these sorts of analogies as we proceed.

So let me state this explicitly: *A city is a natural system, and we can study it in the same way we study other natural systems and how they got to be the way they are.*

Ecosystems are the parts of nature most strikingly analogous to cities. An ecosystem is composed of all the plants and animals that live in a place, together with their physical surroundings. Technically, an ecosystem can be any size, from a small hummock of grass on a hillside to the entire earth. Most commonly, however, the term refers to areas whose sizes range from several acres to several hundred square miles—a lake, a mountain meadow, the Everglades. There are three important features of all ecosystems that we should have in mind before we talk about cities.

First, energy flows through ecosystems. In a forest ecosystem, for example, it enters in the form of sunlight. As it moves through the ecosystem, at each moment there is a choice as to whether or not it will be returned to the environment as waste heat. A portion of the sunlight is used by plants to run their metabolism, and this energy quickly enters the air as waste heat. Another portion is stored in plant molecules, and it may move up the food chain if the plant is eaten by animals. No matter how far up the chain it goes, however, the energy in sunlight is always eventually transformed to waste heat (when the animal uses the energy to move, for example, or when it dies). The only partial exception to this rule occurs when the energy is stored in coal or oil, and even then the same fate awaits it when humans burn the fuel to obtain energy. Sooner or later, all the sunlight that falls on an ecosystem will be radiated back into space. Energy in an ecosystem is always in transit—you can rent it, but you can't own it.

The second important feature of ecosystems is that their materials tend to move in cycles. The next bit of air you breathe out, for example, will contain carbon dioxide created by the burning of food molecules in your cells. That carbon dioxide will be taken in by plants, where, with energy supplied by sunlight, the carbon can be incorporated into plant fibers. In the earth ecosystem, all materials go through cycles, but in smaller ecosystems some materials can be carried in and out—by the air or by water, for instance.

Finally, ecosystems are characterized by the existence of niches. The term, which comes from the latin word for "nest," refers to the role that any species plays in relation to other species and the environment. Thus, there might be a plant that can grow if the temperature stays within certain bounds, if the soil has a certain moisture content and acidity, if there are certain levels of sunlight, and so on. If these conditions exist, the plant will occupy that niche, subject to competition from such things as other plants, diseases, and the presence of herbivores. Every system in nature, from a handful of soil to the entire planet, can be thought of in terms of competition among living things for spaces within ecological niches.

The concept of the ecological niche is a fundamental one, and one that allows us to understand how it is that living systems come to arrange themselves the way they do. It also serves to illustrate one of the most important principles that govern the development and evolution of living things in response to changes in their environment—the principle of natural selection.

It works like this: At any given moment, there is some variation among members of a given species. Some sparrows are bigger than others, some can fly faster, some are lighter in color, and so on. If it happens that one of these traits makes it more likely that an individual will survive in a given environment—if, for example, quickness helps the bird evade its predators—then individuals with that trait are more likely to have offspring. Over many generations, more and more members of the population will carry this trait because their ancestors produced more offspring. Eventually, the entire population will be made up of quick-flying birds.

Plant and animal breeders have known about this sort of process for millennia and have used it to turn wild cattle into placid steers, prickly thistles into artichokes. It was Charles Darwin's genius to see that what humans could do intentionally, nature could do unintentionally.

The effect of natural selection is to produce plants and animals that fit better and better into whatever ecological niche the environment provides. If the environment were stable, then every life form on the planet would eventually be like the orchid—a specialist at exploiting a narrow niche. But environments do change. Old niches disappear and new ones are created. When this happens, natural selection starts to operate on whatever raw material is at hand and mold it to the new circumstances. Those life-forms that have evolved in old niches which resemble niches in the new ecosystem will adapt and prosper. In a sense, then, every surviving form of life on earth carries in its genes the history of the fluctuating environment in which its ancestors evolved.

For it is a simple fact of life that ecosystems are not static.

Change—even drastic change—is nothing special in the natural world. Twenty thousand years ago, for example, much of North America was an arctic ecosystem, covered by a thick glacier. When the glacier melted, the ecosystem on a given spot could change from tundra to lakeside to thick forest in a matter of a few thousand years.

Less dramatic changes happen more frequently. On a local scale, rivers change their courses, making swamps give way to dry grasslands. Forests change from pine to hardwood in a steady progression. Scientists who have traced the evolution of ecosystems in the world have come to one hard conclusion: there are no static ecosystems in nature, there is no perpetual equilibrium or "balance of nature." Nature always changes, even in the absence of human beings, and natural selection allows life to adapt to this fact.

When a city is built, or when a farm or forest is leveled to make way for a subdivision or shopping mall, what happens is that one ecosystem gives way to another. Building a city is just one more example of a process that goes on in nature all the time.

THE CITY AS ECOSYSTEM

Think about downtown areas, for example. They are the places that seem most "unnatural," most unlike regions undisturbed by human beings. From a naturalist's point of view, the most important difference between downtown and the rural countryside is that in the town the soil has been almost completely covered by concrete, buildings, and asphalt: often there is no grass or undisturbed soil to be seen anywhere.

But this isn't really unnatural. There are plenty of places in nature where the soil is replaced by hard surfaces—think of cliffsides in the mountains or along the ocean. From the ecologist's point of view, the building of Manhattan simply amounted to the exchange of a forest for a cliffside ecosystem.

Look at the energy sources of the downtown ecosystem. There is, of course, sunlight to provide warmth. In addition, there is a large amount of man-made detritus that can serve as food for animals. Next time you're walking down the street, look at the number of hamburger buns, apple cores, and partially filled soft drink containers lying around. All of these can and do serve as food sources. Indeed, urban honeybees seem to find sugar-rich soft drink cans an excellent source of "nectar" for their honey—just notice them swarming around waste containers during the summer.

A downtown area, then, possesses cliffside habitats and detritus food sources. Any animal that can take advantage of this ecological niche will be able to live and prosper. In 1385, for example, writers noted that pigeons (descendants of rock doves, who nest on natural cliffs) were moving into London. Today, of course, pigeons are the most visible wildlife in many downtown areas.

The pigeons you see every day, then, are living examples of natural selection at work. They originally evolved to fit into a niche appropriate to high rock cliffs (presumably, the sheer rock provided a degree of protection for their nests that wasn't available to their tree-dwelling cousins). When a similar niche opened up in cities, they were ready to go. There isn't that much difference between the nooks and crannies in a cliff and the nooks and crannies in a church steeple or a skyscraper. This is a rather common scenario for the development of urban wildlife: first it occupies a niche in the wild ecosystem, then it moves in when a similar niche opens up in cities.

The introduction of bird life into the urban environment can follow temporary changes of conditions in the wild. Seagulls, for example, were first seen in London after the unusually severe winters in the late 1880s. Sometimes the introduction is intentional. In the late nineteenth century, there was a movement in the United States to bring all the plants and animals mentioned in Shakespeare to this side of the Atlantic. In 1890, a member of this well-meaning fraternity released the first group of starlings into New York's Central Park. Pigeons, not native to North America, were apparently brought over by early colonists as a food source, similar to chickens. Needless to say, both pigeons and starlings have flourished in the cliffside-detritus zones of central cities.

It is also possible for new technologies to create new niches in the urban ecosystem, albeit unintentionally. When central heating became widespread, for example, the cockroach, a scavenging insect from the tropics, came north, and now is a fixture in our cities.

In recent years, there have been some dramatic events to re-
mind us that the same laws of nature operate in the urban
ecosystem as in any other. By the 1970s, widespread use of DDT
had wiped out the population of peregrine falcons in the eastern
United States. Over the last decade, they have been reintroduced
and are starting to find the tall buildings of large cities an ideal
substitute for their original roosting places on cliffs. There are
now, for example, over ten roosting pairs of falcons with nests in
New York City. Their primary food: pigeons. Some people have
been so upset by this turn of events that they have called for the
eradication of the falcons, but the pigeons themselves seem to
have developed a successful response to the threat: when they
see a falcon, they run under parked cars.

Cities—even central cities—are actually full of nonhuman life,
although we tend not to notice it. Our image of cities involves
wall-to-wall concrete, but in fact there is a surprising amount of
green space even in the most crowded downtown areas. Sometimes this is in the form of large areas set aside for parks, such as
Central Park in New York, Grant Park in Chicago, and Golden
Gate Park in San Francisco. In addition, there are always vacant
lots (perhaps being used as parking lots), little parks, and other
places where animals and plants can flourish.

This fact was brought home to me recently when I was helping
my daughter with her high school science project. It required
going into some of these invisible urban wild spaces—in our case,
into the land enclosed within freeway interchanges. Inside the
loop of cloverleafs, I found small pine forests, wooded creeks,
and wild meadows, all within a few feet of the Washington, D.C.,
Beltway, all supporting their own constellation of life.

In some places, the sheer amount of wildlife can be surprising.
Trafalgar Square in London and the Piazza San Marco in Venice,
for example, can be covered almost solidly with pigeons at times.
The weight of the living pigeons is probably greater than the
total weight of living animals on any comparably sized wild
habitat. Urban ecologists, in fact, argue that the ecosystems they
study are more "productive" (i.e., produce more animal biomass) than any others.

On the other hand, there are only pigeons (and a few other
species) in Trafalgar Square, not the great variety of species you
would find in a woodland or meadow. Birds like quail that nor-

mally nest on the ground, for example, would not be able to survive in cities. In the language of the ecologist, then, urban ecosystems have high productivity but low diversity.

As we move away from the central city, the ecosystems start to change. They become more open, more diverse, and ecologists talk about moving down an urban "gradient" as we approach the open countryside. The suburbs of large cities present a variety of niches into which all manner of plants and animals can fit.

Think about that quintessential suburban reality, the lawn. There are, by conservative estimate, some 50,000 square miles of lawn in the United States, maintained at an annual cost of some 30 *billion* dollars. You could, I think, argue that the greatest ecological effect of urbanization in America has been the replacement of eastern hardwood forest by a lawn that stretches continuously from southern Maine to Miami. The importance of lawns came home to me very strongly once when I was flying into Albuquerque, New Mexico. Coming in over the tan, sagebrush-dotted desert, we suddenly passed over a large square of green, all the more vivid because of the drabness of the surrounding country. Even here in the desert, at great expense, men and women had brought their lawns with them. I turned to my companion and said, "If you ever needed proof that human beings evolved in a savanna, there it is."

Every time you mow your lawn, you are contributing to the maintenance of an ecological niche. Normally, plants in an open field will grow to a height of several feet, then grow seeds to reproduce themselves. The taller the plant, the more energy in the form of sunlight will fall on the leaves and the more likely it is that the plant will reproduce. By mowing your lawn repeatedly, you are creating conditions in which plants that lie low to the ground (perhaps reproducing by sending out runners) will flourish in the absence of competition from their taller brethren. You are, in effect, playing God by deciding which plants will stay and which will not. And, as often happens in natural systems, your attempts to define an ecological niche in which only your chosen lawn grass will survive can have unintended consequences.

Consider, for example, *Taraxacum officinale,* the lowly dandelion. It has evolved a strategy that seems almost tailor-made for areas of mowed grass. It grows with its leaves close to the ground, out of the way of mower blades. When the time comes to produce a flower to attract pollinating insects, a stalk shoots up suddenly, virtually overnight. The flower blossoms for a few days and undergoes pollination. In some varieties, the stalk then becomes flaccid and the flower falls back down while the seeds develop; only when the seeds are ready to be dispersed in the familiar white puffball does the stalk stiffen and lift up again. In this way, the flower is in danger only for short times, when it is absolutely necessary, and safely hidden the rest of the time. No wonder the dandelion is the bane of lawn purists! (I do not include myself in this number, for I long ago learned from my grandfather how to use this flower to make a rather good wine.)

The dandelion's flowering strategy probably developed so that it could compete with taller plants in areas that were heavily grazed. Indeed, the first written records refer to its presence in barnyards. But once that strategy developed, it turned out to be ideally suited for an ecological niche maintained by human effort and preference—the lawn.

The farther we get from the central city, the more its ecosystem fades in response to the open countryside. In the East and Midwest, for example, there can be enormous numbers of trees in the suburbs—flying into a city in the summer, it's sometimes hard to see the houses through the leaves. All sorts of animals can be found in these areas. From my study window in Fairfax County, Virginia, a little over 10 miles from the Washington Monument, I have seen opossums, raccoons, and, occasionally, a deer or two. About once a year or so, a black bear wanders into the area from the surrounding countryside. In the far reaches of the city, in what ecologists call the urban shadow, the wildlife can be even more spectacular. In regions of Pennsylvania, for example, people routinely enjoy watching black bears that have come to feed in their backyards; in Florida, alligators are frequent visitors inside the limits of major cities; and during the past few years, coyotes have started to make their own invasion of suburbia nationwide. Indeed, my son and I recently saw one crossing a road in Indianapolis!

Having made all these points about wildlife in the urban ecosystem, I should emphasize that the whole purpose of the urban enterprise is to provide a habitat for one species: *Homo sapiens*. Other animals and plants are free to hitch a ride, of course, but what distinguishes the urban ecosystem from all others is the massive and persistent intervention of human beings. It is only this constant effort that keeps the city going, and if that effort flags, as it does occasionally, the urban ecosystem dies.

HOW CITIES DIFFER FROM OTHER NATURAL SYSTEMS

Where New York now stands there was once a rocky, wooded island open to the sea. Chicago was a marshy swamp where a river ran into Lake Michigan. Paris, France, was a small island in a river. When cities were built on those places, the kinds of plants and animals that could live there changed, as we have seen.

This process is not unique to cities, of course. When scrub trees invade a meadow, the ecosystem changes as well. And whether the change is initiated by humans or not, one question you can always ask when an ecosystem changes is how the new one differs from the old.

It's a relatively simple matter to measure things in the city and compare them to the same things in the country. Some of the results of such measurements are listed in the table that follows.

Town vs. Country

Feature	Urban Measurement Compared with Rural
Air quality	
· dust	10 times greater
· carbon dioxide	10 times greater
· sulfur compounds	5 times greater
Ultraviolet radiation at ground level	15 to 20 percent less
Fog	50 to 100 percent greater
Precipitation	10 percent more
Annual mean temperature	1 to 2 degrees (F) higher
Humidity	5 to 10 percent less
Mean wind speed	20 to 30 percent less

The causes of most of these differences are obvious. The air above cities is dustier and has more pollutants because of human activities, particularly the use of heating systems and automobiles. There is less sunlight reaching the ground because it is absorbed by that same dust and smog.

Light hitting tall buildings tends to be reflected downward into the concrete canyons of downtown areas. Indeed, such concrete areas retain more of the energy of the sunlight that strikes them than do rural areas. The result is the creation of "heat islands" of higher temperatures in urban areas. The air above the city, warmed by contact with the concrete, rises and pulls air in from the surrounding area. You can see this effect in a large parking lot on any warm day: the heated air above the asphalt creates a shimmering effect as it moves up. In a sense, then, cities create their own weather. The rising, moisture-laden air produces more rain, snow, and fog in the city than in the surrounding countryside.

The rising warm air has another unusual effect. It raises the flight path of insects higher above the ground than normal, making them easier prey for birds. This is another aspect of the urban ecosystem that makes it hospitable to so many avian species.

So when a city is born, a new kind of ecosystem is created, one that operates according to the same principles as any other and comes equipped with its own suite of ecological niches. Plants and animals that have developed strategies in the wild which would allow them to fit into niches created by human beings move into cities and flourish there, while those that do not possess such strategies are forced to move or become extinct. This is how every change of ecosystem, man-made or otherwise, plays itself out.

We should realize, however, that the size of this change isn't all that big—nowhere near as drastic (and a good deal less permanent) as that associated with an ice age, for example. And when cities die (as they do), the urban ecosystem is replaced by another, and the great cycle of life, death, and replacement that characterizes our planet goes on.

But in the meantime, between birth and death, the city functions as a system that can be studied and understood, just like any other natural system. And once we have this kind of understanding, we will be better able to say where the city is headed and what its future holds.

2

You Can't Throw
Anything Away

LIMITS ON THE
URBAN ECOSYSTEM

To what purpose is this waste?

—Matthew 26:8

If we take seriously the notion that a city is part of nature, then we can learn something about possible urban futures by looking at how other ecosystems operate. When we do so, we find that every system in nature has its limits. A mountain can be only so high, there can be only so many trees in a forest. In all of these cases, there is something in nature—some critical factor—that imposes the limit. Understand the limit and you understand how the system can develop in the future.

Consider a forest as an example. If a forest is to prosper and grow, it needs many things. Above all, it needs water, carbon dioxide, and energy in the form of sunlight to serve as the raw materials for photosynthesis. All of these things come into the forest from outside, are brought in across the forest's boundaries; and their availability sets limits on the forest's future. There is, for example, only so much sunlight falling on a square foot of surface, and therefore only so much leaf area that can benefit from it. Once the leaves have absorbed 100 percent of the sunlight shining on a given area of land (a real forest is never this efficient), there is no more to be used. A limit has been reached.

A forest also needs minerals and other nutrients that can be incorporated into its structure. Usually, these are materials that stay in the forest and are continuously recycled. Dead trees and leaves fall to the forest floor and rot, freeing their atoms for reuse in other trees and leaves. But even in situations where some atoms are being recycled, others may be carried in from the outside. There is evidence, for example, that many of the minerals needed to sustain the African rain forests are blown in from the Sahara. But whether the minerals are local or are transported from the outside, they also set a limit on forest growth: if there are only so many atoms to go around, there can be only so many trees.

Finally, a forest is limited by its ability to get rid of its waste products. Photosynthesis produces oxygen, which is carried away by the globe-circling winds that bring in the carbon dioxide. Dead material on the forest floor is broken down by bacteria and other scavengers, which can work only so fast. If waste were to accumulate faster than it could be processed, the forest would choke. This sets another kind of limit on growth.

In point of fact, limits on most forests are set by the availability of water, carbon dioxide, energy, and minerals—by the availability of things that can be brought in across forest boundaries. We will argue in this chapter that, although cities have in the past been limited in much the same way, modern technologies have largely freed us from these constraints. In their place, fundamental limits now seem to be associated with our ability to get rid of wastes and, particularly, with the problems of air pollution and solid waste.

When we talk about large, complex ecosystems, it's not always easy to know where to draw the boundaries. The boundaries of a rain forest, for example, extend far beyond the last tree; you can even (with only mild exaggeration) say that they encompass the entire world. The same is true of cities, especially large cities at the end of the twentieth century. It used to be that a city and its hinterland comprised a fairly well-defined unit, with only minor amounts of commodities being brought in from outside. This is no longer the case—a point I find best illustrated by the New Jersey license plate.

Have you ever wondered why New Jersey is called the Garden State? The question would certainly occur to you if, like many people, your only contact with it has been that stretch of refineries and heavy industry along the northern New Jersey Turnpike. Although New Jersey has many pleasant residential areas, stretches of beautiful coastline, and some rolling farmland, the modern traveler would surely remark on the decided lack of gardens. So why the nickname?

Actually, the name comes from an institution rendered obsolete in the mid twentieth century by advances in technology. At one time, northern New Jersey was covered with truck gardens —huge plots of land devoted to raising vegetables to feed New York City and other nearby population centers. The vegetables had to be grown close to their final destination so that they wouldn't spoil before they were used. With the advent of refrigerated trucks and railroad cars, however, it is no longer necessary to use land near big cities for agriculture, and New Jersey's truck gardens have long been covered over with suburbs, surviving today only as a memory on the state's license plate. Today, New York City's "Garden State" may be California or Florida, or even countries in the Mediterranean Basin and South America. Properly understood, the modern city is a system that extends to the farthest reaches of the globe.

The gasoline you burned the last time you drove your car may very well have been taken from the ground in Saudi Arabia or Mexico. The steel in your car may have been processed in Japan or Belgium. The stone that lines the lobby of your office building may have come from Italy or New Hampshire. The fruit you have at dinner may come from California or Chile, the coffee from Kenya or Colombia. The modern city couldn't exist without this constant inflow of materials.

By the same token, the sulfur compounds emitted by the tailpipe of your car when you drove around yesterday have probably already left your hometown and may someday be part of the acid rain damaging a forest in New England. The garbage you threw away last month has already been hauled away to a landfill, where it may well form a more permanent marker of our civilization than anything else we produce. Not only does the city take things in from all over the world, but at least some of its wastes have a similar global reach.

As with the forest, an examination of the way things move across city boundaries will help us see more precisely the limits of urban development. Before we get into a detailed discussion of these issues, though, there is one distinction that has to be made —a distinction between the effects of large populations and the effects of cities per se. A fixed number of people will require a certain amount of land and energy to live, regardless of whether that population is concentrated in cities or dispersed over the countryside. If the population of the earth were to double, for example, there would be all sorts of negative environmental impacts, but these would occur even if none of the new people moved to urban areas. We have to keep the effects of large numbers of people and the effects of concentrations of population separate in our minds.

ENERGY

Because of the importance of human effort in maintaining the urban ecosystem, scientists customarily distinguish between the properties the ecosystem would have in the absence of human beings and those that arise solely from human activity. Take energy as an example. Sunlight would fall on the area occupied by a city whether or not the city were there. Sunlight, in this sense, is a source of energy independent of human activity. This distinguishes it from something like waste heat from car motors, which clearly is not.

Even in the absence of human activity, the mere presence of buildings changes the energy balance in a city. One effect of this, the so-called heat island, was discussed in the last chapter. Human activity adds to the effect, primarily through the generation of waste heat. During the summer, for example, air conditioners exhaust heat into the atmosphere, making the outside air warmer and more humid even as they cool the interior of buildings. Cars, trucks, and factory machinery add to this heating effect.

So do people. We don't normally think about them this way,

but every human being goes around giving off heat, whose ultimate source is the food he or she has taken in. If you work out the numbers, someone who takes in 2000 calories a day is, from the point of view of energy consumption and heat generation, the equivalent of a continuously lit 100-watt light bulb. In a city of 1 million people, then, body heat alone will generate around 2 million kilowatt-hours of heat, day in and day out. This heat would be there even if everybody just sat on the front porch in a rocking chair all day.

When you add up all these sources of heat generated by human activity, you find that, on the average, it comes to 1 to 10 percent of the energy falling into a city in the form of sunlight. Only in a few very cold places, like Fairbanks, Alaska, in the winter, does the heat due to human activity actually exceed the incoming solar energy. Human activities, in other words, do not normally dominate the urban energy balance, but they are big enough to have an effect.

Almost all of this waste heat starts as energy that comes into the city from outside—in pipelines and trucks, through power lines, and in tankers. The story of how the worldwide energy net developed, as well as a discussion of possible energy futures, is left to Chapter 7. For the moment, we simply note that although cities are great consumers of energy, energy supplies are unlikely to provide more than temporary limits to development.

WATER

Cities need water, and as we shall see, there are some situations where this need may limit further growth. It may, in fact, be doing so right now in places like Southern California.

Cities have a mixed effect on the natural circulation of water. On the one hand, the large areas of paving and roofing keep much of the rain that falls in a city from getting into the soil. Instead, it runs off quickly into sewers and is carried off, without much chance for evaporation. At the same time, human activity tends to put small particles of dust and debris into the air. These particles act as nuclei around which raindrops can form, so that the rainfall is higher in urban areas and in areas downwind of them. Which of these two effects dominates in a given situation depends on the details of urban geography.

There is, however, one aspect of the human need for water that has had a dramatic effect in some cities, and that is the drilling of wells for water supply. In some places, when water is withdrawn from underground reservoirs, the surface land subsides. Because of widespread pumping, for example, about 20 square miles of downtown Tokyo are now below sea level.

WASTES

There is a big difference in the way people and their political systems respond to distant, abstract problems and to those close to home. The average urban dweller is not directly affected by the fact that the carbon dioxide he or she generates is adding to global warming, or that sulfur from the tailpipe of his or her car is destroying a forest 500 miles away. People are, however, directly impacted by pollution that affects the city itself. Photochemical smog (generated by the action of sunlight on nitrogen compounds in automobile exhaust) is nasty stuff, causing the eyes to water and otherwise posing a real health hazard. When it's prevalent (as it is in many cities), citizens suddenly find themselves unable to license cars that don't meet emission standards. In the same way, when a city's landfill starts to run out of space, residents find themselves forced to segregate trash so that it can be recycled—not because of any abstract love of the earth but simply because there's no place to put all the garbage.

Air pollution and solid waste disposal, then, are the real, fundamental limits to urban growth. They affect urban dwellers directly. They are, to a large extent, a consequence of our decision to live together in cities instead of spreading ourselves out across the countryside.

SOLID WASTE

On the interstate highway near Norfolk, Virginia, is one of America's most unusual tourist attractions. It's called Mount Trashmore. A large grass-covered hill, dotted with trees and traversed by walking paths, it provides a welcome respite from the rigors of driving. It is also the end product of the chain of materials that flow into and through our cities, for the entire hill is made of garbage.

Mount Trashmore is what engineers call a sanitary landfill, and as such it represents the future of all the solid wastes we throw away. Trash from surrounding communities was brought to the site, compacted, and then dumped and covered with a layer of dirt. As the garbage is accumulated, the hill grew, layer by layer, until now it is the dominant geological feature on the flat coastal plain on which it sits. When no more trash could be added, the hill was planted with grass and trees and abandoned, like the remains of the ancient cities that archaeologists love to explore. Someday, I suppose, scientists will learn a great deal about modern America by excavating Mount Trashmore.

The amount of solid waste generated in America is staggering. Each year, we produce 10 *billion* tons of the stuff—enough to fill a line of dump trucks that would stretch to the moon and back a dozen times. Every five years, on the average, each American generates a mass of garbage equivalent in size to the Statue of Liberty. This is a lot of waste, and like most past civilizations, we deal with it by finding a convenient dumping ground.

So long as towns stayed small, this haphazard approach to waste disposal didn't create many problems. Organic waste (including human waste) was either used directly as fertilizer or composted; other wastes could easily be burned or discarded. Anyone who has lived in the country or in a small town knows that there are always places where people throw trash, whether they're supposed to or not. This is why you see so many NO DUMPING signs when you drive on rural roads. But when people moved into cities, their garbage moved with them, and space had to be found to dump more garbage of all kinds in a much smaller area. With more and more waste being generated by more and more people, and with less and less prime real estate near large cities available for dumping, it's not hard to see that a crisis situation would develop.

At least, it's not hard to see in retrospect. In fact, few city planners thought very much about where to put the garbage until we started to run out of space. Only then, belatedly, did we come to see this as a major urban problem.

Every natural ecosystem generates some sort of solid waste. Any suburban homeowner can tell you, for example, that trees produce tons of solid waste every fall in the form of dead leaves —leaves we rake up and consign to the city landfill. In a forest, these leaves lie on the ground and, subject to the action of weather and bacteria, eventually decay to form a rich, black soil that, in turn, nurtures the plants around it. In our modern language, we say that the atoms and molecules in the leaves are recycled.

In fact, any organic material on the ground can be thought of as a rich source of complex molecules—molecules that can be used by other living things for food and structural material. Over the millennia, bacteria have evolved to occupy the ecological niche created by this opportunity. Excreting chemicals expressly designed to break down the long molecules in the detritus, they live a fat and happy life on the forest floor, gorging themselves on the dead leaves.

To carry out their job, most of these bacteria require oxygen to maintain their own metabolism. Like human beings, they breathe in oxygen and use it to "burn" complex molecules to produce energy. If for some reason waste materials end up in a situation where there is no oxygen—by being buried in a bog or enclosed in a glacier, for example—the bacteria can't get at them and the materials don't decay. (There are some so-called anaerobic bacteria that don't require oxygen, but they play only a minor role in the breakdown of solid wastes.) This is why we occasionally find prehistoric human beings preserved whole in peat bogs around the world.

Sometimes this removal from oxygen can have unexpected consequences. About 500 million years ago, for example, a group of strange critters (some of the first living things to have developed exoskeletons) were living in shallow, oxygen-rich water on the shelf of an ancient continent. An undersea landslide carried a small part of this shelf down to the depths of the sea, far from scavenging bacteria and the oxygen needed to keep them going. Over the ages, while their skeletons were being buried and fossilized, the ocean-floor ooze turned to rock and was lifted up to form part of the Canadian Rockies. Today, those fossils are part of the Burgess shale, one of the best records we have of how complex life began on our planet.

One limit on a forest's rate of leaf production requires that the leaves on the forest floor not accumulate faster than the bacteria can break them down. In particular, this means that the lower layer of leaves must have time to decay before more leaves are added, thus cutting off the supply of oxygen to the bottom. In a forest ecosystem, you can't go on creating waste faster than it can be recycled.

This is the lesson we haven't learned about the urban ecosystem. In fact, our response to the mountains of waste we generate has traditionally been to find bigger and bigger places to dump the garbage. The world's largest landfill is located on Staten Island, within the city limits of New York. Located on Fresh Kills (*kil* is the Dutch word for "stream"), it covers over 3000 acres of land. As the layers of trash and dirt have accumulated since it opened, in 1948, it has grown to hold 2.4 billion cubic feet of refuse—25 times the volume of the Great Pyramid at Giza.

Huge garbage dumps aren't like ordinary garden compost piles or leaves on a forest floor. When material is compacted and buried in a landfill, it is cut off from contact with both water and oxygen, and in these conditions the bacteria never have a chance to get at it. Consequently, the material never rots—it just accumulates.

As it turns out, we know a surprising amount about what's in America's landfills because some archaeologists—most notably William Rathje of the University of Arizona—have already started to study modern American culture the way their fellow archaeologists study those of the past—by digging through garbage dumps. When Rathje does his excavations, he routinely turns up 50-year-old newspapers, still undecayed, still legible. In fact, he often uses the papers to date the material at a given level in the landfill. He has found 30-year-old guacamole salads, 20-year-old steaks, and innumerable hot dogs. ("The preservatives really work.") These findings tell us that for all practical purposes, we have to think of landfills as permanent structures. What we bury today will, in all likelihood, still be in its pristine form (if that's the right word) half a century from now. We can't assume that it will just go away if we leave it alone. We can't really throw the garbage away. As in every other ecosystem in the world, waste products (in this case, urban solid wastes) are going to have to be recycled.

You can get a sense of how important recycling might be by looking at the following table, which summarizes Rathje's excavations.

Contents of American Landfills

Material	Percent of Volume Occupied
Paper	50*
Plastic	10
Organic (includes yard waste)	13
Metal	6
Glass	1
Miscellaneous (tires, rubber, debris)	20

*10 to 15 percent of the total volume is newspapers; the rest is packaging.

One way of thinking about modern urban landfills is to see them as logjams in the recycling process that goes on in natural ecosystems. Take the paper that clogs our dumps as an example. Using solar energy, trees take carbon dioxide from the air and assemble it into long molecules of cellulose—the raw material from which paper is made. In the normal course of affairs, the actions of bacteria would return these atoms to the air when the tree died. Instead, they are made into paper and buried, delaying the return until some far-off time when geological weathering again exposes the paper to the air and the decay process can begin. The same comment can be made about the organic wastes, except that in their case we eliminate the intermediate step of paper manufacturing and proceed directly to the burial.

Similarly, plastics are made from petroleum, which represents a stored and processed version of those same vegetable fibers. From the point of view of ecosystem operation, then, we seem to be filling 10 percent of our dumps with carbon chains taken from deep reservoirs of oil and coal around the world, used briefly, and then reburied.

Having made these points, I have to say that the burial of paper, plastic, and organic waste is not without its beneficial effects. The carbon in the buried paper, plastic, and grass clippings at Fresh Kills, however many problems it creates for sanitation engineers, isn't in the atmosphere in the form of carbon dioxide, thus adding to the greenhouse effect. From the point of view of global warming, burying these materials may be the best thing we could do.

But there are other possible solutions to the problem of waste disposal. Just glancing at the table should convince you that a lot of what we put into our landfills needn't be thrown away. Paper, glass, and metal can all be recycled; yard and organic waste can be composted. Our descendants will surely do a lot more recycling than we do today—if not for economic reasons, then because they'll have no place to put the stuff if they don't.

AIR POLLUTION

The most acute (and most visible) negative effect of urbanization is air pollution. How many times have you flown into a city, looked at the brown layer of crud hovering above the ground, and thought, Am I really going to be breathing that stuff in twenty minutes?

Urban air pollution is not a new problem: cities have been described as "stinking" from ancient times. Up until the late 1950s, coal stoves in London created huge amounts of sulfur and nitrogen compounds in the form of tiny droplets suspended in the air. As they floated around, these droplets acquired an oily coating and produced the worst episodes of air pollution in history—pea-soup fogs that lasted for days at a time and killed thousands of people. The fact that these episodes no longer occur testifies to the fact that we can eliminate air pollution—even severe air pollution—if we want to.

Actually, London's pea-soupers were an example of what scientists call classical smog. This is a mixture of smoke and fog that forms over cities in the winter, when large quantities of fossil fuels like coal are being burned. There are extended descriptions of this phenomenon going back to Elizabethan England, when coal burning became widespread. It's different from photochemical smog, which is characteristic of places like modern cities that have come to depend on the automobile. It is at its worst in the summer, when there is lots of sunshine.

Some urban air pollution comes from mundane sources—dust kicked up by construction, tiny bits of rubber that concrete rips from tires. But by far the greatest amount of pollution comes from the burning of fossil fuels. There are two major contributors here: stationary sources like power plants, factories, and home heating plants; and moving sources like cars and trucks. All of these sources emit a cornucopia of chemicals and particles into the air every day.

We can identify three classes of pollutants: the dust and particles discussed above; chemicals that come from fuel, either from
impurities or from incomplete burning; and chemicals made
from the air itself.

Dust and Particles. In urban areas, dust and particles fall out
of the air at the rate of 10 to 100 tons per square mile every year.
Particles include everything from pollen to droplets of sulfuric
and nitric acid to smoke. Most come from stationary sources,
particularly those that burn large amounts of coal.

Sulfur dioxide. Every fossil fuel, from coal to gasoline, contains some impurities in the form of sulfur atoms. When the fuel
is burned, the sulfur combines with oxygen to form sulfur dioxide (SO_2) and, occasionally, some other combinations of sulfur
and oxygen. Sulfur dioxide is not stable, and when there is moisture present, it forms droplets of sulfuric acid in the air. This
acid can cause damage to the lungs when it is inhaled. When it is
washed out of the air by rain, it is one component of acid rain.

Hydrocarbons and carbon monoxide. Fossil fuels are made
from long chains of hydrogen and carbon atoms. If they burn
perfectly, the only by-products (aside from impurities) will be
carbon dioxide and water. Burning is almost always imperfect,
however, and the result is that small molecules—pieces of the
original chains—enter the atmosphere. There are a wide variety
of these molecules in the air, and we refer to them collectively as
hydrocarbons. In addition, it often happens that not enough oxygen gets to the fuel. In this circumstance, carbon monoxide
(CO) is given off instead of carbon dioxide. Carbon monoxide is
a lethal substance: it binds to hemoglobin in the blood and, in
effect, deprives the body of oxygen. Carbon monoxide is impli-
cated in many deaths during episodes of severe pollution.

Nitrogen oxides. The air is about 80 percent nitrogen. Whenever the temperature of the air is raised above about 900 degrees
Fahrenheit, the nitrogen in the air burns to form nitrogen oxide
(NO), which is quickly converted into nitrogen dioxide (NO_2).
This gas is toxic on its own and, in the presence of water, forms
droplets of nitric acid, the other component of acid rain. It is
nitrogen dioxide that gives the city sky its brownish color.

Most of the nitrogen oxides in urban environments come from
the burning of fuel in cars and trucks. You should note, however,
that they originate in the air, not in the fuel. You can clean sulfur

from fuels before burning, but nitrogen oxide will always be a by-product of any process that produces high temperatures. It is, for example, found in cigarette smoke.

Sunlight hitting hydrocarbons and nitrogen compounds in the air initiates a series of chemical reactions that produce ozone, a molecule made from three atoms of oxygen. When ozone sits in the stratosphere, 20 miles up, it forms a shield against ultraviolet radiation. This is "good" ozone, whose continued existence is one of the world's major environmental preoccupations. When ozone is made at ground level, however, it is a sharp-smelling, corrosive gas that can cause extensive damage to the human respiratory tract. Many cities already have emergency laws that shut factories and highways down when ozone levels get high.

Because both stationary and mobile sources contribute to air pollution, the means of combating it split into two categories. Emissions from stationary sources are governed by devices like smokestack scrubbers (which remove chemicals and particles from the smoke before it is released into the air) and by the removal of sulfur from fuels. Since stationary sources tend to be concentrated in large industrial plants, control is a relatively simple (if expensive) procedure.

The control of automobile exhaust, on the other hand, is more difficult because there are so many sources and they are scattered all over the city. Catalytic converters, the banning of leaded gasoline, and annual emission inspections are already used in many cities to deal with the problem. In 1998, California will require that a percentage of the cars sold in the state emit no pollutants whatsoever, a law that will, in effect, mandate the introduction of electric cars.

I will argue later that the only long-term solution to problems of air pollution will be to develop energy sources that don't depend on the burning of fossil fuels. What this requirement will do to cities in the future is something we'll have to explore.

3

The Fabric of Cities

Climb upon the wall of Uruk; walk along it, I say. . . . Is it not burnt brick and good?

   —Epic of Gilgamesh

Atoms are destiny.

Or, more precisely, the ability to shuffle atoms around is destiny. Walk down any city street and you'll see dozens of different kinds of materials—stone, metal, wood, steel, asphalt, glass, and so on. The kind of city you build—whether you live in a skyscraper or a mud hut, whether you get around it by walking or riding, whether or not you have indoor plumbing—depends to a large extent on your ability to make materials like these, on how good you are at shuffling atoms around.

Making any material is a lot like baking a cake according to a recipe. You get the ingredients together, you heat or stir or freeze according to the recipe, and in the end you get something whose properties are totally different from the stuff you started with. A cake, for example, isn't anything like an egg or a handful of flour. In the same way, materials made from atoms don't have to resemble the initial ingredients. If you combine silicon (a shiny metal) and oxygen (a gas) in one way, for example, you get glass. Cook the ingredients a little differently and you get quartz, a hard white rock. There's no limit to the recipes for putting atoms together, no limit to the kinds of materials that can be made. And, among all this diversity, there are bound to be a few materials that humans can use to make their cities.

So the real questions you should ask when you walk down a city street are these: How did our ancestors learn to shuffle atoms around so that they could move from mud huts to skyscrapers, and what new recipes will our children find to change the face of our cities in the future?

For the fact is that what people know how to do has a direct bearing on the kinds of cities they build. If people in a given society know how to cut down trees and work with lumber, then their buildings will be low and rambling, no more than a few stories high. If they know how to use stone (or, better yet, how to use concrete and brick as substitutes for stone), the buildings will be taller, more monumental, more in keeping with our image of a city. If they can make steel in quantity, yet another kind of city will emerge. Each of these materials has its atoms arranged in a different way, and hence responds in a different way when it is required to hold up the weight of a building.

Any structure, from bungalow to office tower, has to stand up. The force of gravity, inexorable and eternal, pulls downward on every member of every building, striving to reduce the structure to a pile of rubble. The fact that the building doesn't collapse means that there is another force at play, counteracting the downward pull. In all structures, from bicycles to the human body, that countervailing force is the electrical interaction of one atom with another.

Look at any building on your street. Try to *see* the force of gravity attempting to pull every atom down to ground level, and then imagine a network of upward forces between those same atoms that holds the whole thing in stasis. From the foundations to the topmost brick, these interatomic forces create a web that holds everything in place. It is this constant interplay between the atoms and the force of gravity—this continuing miracle, if you will—that allows us to raise permanent structures in our cities.

Not all materials are good candidates for being incorporated into the fabric of a city. The paper on this page, for example, would make a very poor building material. It's not very strong and has very poor weather-resistance properties. On the other hand, it has very good properties for use in a book—lightness, flexibility, the capacity to take ink easily. Whether a material has properties that are "good" or "bad," then, depends on the use to which it is to be put.

WOOD

Take wood as an example. Wood gets it strength from fibers of cellulose, which is made from long chains of sugar molecules locked together like elephants parading tail-to-trunk in a circus. Think of a tree trunk as being something like a fistful of plastic drinking straws glued together, with the straws going up and down the trunk. The actual binding of one atom to another in wood fibers is usually accomplished when neighboring atoms share electrons. This is the same sort of "glue" that holds the tissues of your body together.

Humans didn't create wood, of course, but probably used it in their first artificial dwellings. Even today, most construction in America—even construction in cities—uses wood as the main material. Single-family houses and small apartment buildings usually have a wood frame, although it may be covered by a layer of brick to shield against the weather.

Because it is made of long fibers, wood has properties that make it ideal for use in construction. For one thing, it's flexible. When you pound a nail into it, the fibers can bend around, letting the nail through without seriously weakening the board. The flexibility also allows wood to withstand forces exerted from the side—what engineers call shear loads. You have surely seen trees demonstrate this property when they bend and sway in a strong wind. The force of the wind makes the tree bend, but then forces between atoms in the wood come into play and make the tree snap back. These counteracting forces can be quite large.

I was surprised to learn, for example, that pound for pound a wooden beam has as much stiffness as metals like aluminum.

The ability to resist shear explains why wooden beams are so often used to hold up floors in residential structures, where the main load is a downward weight exerted across the grain. Like a tree swaying in the wind, the floor beam gives a little, then holds as its atomic forces come into play. You may well be sitting on a floor held up by wooden beams as you read this, prevented from falling through by those same forces.

In general, the "fistful of straws" is able to resist a force exerted across the straws (perpendicular to the grain) more easily than a force exerted along them. This is why the standard demonstration of prowess in karate—board breaking—is actually less impressive than it looks. If you watch carefully, you'll note that the blow is always delivered along the grain, in the wood's weakest direction. (I have to confess that the reason I know this trick is that I exploited it shamelessly in my days as a brown belt.)

But there are limits to what can be done with wood. When you want to put up something more than three or four stories high, the weight of the upper stories begins to be too much for the wood beams and posts at the bottom to support. You can convince yourself of this fact by doing a simple experiment. If you take a single plastic drinking straw, you can balance an orange on it (at least with a little practice). If you take several straws and join them end to end, however, you find that they cannot hold up the orange. The column of straws will always buckle as the weight is put on it.

In just the same way, a tall column of wood will buckle if it is loaded too heavily—the taller the column, the less weight it can carry. The reason for this failure is inherent in the structure of the wood itself. When one "straw" in the wood fails and buckles, it pushes sideways on its neighbors, so that they, too, are forced to buckle. Eventually, the whole column fails.

Incidentally, this same kind of process goes on when wood "creeps" over time—when a bookshelf sags after years of use, for example—and you can actually hear it happening in the nighttime creaking of old houses.

So the very thing that makes wood an ideal material for floor beams limits its usefulness in supporting tall buildings. Ancient builders learned this fact about wood early on, probably by trial and error. It explains why even today wooden structures are generally limited to a few stories in height.

BRICK, ROCK, AND CONCRETE

The use of stone, either natural rock or artificial "stone" like brick and concrete, was the next step in the quest for height in buildings. Referred to collectively as "masonry materials," they were used in most of the great monuments of the past, from the Egyptian pyramids to the Gothic cathedrals.

These materials have a complex structure, one that you can understand best by thinking about how a rock forms from a pool of molten magma. As the magma cools, solid material starts to coalesce around nucleation points within the liquid. Each nucleation point is a growth center for a tiny crystal. Within that tiny crystal, the atoms are locked together into a rigid Tinkertoy structure. Occasionally, if the conditions are just right, there will be only a few such growth centers and the molten mass will produce the sort of large crystals so beloved by New Age aficionados. Normally, however, there are many nucleation centers in the melt. In this situation, each crystal grows until it bumps up against its neighbors. The result: a system of interlocking crystals, called grains. The properties of the stone are then determined not only by the atomic bonds within each grain but by the forces at the boundary between grains.

Common building materials like granite are actually formed in this way. Others have a slightly different (and perhaps more interesting) story. For example, 100 million years ago, there was a range of mountains in Central Africa. As the rocks weathered, individual grains became detached and were washed downstream into large sand beds in what is now Egypt. As time went by, the pressure of overlying sand and the effect of water running between the grains eventually fused the grains into a new kind of rock called sandstone. (Think of it as being like something you'd get if you poured a bottle of glue on a pile of sand.) A few thousand years ago, Egyptian builders took the sandstone —the remains of the ancient mountains—and made them into the temples and pyramids that we wonder at today.

Bricks are a kind of artificial stone that has much the same sort of interlocking grain structure as natural rock. The kinds of clay that are used in ordinary bricks are made up of grains held together very loosely by electrical forces. (The fact that you can crumble clay in your hand tells you the intergrain forces have to be weak.) Inside each grain are atomic Tinkertoy structures containing aluminum, silicon, and oxygen, with water molecules jammed in here and there between the junction points of the Tinkertoys. When the clay is shaped and heated, the water is driven out and the larger atomic structure is broken down and rearranged. The result: a material composed of interlocking grains which is much stronger than the original clay and which will no longer absorb water. Such an arrangement of atoms can be very strong, particularly when it comes to carrying weight.

We can appreciate the ability of masonry to support heavy loads by calling up a few numbers. Brick and stone weigh about 120 pounds per cubic foot, and it generally requires a weight of about 6000 pounds on each square inch of surface to break down the grain structure and initiate crushing. Thus, you could stack bricks a mile and a half high before you would have to worry about the bottom layers failing—a height some five times greater than that of the world's tallest buildings.

This little exercise points to an important point about tall buildings: you almost never have to worry about the ability of masonry to support the weight of the building itself. Even the Egyptians had materials that could easily carry the weight of their tallest structures.

So what limits the height of a building made of brick or stone if the weight doesn't? The limit is set by shear, the Achilles' heel of masonry. It may be true, for example, that you could make a wall of bricks over a mile high *provided* you stacked the bricks in an absolutely vertical line. But in the real world, there will always be a tilt in the wall somewhere, some shaking when the wind blows. When this happens, the weight of the wall will no longer be centered, and will act to twist the wall around and make it fall. This sort of sideways twisting is precisely the kind of force inimical to masonry. The forces that hold the Tinkertoy structure of atoms in place are strong, but they are also rather brittle. Like a china plate that, once dropped, cannot be put together again, so masonry materials, once twisted too far, break for good.

Provided the wall isn't too high, it will probably stand even if things get a little out of line. Build it too tall, though, and it will come down, regardless of how solidly the bricks are mortared into place. Gothic cathedrals, the tallest old masonry buildings in the world, typically have steeples several hundred feet high. In general, masonry buildings that have to support more than their own weight don't rise more than 10 to 12 stories above the ground. For our purposes, we can take this as a practical limit to heights achievable with stone and brick. If you look at the old buildings in cities like London and Paris, you will see that they all fall comfortably under this limit.

Having said this, I should point out that brick and stone structures do, in fact, have some limited ability to bend and flex. In Salisbury Cathedral, for example, the four stone columns that support the great central tower are visibly bowed out. They weren't built this way—they flexed (but didn't break) as the weight of the tower was added on top of them.

At a more homey level, I saw this same property in a double fireplace I built. The first time I used it, I had a fire going on one side only. Imagine my surprise (and consternation) when I looked up to where the chimney went through the ceiling and saw a 1-inch gap between the brick and the plasterboard. What had happened, of course, was that one of the two flues inside the chimney had heated up and expanded because of the fire, while the other had not. The result: the whole 16-foot chimney bent over like a tree in the wind. When the fire went out, the chimney bent back. Over many years of use, the repeated bending seemed to have no harmful effects; nonetheless, the experience was such a shock that I had nightmares about it for months!

Concrete, the last of the masonry materials, has, like brick and stone, an ancient lineage. Concrete goes back to the Romans, and it may very well be the modern city's most common construction material. It is universally used for floors, stairwells, and elevator shafts in high-rise office buildings, and is often used for all the important parts of low-rise buildings as well.

Concrete is a mixture of sand and gravel held together by cement. The main working ingredient of modern concrete, called portland cement, is a mixture of ground limestone and clay that's been baked in an oven—think of it as dehydrated rock. When water is added to the cement, it forms a pasty slurry that can be poured into molds and allowed to harden over time. (Portland cement gets its name from the fact that the Englishman who invented it in 1824, a man named Joseph Aspdin, thought the final product looked like a type of limestone found near Portland, England.)

The setting of cement is one of those mundane processes that turn out to be so complex that scientists still haven't fully worked out how they happen. (The fermentation of wine is another.) Basically, what happens when water is added to cement is this: Minerals formed from calcium (which comes from the limestone) and silicon (which comes from the clay) absorb some water and lock themselves into a new structure. Initially, these minerals form a kind of gel (the wet cement), but an interlocking set of long crystal fibers precipitates out as the rest of the water evaporates. It is this web of interlocking fibers that holds everything together and gives it its strength. You can get a good picture of how cement sets by holding your hands out flat with fingers spread, then interlocking the fingers.

By itself, concrete has the strengths and weaknesses of other masonry materials. It's good against compression, not too good against shear. To overcome this weakness, steel rods are placed in the area where the concrete is to be poured, and they become embedded in the concrete when it hardens. The result is reinforced concrete, in which the steel provides strength against shear and the concrete provides strength against compression. Virtually all concrete used in buildings is reinforced in this way.

Today, there is a great deal of research going into the production of stronger concrete for buildings and highways. Most high-strength concretes now contain long molecules called plasticizers that make it possible to use less water in the mixture—the less water used, the stronger the final product. At the moment, it requires about 3 square inches of high-strength concrete in a column to equal the strength of 1 square inch of steel, with the concrete costing half as much per square inch. Thus, steel still enjoys an economic edge for use in tall buildings. Nevertheless, some very tall buildings have been put up using only high-strength reinforced concrete. Water Tower Place in Chicago (859 feet) and Norwest Corp. headquarters in Minneapolis (950 feet) are examples.

The story of concrete illustrates an important point about the interplay of craftsmanship, technology, and science in the modern city. A Roman engineer pouring the foundations of a pier would not have thought about the structure of grains in the finished concrete; indeed, he wouldn't even have known about their existence. He was a craftsman, someone who had learned by trial and error how to mix the ingredients of his materials together to get a desired end product without necessarily wanting (or needing) a deep understanding of why his procedures worked. This kind of hands-on, empirical approach worked quite well for centuries, producing a good deal of the infrastructure of the industrialized countries.

Eventually, however, the time came when simple craftsmanship could carry us no further. To develop a modern high strength concrete, engineers have to think about atoms and molecules, about the fundamental science involved in the way things bond together. The "rule-of-thumb" craftsman, the "seat-of-the-pants" engineer had to be replaced by a white coated technician in a gleaming laboratory.

We shall see this progression over and over as we examine our cities. Clever techniques will get you only so far in this world—after that, you have to understand as well. And understanding, for better or worse, requires a knowledge of the fundamental laws of nature.

STEEL

The real breakthrough in building height was the start of the skyscraper boom at the end of the nineteenth century. The surge in building height gave us a number of landmark structures—the Woolworth Building (55 stories, 792 feet) in 1913, the Chrysler Building (77 stories, 1046 feet) in 1927, the Empire State Building (102 stories, 1250 feet) in 1931 and the Sears Tower (110 stories, 1454 feet) in 1973. The radical change in our cities brought about by the skyscraper was made possible by the introduction of a single new material—steel—into the building process.

Iron and steel have long been familiar to human technicians. Indeed, the start of the Iron Age is generally reckoned to be about 1000 B.C. Scholars speculate that iron was discovered by accident, perhaps when campfires were inadvertently built on rocks containing iron ore. Steel also has ancient roots. One of the earliest known steels was made by Indian metalworkers and had the wonderful name of *wootz*. But until fairly recently, both iron and steel were available in small quantities only, so they were used almost exclusively to make tools and, of course, weapons.

To understand why the development of abundant supplies of iron and steel had such a profound effect on the fabric of cities, you have to know a little about what gives iron and steel their unique properties. Unlike the long fibers of wood or the Tinkertoy bonds of stone, atoms in a metal are held together by bonds that are both strong and flexible. You can imagine how a metal is constructed by thinking of a pile of marbles immersed in sticky molasses. The marbles are the metal atoms, the molasses a sea of loose electrons that holds them together. The stiffness and stickiness of the molasses vary from one metal to another, depending on the particular way things are put together. The point about this so-called metallic bond, however, is that there is a resiliency built into it. Push on one part of the metal and the atoms shift around a little to resist the force, but the bonds themselves do not break.

Pure iron, like most metals, is not particularly strong—the atoms are too free to move around. The way to remedy this weakness is to add small amounts of other atoms to the iron. These atoms can form other kinds of bonds to their neighbors and, in essence, "pin down" some locations within the marble-plus-molasses system. Pinning down a few locations serves to strengthen the material, but pinning down too many makes the whole system brittle, like a rock. The trick, then, is to figure out how to add just enough extra atoms to make the metal strong without making it brittle at the same time.

Iron-based building materials involve the addition of tiny amounts of carbon to pure iron. Depending on how much carbon is added (and under what conditions), you can get a whole panoply of useful materials—wrought iron, cast iron, and all the immense variety of modern steels.

The reason these materials were so late arriving on the scene (at least in large quantities) is that, except for the occasional meteorite, pure iron tends to be pretty rare on the surface of the earth—it rusts if it's left around too long. Thus, most of the iron available to us is locked up in chemical combinations we call ores, and it has to be separated from the other atoms with which it has combined, usually by heating the ores to a high temperature.

The central problem of metallurgy throughout most of human history was simple: how to build a furnace capable of sustaining temperatures above 2700 degrees Fahrenheit—the melting point of iron.

Take wrought iron as an example of how crucial a good furnace is in making things from iron. Wrought iron is a black metal much used in decorative ironwork these days—you've probably seen it in balcony railings. In the past, however, it was the main working material of blacksmiths. It became one of the first forms of iron in widespread use because it allowed manufacturers to sidestep the requirement of a high-temperature furnace and to produce large quantities of material.

During the eighteenth century, wrought iron was made by "puddling," a process involving the heating of iron ore and refined iron until impurities like sulfur and silicon combined with oxygen to form a slag. After removal of most of the slag by hand, the temperature was raised until the carbon still left in the mix started to combine with oxygen and burn.

As you visualize the process, at this point you can think of the material as a sponge, with the iron being the sponge and the slag filling the holes. If the mass is taken from the furnace and hammered or worked in some way, the slag squishes around among the grains of pure iron, giving the metal a strength and flexibility far superior to those of iron alone.

This illustrates one way that different materials can combine in a metal: they can simply exist side by side, without any chemical combination. You've probably seen an analogous process, perhaps without realizing it. Have you ever had a carton of ice cream melt and then be refrozen? If so, you probably noticed that the refrozen ice cream was different from the original, even though they both had precisely the same chemical composition. What happened was this: When the ice cream melted, water that had been mixed in with the main body liquefied and separated out. Upon refreezing, the free water froze into ice crystals.

Thus, without changing the chemical composition of the ice cream at all, simple heating and freezing produce a different material—different texture, different look, different taste. In a similar way, the slag in wrought iron produces a totally new material even though it doesn't combine chemically with the iron.

Puddling, even though tedious, was once used to make large

batches of wrought iron. The material found its way into many nineteenth-century buildings, the most famous of which is the Eiffel Tower in Paris.

To go from wrought iron to steel, it is necessary to provide a milieu in which carbon can combine chemically with iron atoms, not just sit next to them, and this requires melting the iron. In 1856, the English industrialist Henry Bessemer, in his quest to develop stronger cannon barrels, patented a process in which air was blown through molten iron, supplying oxygen that combined with impurities like manganese, silicon, and carbon. In effect, these impurities were burned, and the heat supplied by the burning raised the temperature of the molten mass to about 2900 degrees Fahrenheit—more than enough to keep even pure iron molten. By careful control of the air blast, just enough carbon could be left to produce the correct mix for steel.

In the Bessemer "converter" (so named because it converted iron to steel), this whole process took place in a cauldronlike vessel that was tipped over once the steel was made. The operator kept track of the "blow" by watching the flames coming out of the top of the cauldron. As the manganese and silicon burned, the flames were short and reddish brown; as the carbon was removed, they became white and shot out a long way; and finally, as the carbon was burned off, they died out.

At about the time the Bessemer process was gaining an industrial foothold, Karl Siemens patented another way to produce steel. In his open-hearth process, scrap steel, iron, and limestone were heated together in a furnace to burn off impurities. Although the Bessemer process was the first to catch on, probably because it was simpler, the open-hearth process dominated American production throughout the first half of this century. Modern steel production uses a variation on the open-hearth scheme—a furnace that blows pure oxygen instead of air through the molten iron.

The details of how these early processes worked is much less important than what they accomplished. For the first time in history, steel could be made not by the pound by a blacksmith, but by the ton. A single 15-minute "blow" in a Bessemer furnace could produce 10 to 25 tons of finished steel—more steel than was available in the entire Roman Empire in its heyday. And it was the availability of plentiful supplies of cheap steel that transformed our cities.

For steel is truly a miraculous material. It is strong, capable of holding up the weight of tall buildings without buckling like wood. It is flexible, so it won't crack if it bends, as brick and concrete do. It is the heart of the modern skyline, what makes the modern metropolis possible. We'll talk more about how it works in present-day buildings and its effect on the city of the future in later chapters, but for the moment let's look at steel a little more closely to see how it works.

Adding as little as 0.5 percent carbon produces a metal that has over twice the tensile strength of pure iron. The steels used in buildings—the so-called mild steels—contain less than 0.25 percent carbon, yet they suffice to hold up the tallest skyscraper. Adding more carbon makes the steel stronger up to a point, but when the carbon gets to be more than a few percent, the metal gets brittle. This hard, brittle metal is what we call cast iron.

There are many ways to shuffle atoms around in steel, and the arrangement that actually exists in a given piece of metal depends on the amount of carbon it contains, the temperature to which it has been heated, and the way in which it has been cooled. For example, in your kitchen you may have expensive knives with "high carbon steel" in their blades. This metal is roughly 1 percent carbon and is quenched by being plunged into a cold bath. The result: "hardened steel," which is used extensively for things like knife blades and machine tools. Hardened steel gets its properties from the fact that its grains are forced to come together quickly in the quenching process, so that they have a different arrangement than they would have if they had been allowed to cool slowly.

A new level of complexity can be added to the picture if atoms other than carbon are added to the melt to produce so-called alloy steels. If a mixture contains chrome and nickel (typically 18 percent of the former, 8 percent of the latter), the resulting steel will not corrode when exposed to the atmosphere. It will be considered a "stainless" steel. If, on the other hand, 11 to 14 percent manganese is added to the molten steel, the result is a metal unparalleled in toughness—one that finds common use in railroad tracks. The addition of tungsten (with smaller amounts of chrome and vanadium) produces a steel that takes a good edge and doesn't lose it when the metal is red hot. This alloy is used to make cutting edges in machine tools.

And so it goes. There are literally thousands of recipes for making steel, each producing a final product exactly suited to some specialized use. There are even "steels" in which there are more "extra" materials than underlying iron.

Given this complexity, it's not too surprising that a large folklore grew up around steel. The famous samurai swords of Japan, for example, started as blocks of wrought iron that were pounded out, heated, folded over, and pounded out again like pastry dough. During this process, which could take a master smith and his crew up to a year to complete, impurities were removed from the iron, and the carbon underwent a slow chemical bonding that eventually turned the blade into steel.

The process of quenching, in particular, seems to have more than its share of mythology, probably because it was used extensively in making sword blades. There is, for example, a set of instructions for the making of Damascus steel (particularly prized for its sharpness and beauty) in which the smith was instructed to quench the hot steel in a bath made from the urine of red-headed female virgins.

It's a good thing you don't have to do that with skyscraper beams! (I jokingly mentioned this legend to a metallurgist friend, and he told me there was probably something to using urine for quenching. It turns out that the nitrogen compounds in urine form crystals along the hot metal and conduct heat away, aiding in the cooling process. He ventured no opinion on the effects of red hair or virginity.)

The Japanese and Arab swordmakers were like the Roman engineer we talked about earlier—men who learned their craft through long experience. Even Henry Bessemer, who revolutionized industry, was more of a tinker than a scientist. But as you may have gathered from the description of the different kinds of steels now being made, the creation of steel has moved away from the domain of craftsmen. When we want to make new kinds of steel to put in our buildings today, we have to *understand* how atoms work and how to put them together to get what we want. Once again, the technician in a lab replaces the craftsman.

4

Letting the Light In

Don't throw stones at your neighbors', if your own windows are of glass.
—BENJAMIN FRANKLIN, *Poor Richard's Almanack*

As it went with iron and steel, so has it gone with a host of other materials in today's city. Plastics, ceramics, lightweight composite substances, and many other materials are all just exercises in shuffling atoms around until you have a final product whose properties you value. I'm going to look at one of these common materials—glass—to give you a sense of how much history, how much technical virtuosity, lies behind everything you see in your everyday life.

Next time you're walking down a city street, look around and see how much of the surface area of the buildings is taken up by glass. If you're in a downtown area that has seen a lot of construction recently, it may well be that almost everything you see is glass of one sort or another.

It wasn't always this way. Through most of recorded history, glass was something of a rarity, used more for decoration and tableware than for buildings. Indeed, there is probably more glass contained in a single modern skyscraper than there was in the entire Roman Empire.

Glass really came into its own as a structural material during the 1960s and '70s, when the squared-off, unadorned glass-walled structures of the international style were being erected. Aesthetic opinions on this style can differ; Tom Wolfe, for example, calls Sixth Avenue in New York (a centerpiece for the international style) the "Rue de Regret." I have to admit I'm not wild about these structures, but they do emphasize how we have gone from building cities of stone to building cities of glass.

There are many reasons for this change. Glass is a wonderful material. For one thing, it's cheap. For another, it doesn't rust or corrode—it just needs to be cleaned off occasionally. It lets light into the interior of buildings, allowing people to get by with less artificial illumination and thereby cutting down on electricity bills.

But until recently, glass was little used in buildings, a fact that can be traced to some of its other properties. It can't carry weight or withstand wind force very well, which makes it difficult to use unless something else (such as a steel skeleton) holds the building up. And for quite a while, glass was a real energy hog, dumping heat into the outside air in winter and letting heat in during the summer. How modern technology was able to make enough glass to cover a skyscraper, and then turn around and modify the material to overcome its weaknesses, makes a fascinating story.

But let me be honest with you. As important as glass is in the fabric of the city, as important as its economic impact on the economy may be, what really interests me about it is its atomic structure. In fact, glass is one of the weirdest materials known to science.

THE STRUCTURE OF GLASS

Although glass is to all appearances a solid, like rock and metal, from the atomic point of view it doesn't have the grainy, crystalline structure of other solids. Glass is, in fact, much more like a liquid, with an essential disorder among its constituents. It is a liquid that flows very slowly, of course—it may take millennia to "pour" glass—but at the atomic level it is a liquid nonetheless.

The basic atomic building block of most glasses is a single atom of silicon surrounded by oxygen. These collections of atoms are connected in a chainlike structure around scattered atoms of sodium (see Figure 1). There is, therefore, a kind of order among the atoms in glass. If you find a silicon atom, you know you will find oxygen atoms in close attendance. In this respect, glass is like a solid.

The arrangement of the silicon-oxygen building blocks, however, is more or less random. If you find a silicon atom, you know that if you move over one atom, you'll find oxygen; but if you move over a thousand atoms, you may find anything. In this sense, the arrangement of the atomic building blocks is totally unordered, as it is in a fluid. In the language of the physicist, glass is a material that exhibits short-range order and long-range disorder.

There are other systems in nature like this, such as the liquid crystals in the display of your hand calculator. In another system studied by scientists—"spin glasses"—the spins of neighboring atoms tend to be aligned with each other but have no correlation with the spins of atoms far away.

It's hard to overstate the attraction these sorts of systems, delicately poised between solid and liquid, have for scientists who study the structure of matter. I remember an occasion when I was asked to help put together a report on a decade's worth of progress in American physics. The first draft I received devoted one page to studies of the origin of the universe, and four to spin glasses!

The notion of glass as a "frozen" liquid explains at least one unusual observation. In old cathedrals, glass at the bottom of window frames is uniformly thicker than it is at the top—a result of the glass's sagging down over time. Glass can, indeed, flow if you're willing to wait long enough.

Another interesting feature of glass is its strength. Although glass is brittle and easily broken by small shocks, fibers of glass can support a surprising load. If, for example, you had a thin glass fiber and an equally thin steel fiber and you pulled on both with an equal force, the steel would break before the glass! This

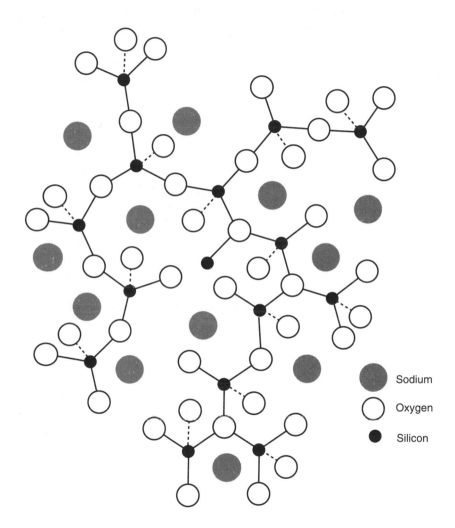

Figure 1. The atomic structure of glass

is why fiberglass, a material in which glass strands are held together by a strong glue, is used to build everything from boats to automobile fenders.

MAKING GLASS: SHUFFLING THE ATOMS

To make a glass, you have to coax the silicon and oxygen to form the kind of disordered network described above, and this, in essence, means that you have to melt sand (which is composed mainly of silica—a silicon atom attached to two atoms of oxygen) and let the chemical bonds rearrange themselves. Unfortunately, the melting point of silica is over 3000 degrees Fahrenheit, far above the temperatures available in the furnaces of early craftsmen and much too high to allow glass to be made economically even today.

To lower the melting point of the silica, soda (a compound of sodium and oxygen) is added to the mixture. This has the same effect as the salt you use to clear your sidewalk of ice in the wintertime. It allows the silica to melt and reform as a glass. Unfortunately, the so-called soda glass that results from this mixture is soluble in water—fill a bottle with water and the glass eventually turns cloudy and crumbles away. Needless to say, this makes soda glass inappropriate as a building material.

It turns out that the solubility problem can be solved by the addition of a third substance to the molten mixture. A mixture of silica (for the main glass structure), soda (to lower the melting temperature), and lime (calcium oxide—usually added in the form of crushed limestone) produces a glass that won't dissolve yet is easy to produce in a furnace. This so-called soda-lime-silica glass, which was discovered in antiquity, is the basic formula for almost all the glass used today.

There are, of course, other kinds of glass. Just as the properties of steel can be altered by the addition of small amounts of other materials, so, too, can the properties of glass. The addition of small amounts of boron to the melt will produce pyrex, a glass capable of resisting high temperatures. You may remember the pyrex test tubes in your high school chemistry lab, and you probably have cookware in your kitchen made from pyrex. The addition of small amounts of extra materials will also change the color of the resulting glass. Copper, for example, can produce either a green or a red color, manganese creates a purple color, and the addition of tin produces an opaque white glass. The art of coloring glass was important for decorative tableware as well as for stained-glass windows.

THE STORY OF GLASS

Glass and human culture go back a long way—there are 5000-year-old glass beads adorning tombs in both Egypt and Mesopotamia. But early work with glass was strange by modern standards. For almost 2000 years, craftsmen seemed unaware that glass can be worked when it is molten. Many early dishes, for example, seem to have been made by taking a chunk of solid glass and laboriously carving it into the desired final shape, as if it were a piece of marble. Alternatively, a thin layer of molten glass was poured over a form made of sand and allowed to cool. When it had, further layers were added until the glass was thick enough to support itself. It was almost as if the craftsmen were making bottles the way people made candles—by repeatedly dipping a wick into hot wax.

Sometime around A.D. 200, someone discovered that molten glass could be shaped by putting a blob on the end of a pipe and blowing into the other end. Whoever discovered this technique did a great service to humanity, initiating an art form that has produced countless treasures and persists to this day.

You are probably wondering why, if all you have to do to make glass is mix three common materials together and heat them, the ancient Egyptians didn't have picture windows. The reason is simple: it's a long way from a molten material that will harden into the disordered atomic structure of a glass to a smooth, uniform, transparent sheet suitable for a window. As the Romans discovered, just pouring the mixture out won't do—the glass will too likely crack as it cools and will have a rough surface that needs to be polished. (This problem of cooling is still with us. When the telescope mirror at Mount Palomar was cast in the 1930s, its cooling had to be carefully controlled for a full two years to avoid cracks.)

But the fact that it wasn't possible to make large sheets of glass didn't stop people from making large windows. As anyone who has visited a medieval cathedral knows, such windows can be made by piecing together small bits of glass within a lead frame-work. ("Stained glass" is actually something of a misnomer for this technique, since each piece of glass is actually colored all the way through.) This old art form has survived advances in technology quite nicely and is widely practiced by artisans today.

The first modern attempts to produce window glass (in the 1700s) involved an incredibly complex set of operations, requiring teams of up to ten craftsmen. It worked like this: Blobs of molten glass were taken from a furnace, and while one man blew into a pipe to expand the mixture, others rolled it on a metal plate to get it into a generally conical shape. During this operation, the glass would be reheated from time to time to keep it at the right consistency. Finally, a skilled glassmaker dressed from head to toe in thick leather took the glass, put it into a furnace, and started spinning it. When the glass got to a critical temperature, its viscosity would drop and centrifugal force would cause it to flash out into a flat disk. While still spinning the sheet, the glassmaker removed it from the furnace and allowed it to cool. The glass was then cut from the point of attachment to the pipe.

By the start of the nineteenth century, English glassmakers could produce sheets of glass up to 5 feet across by this process. Each sheet had a bump (or "crown") at the center where the pipe had been attached, and the final product was known as crown glass. You can see the characteristic bull's-eye glass patterns in old buildings in Europe and, of course, in places with names like Ye Olde Towne Pub throughout the United States. (I am reminded of syndicated humorist Dave Barry's facetious suggestion that there should be a fine of $1000 for each extra *e* used by restaurateurs and shopkeepers, with the use of four *e*'s being a capital offense.) After 1830, the crown process was replaced by one in which a large cylinder of glass was blown, then slit down one side and laid out flat while the glass was still malleable.

Large amounts of glass were produced this way throughout the nineteenth century, but both crown and cylinder glass shared a defect: they were made by what engineers call batch processes. After molten glass was taken from a furnace to be worked, the furnace had to cool off and then be reheated with a new mix, so it was in use only a fraction of the time. Of course, it would have been much more efficient had the workers been able to pull the molten glass right from the furnace while the new mix was being fed in.

It wasn't until the first decade of this century that mass production of glass became a reality. The stumbling block was something you can see for yourself in your kitchen tap. If you adjust the flow of water so that just a thin stream is coming out, you'll notice that the water "necks down." The stream is less thick when it is an inch or two from the tap than it is higher up. This is an effect of what physicists call surface tension. It arises from the attractive force that exists between molecules in the water, a force that tends to pull the stream in tightly as it falls. The same force is what makes raindrops "bead up" on the surface of a freshly waxed car.

Surface tension operates in all liquids, including molten glass. This means that when a glass sheet is pulled out of a melt, its thickness will change as it emerges. It was only after they learned how to control this process that engineers could make glass continuously. By the early decades of this century, however, the problem had been solved. Sand, limestone, and soda were fed into furnaces several stories high, then sheets of glass were drawn from the melt and run through a production line in which they were ground, polished, and cut to size.

Today's glass is made by an interesting variation of this continuous production technique called floating, in which glass is melted, then poured onto a pool of molten tin. The glass floats on the metal, hence the name of the process. Near the furnace, the glass is heated from above to keep it fluid, and as a result it flows into a uniform thin sheet. As the ribbon gets farther away from the furnace, it cools slowly to about 1100 degrees Fahrenheit, at which point it is hard and can be pulled out to be finished and cut. This process has the advantage of never having the molten glass come in contact with rollers, so that it doesn't have to be ground or polished after it comes out of the furnace. About 95 percent of the flat glass made in the United States today is made by floating.

For completeness, here are some other types of glass you may have heard of, together with a description of how they're made and what they do:

Annealed glass. Chances are the windows in the room where you're sitting are made of this type of glass. Annealing is a process by which the glass is heated a bit after it has formed, then allowed to cool slowly. The heating allows minute cracks and imperfections in the glass to work themselves out, so that the end product is stronger.

Tempered glass. Heated, then cooled quickly with air jets, tempered glass is three to five times stronger than regular glass and is often used in situations where people are likely to bump into it. Patio doors, for example, are usually made of tempered glass, as are floor-to-ceiling windows in skyscrapers.

Shatter-proof glass. Also called laminated glass, it is made by bonding two pieces of glass to a tough plastic sheet. This sort of glass is used in automobile windshields and in buildings where safety is important. If the glass breaks, the pieces stick to the plastic and don't fly around.

Bullet-proof glass. It resembles safety glass except that it has four or more layers in the glass-plastic "sandwich." The windows in the presidential limousine and some teller cages in banks are made from this sort of glass.

THE CRYSTAL PALACE

The first all-glass building was not part of the twentieth-century skyscraper boom, but part of the first world's fair, in London in 1851. This was the Great Exhibition of the Works of Industry of All Nations of the World, and it required a large exhibition hall that could be put up in Hyde Park in central London, then taken down and reconstructed somewhere else after the fair. A competition for the design was announced, and after a certain amount of political maneuvering, the winner was one Joseph Paxton, the son of a farmer and the superintendent of gardens to the duke of Devonshire.

The winning design, which became known as the Crystal Palace, was the precursor of the modern glass-walled skyscraper. Covering about 19 acres, with a central avenue over 60 feet high, the building resembled nothing so much as an overgrown greenhouse—not too surprising, considering the architect's occupation. The building was held up by a series of cast-iron columns, which supported the weight of the roof, so that the walls and ceiling could be made of glass. All told, there were some 900,000 square feet of glass in the Crystal Palace, an appreciable fraction of England's glass output in the mid nineteenth century.

What Paxton and the builders of the Crystal Palace had done, a half century before the first skyscraper, was to show that it is possible to put together a large structure in which one material carries the weight while the other keeps out the elements. And what better way to make their point than to use glass—brittle, thin panes of glass—for walls and ceilings? With this aspect of the Crystal Palace, they prefigured the modern steel-frame building.

As a footnote, you might be interested to know that after the fair the palace was indeed moved to a hill on the outskirts of London, where it continued to serve as an exhibition hall until a fire in the interior destroyed it in 1936. When I was a student in England in the 1960s, the site of the Crystal Palace was occupied by a campground, and, unknowingly, I often pitched my tent on its ruins.

GLASS IN THE MODERN CITY

The main reason the Crystal Palace didn't usher in a boom in glass-walled buildings is that ordinary single-pane window glass is a terrible insulator. Chances are that in your home a good fraction of your heating dollar goes to generating heat that leaks out through the windows. It is estimated, in fact, that such heat loss accounts for a third of American home heating costs, an amount of energy roughly equivalent to half the energy production of Alaska's North Shore. A similar kind of inefficiency occurs in the summer, when the direction of unwanted heat flow is from the outside to the interior of the building. Ordinary glass lets heat in, pushing up the cost of air-conditioning. Before glass could be used widely in construction, a way had to be found to stop heat from leaking through it so easily.

The first step in solving any problem is understanding where it comes from. In the case of heat loss through glass in winter, air molecules in the heated building are moving quickly, and when they collide with the window, they give up some of their energy and set molecules in the glass into faster motion as well. Vibrating molecules in the glass pass this captured energy from the inside surface to the outside—in effect, heat from the interior air flows through the glass easily and warms up the outside surface.

There, the molecules in the glass collide with slow-moving molecules in the exterior air, sending the energy off to heat the great outdoors. In summer, of course, the process is reversed and heat flows in.

In addition, a lot of heat enters and leaves buildings in the form of ordinary light and infrared radiation ("light" to which the human eye is not sensitive). If you have ever started to sweat sitting next to a window on a sunny day, you know how significant this sort of heat flow can be.

The most common way of blocking the energy flow is to make the window out of two or more layers of glass, with an air pocket or partial vacuum trapped between them. It's harder for the collision process to transfer heat through the air or the vacuum than through solid glass, so the energy loss is reduced. These "insulating," or "thermopane," windows are widely used today—you may have some in your own home. They're also important in high rise buildings.

This simple technique has led to other improvements in window glass. If heat enters buildings in the form of light, then one way to proceed is to modify the atoms in the glass to make it reflect more light. If heat flows through ordinary glass too quickly, then the arrangements of atoms can be changed to slow it down. The last 20 years have seen enormous changes as the kinds of science that led to high-strength concrete and modern steel began to be applied to windows, the weak link in a building's energy chain.

In the 1960s, for example, tinted glass came into widespread use. Colored all the way through, it is made by adding metallic oxides at the melting stage. Tinting the glass cuts down on glare, reflects or absorbs some sunlight, and reduces air-conditioning costs. A building with tinted glass will have a colored wall, but you'll be able to see through it. You can probably think of a building with this sort of glass in it.

More recently, engineers have started to modify window glass by coating its surface after it is made—usually by putting the glass in a vacuum chamber and then heating some of the coating material. When this material condenses out, it will form a thin, uniform layer on the glass.

The simplest sort of coating involves a single layer of material that either reflects light (if the goal is to keep the light from passing through the glass) or absorbs it (if the goal is to move energy through the glass). Buildings made with glass designed to lower air-conditioning costs often look shiny, like silvered sunglasses. A common technique is to choose the coating so that it allows visible light to pass through but reflects infrared light. This kind of window looks normal to the eye but keeps the invisible infrared radiation from passing through.

This is accomplished by putting different coatings on different surfaces of the glass. You can use a reflective coating on the outside and a transmitting coating on the inside, for example, in a situation where air-conditioning costs are high and you want to transfer heat out of the building. Just the opposite design may work for a building in the north, where the main cost is winter heating. When you realize that there are four surfaces in a thermopane window, you can imagine the various effects you can achieve by playing with coatings.

The energy savings from window coatings can be truly prodigious. It has been estimated, for example, that a single factory building whose windows were replaced with coated windows will save as much energy as that generated by an entire offshore oil drilling platform.

Recently, windows with up to five different layers of coatings have been tested. The atoms in these coatings are arranged so that electrons flow back and forth between the layers in the coating when the level of light or heat flow goes up or down. These "smart windows" can respond to changes in the environment (they may become more opaque as the sunlight gets brighter, for example) or to electrical controls (you can change the way a window transmits light and energy by turning a knob). Smart windows are still being tested, but I expect to see them in wide use before long.

Finally, the quest for the "superwindow" has driven scientists to take another look at glass itself. I have seen glass, for example, with tiny air bubbles deliberately included—in effect, glass with built-in thermopane. It is a little cloudy (the effect is much like looking through a dirty window), but a half-inch thickness of this glass has as much insulating capability as one of those huge fiberglass batts that people use to insulate their attics. I wouldn't be at all surprised to see a demonstration house built in the next few years in which the walls, rather than the windows, were the weak links in the energy chain.

There is, in short, a bewildering variety of glass available to people who want to build glass-covered skyscrapers, 20-story hotel atria, and the all-glass office buildings you see on your morning commute. And this variety is growing all the time—a fact brought home to me very forcefully between the time I wrote the first draft of this chapter and the time I revised it. Walking in downtown Chicago, I came upon a sign announcing that the building under construction on the neighboring lot was using a new kind of glass—glass whose atomic structure has been modified so that it has the properties of tinted or coated glass but still looks like an ordinary clear window.

So the story of glass is far from over. I often wonder, when I drive by one of the futuristic glass-walled buildings in my neighborhood, what those ancient craftsmen, chipping patiently at their glass bowls, would think if they could see what I see.

5

What Goes Up Must Come Down —Eventually

HOW A BUILDING WORKS

A building starts to fall as soon as you put in the last brick.
—TOMÁŠ TREFIL, *stonemason*

We pulled onto the freeway entrance ramp in downtown San Francisco and started to climb. My companion was one of that select fraternity of engineers licensed to design buildings in earthquake zones. Looking out the window, she commented, "This is the worst place you could possibly be in an earthquake, you know."

"Really?" I said, mentally calculating the time it would take us to get back onto solid ground. "Why is that?"

What followed was a short description of how structures respond when the ground under them shakes. My companion pointed out that an elevated freeway—essentially a heavy weight balanced on a series of sticks—could be particularly vulnerable.

Her chance remark stuck in my mind, particularly after the

1989 earthquake, in which, as you know, the major loss of life occurred during the collapse of just such an elevated highway. But her comment spoke to a deeper point about man-made structures. No sooner do we put something up than natural forces try to tear it down. It's not just occasional events like earthquakes and hurricanes, but everyday things like wind and the downward pull of gravity. The life of every man-made structure is a battle against these forces, and every engineer feels in his or her bones the vulnerability of what he or she builds. Such a vision of the battle between builder and destroyer, between mankind and the raw forces of nature, is in the mind of every engineer, and if you are to understand how a city is built, you'll have to share a little of it too.

When most of us look at a building, we see the outside—the stones and bricks and glass that form the outer skin. When an engineer looks at a building, however, he or she sees something else. In response to the forces trying to pull it down, the materials in the building deform, shift around, and exert their own countervailing influences. They resist the destructive forces of nature, and for the time being, the building stands.

Eventually, of course, the forces of nature must win. Our greatest monuments, our cities, even the Egyptian pyramids will someday be nothing more than piles of rubble. But in the meantime—between the time when mankind builds and nature destroys—the monuments shine out as the greatest glories of our civilization.

So what is it, to paraphrase Robert Frost, that "doesn't love a building"? I will talk about three dramatic kinds of building killers—gravity, wind, and earthquakes—and then about the less dramatic (but often more effective) forces that we see around us all the time. You can think about the three dramatic forces in terms of a simple analogy. Suppose you took an ordinary kitchen knife and stuck it into a cutting board: the effect of gravity would be analogous to the weight of the knife pushing down into the board; the effect of wind, to pushing on the top of the knife and letting it vibrate back and forth; and the effect of an earthquake, to grabbing the cutting board and giving it a yank. Each of these effects presents its own problems to the builder, and each is met by a different kind of strategy.

GRAVITY

The most obvious force that a building must overcome is gravity. It is so much a part of our lives that we tend to forget that it's there, always working, always pulling. We've become so used to building structures in defiance of gravity that when a building collapses under its own weight, it's big news. But this aura of safety is an illusion, something like the illusion that only good movies were made in the 1930s and '40s. We forget that for every *Casablanca* there were hundreds of pieces of schlock that we don't see anymore. In the same way, buildings that are still around are those that, by definition, haven't collapsed. The long history of trial and error, the thousands of buildings that *did* collapse, are invisible to us today. All the rubble has been cleaned up, and the knowledge that each collapse gave us is safely stored in our collective memories. But the first requirement of every design for a building is still that it stand against the tug of gravity.

You can picture the action of gravity as a kind of cascade running down from the top of a structure to the bottom. Most buildings have a roof of some sort to keep out the weather, and the weight of this roof constitutes the first few drops of the cascade, way up near the top. As the cascade descends, it swells with the weight of the walls and floors that it passes. When it reaches an opening—a door or window, for example—it is diverted to the sides. Depending on the height of the building, the cascade can reach truly torrential proportions by the time it reaches the bottom. (You can get some idea of the huge gravitational forces at work in a modern building when you realize that the weight of a 70- to 80-story structure will compress the huge steel columns at the base of its skeleton by a full inch by the time construction is finished.)

The cascade has to go somewhere when it reaches the ground, and the first question we can ask is simple: Will whatever is under the building hold it up? As it happens, you can learn a lot about cities by looking at the geological history of the ground on which they stand.

On the island of Manhattan, for example, the tall buildings are supported by a 500-million-year-old geological formation made up of sediment deposited by a long-vanished ocean—sediment then subjected to enormous pressures and temperatures in the heart of mountains now long eroded. This stuff is now the hard, dark rock that pokes above the surface in Central Park.

The shape of this particular geological formation explains some of the features of the New York skyline. Tall buildings in Manhattan are clustered in two locations: near the southern tip of the island, around Wall Street, and then again in Midtown, near Central Park. Between these two clusters lies a region of smaller buildings—a gap in the skyline. I used to think the reasons for this arrangement were economical, that somehow the intermediate area just wasn't a desirable location for offices. It turns out, however, that the reasons are geological. The hard rock is near the surface at the lower tip of the island, dips down as it comes north, and then approaches the surface again. Where this rock is at or near the surface, tall buildings stand. Where the rock dips down and the surface is made up of loose gravel and rock deposited by glaciers, the buildings are shorter. The Manhattan skyline, in other words, traces out the contour of underground Manhattan geology.

But you can build a city without rock formations if you have to. The John Hancock Center in Chicago rests on steel-and-concrete caissons sunk down into the mud of the Lake Michigan shoreline, and many other cities have similar situations. Most of the historic buildings in Venice, Italy, rest on a foundation of tree trunks driven into the swampy soil. In the words of structural engineer Joe Colaco, "In Houston, [the foundation is] only thick clay, and in New Orleans—they don't like me saying this—it's like mush." The solution? In Houston, buildings can be floated on the clay like buoys on the ocean; in New Orleans, pilings can be driven through the "mush" to firmer footing. My sense is that there's almost no place on the surface of the earth where you can't run the gravitational cascade harmlessly into the ground if you want to badly enough.

As the gravitational force flows down through the building, it must occasionally be diverted. If you want to make an opening for a door or a window, for example, you have to do something with the flow that would ordinarily go through that space. Even when you walk through the door of a one-story bungalow, you should be aware that a certain fraction of the roof's weight is being carried away from the region just over your head.

The easiest way to divert the downward flow of force is shown on the left in Figure 2. A block of material (called a lintel by architects and a header by construction workers) is simply placed across the flow like a dam in a stream, and the force is carried around it, leaving the space immediately downstream free for other uses. Next time you drive by a place where a wood-frame building is going up, look at the walls. You'll see the horizontal beams stretching between the uprights, ready to divert the weight of whatever is built above them.

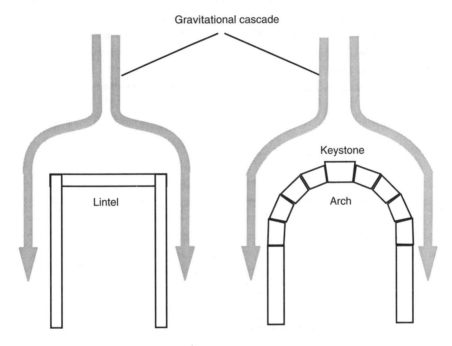

Figure 2. Flow of force on a lintel and an arch

Another time-honored diversion technique is the arch, shown on the right in Figure 2. Here the diversion of the flow of force is used to press wedge-shaped stones together, keeping the structure intact. The arch was used for stone bridges by the Romans and can still be seen in surviving medieval structures all over Europe. The same principle of using the flow itself to wedge things together is the basis for the great stone domes found on buildings like St. Peter's in Rome and the Hagia Sophia in Istanbul.

Incidentally, the topmost stone of an arch, called the keystone, is often made bigger than the others for aesthetic reasons and, therefore, has acquired a kind of mythical importance. In fact, the keystone is no more important than any other stone in the arch, just as one link of a chain is no more important than any other.

Occasionally, you see an interesting effect in old buildings. The Parthenon in Athens is a good example. When the building was put up, a slab of stone was laid across some columns as a lintel (as shown on the left in Figure 3), carrying the force due to the weight of the stone to the side and leaving the space underneath open. Over time, however, such stones often crack, and then you get the configuration shown on the right. In effect, the broken stone has become a de facto arch. In most cases, the arch is stronger than the slab from which it was made, so that the building is actually better off after it's been "wrecked" than it was before.

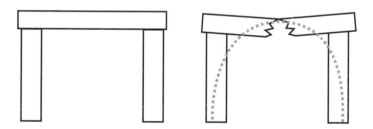

Figure 3. The Parthenon: from lintel to arch

Arches and lintels can divert only so much weight. As a building gets taller, the sheer magnitude of the downward flow starts to put restrictions on how big a space can be freed up. The lower walls have to be made thicker and thicker to hold the weight, and it gets harder and harder to put in windows. The dark Romanesque churches of the early Middle Ages, with their arched roofs and tiny openings for light, are examples of what these sorts of restrictions can do to a building. The Monadnock Building in Chicago—at ten stories the tallest of the masonry skyscrapers of the nineteenth century—has walls as thick as 12 feet at its base, just to carry the weight of the upper floors.

To build a true skyscraper, you have to develop a totally new plan for dealing with the flow of gravitational force. Instead of letting it spill down the sides of a building like a waterfall, it is channeled into specific paths—through steel columns, for example. In this way, a division of labor between the building parts is set up. The steel (or concrete) skeleton carries the weight of the building to the ground, while the outer skin keeps out the weather and looks pretty. This trend was prefigured in medieval cathedrals, where the weight was channeled to flying buttresses outside the building proper, leaving the walls free for large windows. The magnificent stained-glass rosettes of Chartres and Notre-Dame de Paris, for example, were made possible by such a division of labor. So, too, were the Crystal Palace I described in Chapter 4, the glass-walled skyscrapers that line our streets today, and in all likelihood, the great buildings in our cities' future.

In a sense, then, a modern building bears the same relation to an old one as a human being does to a beetle or lobster. In old buildings, insects, and crustaceans, the weight is carried by the external walls, or exoskeleton. The important stuff—organs or office space—is buried inside those walls. In humans and skyscrapers, on the other hand, the weight is carried by an internal skeleton designed especially for that purpose. Not only can the skeleton be lighter than the walls, but the outer covering can be designed in such a way that there is no indication of how the gravitational cascade is actually flowing on the inside.

One interesting historical sidelight: when steel-frame buildings first started going up in Chicago in the late 1800s, the buyers and renters were much too conservative to jump to a new architectural style immediately. Instead, they clothed the steel skeletons of their buildings in stone, producing buildings that looked for all the world like tall versions of Italian palazzos and Gothic cathedrals. This human tendency to hold on to traditional forms is best illustrated today by the decoration on some station wagons, whose sides are painted to resemble the wooden coaches and wagons that were their distant ancestors.

The enormous weight of even the biggest building is eventually brought safely home to the earth. When the wind blows, however, there's nothing for the building to lean against, nothing to support it. It has to be put together in such a way that it will itself generate the force to counteract the sideways push of the wind. Like a tree, it must find within itself the means to stay erect.

At one level, the problem of wind and tall buildings is simple to visualize. As you go up in height, the velocity of the wind (and hence the force it exerts on a building) goes up geometrically: it's four times stronger 50 stories up than 25 stories up, nine times stronger 75 stories up, and so on. In the supertall buildings we'll describe in Chapter 11, this force can become truly prodigious. In a hurricane-strength storm, for example, the wind could exert as much as 4000 *tons* of force against one side of a 200-story building. (To get some idea of how big a force this is, imagine that you could take the building and fasten it to the side of the Grand Canyon, so that it stuck out horizontally. The wind force would then be equivalent to what you'd get by parking several hundred fully loaded dump trucks on the upper side.)

The most obvious threat posed by the wind is that it will topple a skyscraper (or "overturn" it, to use the engineer's innocent-sounding phrase). In fact, given the strength of modern steels, this sort of brute-force scenario is pretty unlikely, but there are other things wind can do—blow out windows, for example, or tear decorative trim off the sides and dump it on the sidewalks below.

In New York, designers have to assume that their buildings will be subjected to 100-mile-per-hour winds (something that would happen, on the average, about once a century). In a typical skyscraper, this might translate into a maximum force of 50 pounds per square foot on the building's surface. But, of course, engineers never design anything to be barely capable of withstanding the greatest load it will have to bear. They know that something will always go wrong somewhere—a bolt will have a crack in it, a weld won't be up to snuff, or whatever—so they always add in a "safety factor." In building skyscrapers, the accepted safety factor is 50 percent—that is, the building is designed to carry 50 percent more load than it can ever imaginably face in the real world. For the wind load, then, the wall has to be designed to withstand 75 pounds of force per each square foot of area (50 pounds' actual load plus 50 percent of 50, or 25 pounds, as a safety factor). This number determines the kind of wall surface you can have, how you fasten it to the frame, what the windows will be like, and so on.

Dealing with this sort of direct, head-on wind force is usually pretty straightforward (if often expensive). For very tall buildings, however, the main threat of wind comes from a rather more subtle phenomenon called vortex shedding.

Have you ever been on a tree-lined street in autumn and watched a car go by? If so, you may have noticed that the leaves in the car's wake don't just blow to the side—they form themselves into circular patterns like those shown at the top in Figure 4. As the car passes through the still air, it leaves behind it ("sheds") self contained circular swirls of air called vortices, and the leaves trace these vortices so that we can see them.

The production of vortices is not confined to cars on suburban streets. It's also a feature of the turbulent flow of almost any fluid past a solid object. You can see it, for example, in the white water generated by rocks in mountain streams (in which case it is bubbles in the water that trace out the flow). It explains why paper on a city street usually swirls around, rather than simply blowing by in a straight line. You can also hear (but not see) the effect of vortex shedding in power lines. When there is a high wind, these lines often hum. What happens is that as each vortex is shed, the line is plucked like a guitar string, resulting in the sound you hear.

Wind blowing by a skyscraper behaves in the same way. What actually happens is shown at the bottom in Figure 4. As the wind blows by, a vortex is shed first from one side of the building, then from the other. Like the power line, the building is "plucked." And like the power line, the building vibrates in response to the plucking. It's one of those odd but true facts that the plucking produced by the vortices causes the building to vibrate perpendicular to the direction of the wind: a north wind produces an east–west motion in the structure.

The problem with this sort of motion isn't the vibration per se —it's the possibility of what engineers call resonance. Like any

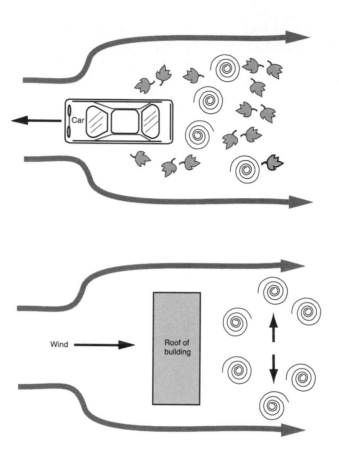

Figure 4. The shedding of vortexes

physical structure, a skyscraper will, if left to itself, vibrate at a
single frequency. Think of our analogy of the carving knife stuck
into a piece of wood. If you pulled the knife over and let it go, it
would vibrate at what physicists call its natural frequency. If you
were then to push on the vibrating knife, and time your pushes
just right, you could get it to swing through a very large arc
indeed, perhaps even shake it loose from the board. In the same

way, if vortex shedding is timed to give the building a push each time it starts back along a swing, it can induce larger and larger swings in the structure, even to the point of causing it to collapse. And while this hasn't happened (yet) in a skyscraper, it has happened often enough in bridges for engineers to know that it isn't just a theoretical possibility.

In 1941, just four months after it was put into operation, the Tacoma Narrows Bridge in Washington was hit by a wind that shed vortices at the natural frequency of the bridge. The results were dramatic, to say the least. There is a film showing the bridge's roadbed heaving up and down 6 feet or more and eventually collapsing—eloquent testimony to the power of properly timed vortex shedding. I never fail to show this film when I teach physics to engineers—it induces a proper sense of humility. I wish there was something analogous I could show physicists!

In the old days, design for what engineers call wind loading was pretty primitive, and architects tended to stick to things that had worked in the past. They were, in many ways, like the Roman concrete workers we talked about in Chapter 3. Today, however, we have sophisticated computers that can test hundreds of different designs in all sorts of wind situations before a single I beam is bolted into place. It is now common to go even one step further by putting scale models of buildings representing the final design choices into a wind tunnel and actually measuring forces. This means that long before the first shovelful of earth is turned on the building site, designers have worked out a detailed picture of how the wind will affect their building, as well as taken steps to deal with it.

A WAR STORY

One of the more intriguing aspects of thinking about buildings is the large collection of "war stories"—legends that surround classic failures. One of these, directly related to wind force, concerns the John Hancock Tower in Boston. A 790-foot structure that dominates the Boston skyline, the building contained 10,344 large panes of glass in its outer skin. On January 20, 1973, when the building had almost been completed, a major storm swept through Boston, dislodging dozens of these panes and sending them down to the pavement below. Through the spring and summer, hundreds more of the panes came out on their own, until fully a third of the building was covered with plywood replacement panels, earning it the nickname Plywood Palace. Eventually, every pane of glass had to be replaced, at a cost that is estimated to have exceeded the building's entire $95-million-dollar budget.

This incident created one of the most unusual jobs in the American construction industry. At one point, men were hired to stand in the street and look up at the building. When a window was about to go, numerous small cracks would start to appear on its surface. The men would then warn people to get out of the way before the pane fell.

For a long time, the cause of the great Hancock disaster was unknown because all the parties to the innumerable lawsuits that followed were sworn to secrecy. Recently, however, two of the consultants who analyzed the problem (and who never signed the secrecy agreement) gave an interview to *Architecture*, a prominent professional journal. Here's what they say happened: All the glass panels in the building were sandwiches. They had two panes of glass separated by a lead frame, with air in between. The inner pane had a reflective coating, and the solder that held the glass to the lead formed an unexpectedly strong chemical bond that, in effect, fused the whole frame into a single unit. When the wind blew, the windows deformed and the air between the panes acted as a kind of bellows, puffing the glass frames in and out. Eventually, ordinary metal fatigue started to break the lead and solder, but the bond to the glass was so strong that when the metal went, the glass went with it. The entire pane shattered and came raining down. (In fairness, I should point out that this was the first time anyone had used a double-paned panel with coated glass, so there was really no way to anticipate this particular problem.)

EARTHQUAKES

Wind and gravity are forces with which we are all familiar, having dealt with them in our everyday lives. Fortunately, the third great destroyer of buildings—earthquakes—is not encountered so often.

When a building vibrates in the wind, there is one fixed point: the bottom of the building is stationary, attached to the solid earth. When an earthquake strikes, on the other hand, the situation is more complex. The first jolt moves the foundations, but inertia keeps the top of the building fixed. Eventually, the vibrations move up the structure until it is all swaying, without any point being fixed.

Earthquakes, as you know, are caused by the sudden release of tension in underground rocks. In California, this tension builds up along the San Andreas Fault because the two sides of the fault are being dragged past each other. For long periods of time the force of friction keeps the rocks from moving, and energy builds up, much as it does in a compressed spring. When the strain gets too great, there is a sudden release of tension. The sides of the fault slip past each other—perhaps by as much as tens of feet— and the stored-up energy is released. Waves travel out through the solid rock surrounding the fault, and it's these waves we perceive as the earthquake.

When that wave arrives at a building, the most crucial factor— the thing that determines what happens next—is the kind of ground the building rests on. This was apparent during the San Francisco earthquake of 1989, when some areas were heavily damaged and others were hardly touched, even though the same waves passed through them. You can understand one reason for this difference by imagining that you have a cement birdbath filled with jello. If you tap on the outside with a hammer, the energy you deliver will travel through both the cement and the jello in the form of waves. The response of the two materials will not be the same, however. When the waves pass through the cement, almost all the movement will be at the molecular level. The jello, on the other hand, will quiver and toss around as the waves pass through. The same amount of energy passes through both materials, but because of the way the molecules in them are connected to each other, the motion associated with the wave is markedly different.

In just the same way, earthquake waves pass through solid rock without generating much motion, but when they hit loosely packed soil (in land that has been filled in, for example), the oscillations get very large. This is why the Marina District of San Francisco, built on land reclaimed from San Francisco Bay, suffered such heavy damage, while homes a few blocks away, on rocky hills, were unscathed.

I have to admit that the hills of San Francisco have always been a little frightening to me, especially when I'm driving on them. I have always assumed that they'd be bad places to be in an earthquake—I suppose because there's such a long way to fall. When I bring this up with engineers, though, they just laugh. One pointed to a high rise towered above a nearby hill and said, "I'd much rather be up there than down here in an earthquake." The high rise, I was told, had its foundation securely anchored in solid rock and, like the solid birdbath, simply wouldn't shake very much.

So much for appearances.

But the ground under a building isn't the whole story of what happens during an earthquake. The way the building responds to having its foundations shaken depends on how it's designed and what it's made of. In general, there are two strategies to minimize the damage earthquakes do—strategies we can categorize as "make it stiff" and "make it flexible."

An oak tree swaying in the wind is an example of a flexible structure: it bends under stress but goes back to normal when the trouble is over. Steel-frame skyscrapers operate in much the same way in an earthquake. They shake, bend, and whip around, but they don't collapse. To a large extent, the same sorts of things that allow such a building to resist wind force will make it earthquake-proof (or at least earthquake-resistant) as well.

In the "make it stiff" approach, the basic idea is to make the building as rigid as possible so that when the earth shakes underneath it, it moves as a unit, like a solid box floating on the waves. The rigidity of the building itself prevents collapse, regardless of what the ground does.

Concrete buildings are usually built to be stiff, but, surprisingly enough, so are wooden houses. The basic technique for stiffening a house is to nail plywood sheets all around the outside. When the house starts to rock, the plywood keeps all the corners at 90 degrees so that the whole house moves together.

Bridges and freeways, like the one I was on when I was warned about earthquake damage, present their own problems. Large steel bridges (like the Golden Gate, for example) may look unsafe, but they aren't. They are flexible enough to sway and survive; indeed, anyone who has driven across the Golden Gate in a high wind probably remembers the feeling of movement as the bridge deformed in a particularly strong blast.

Concrete freeways, on the other hand, tend to be reinforced and stiffened so that they move as a whole and don't come apart. Modern building codes have added a new wrinkle to freeway design, even though it's not visible to the naked eye. Inside the concrete columns holding up the roadway, steel reinforcing rods are wrapped around in circles, forming a kind of basket. In mild earthquakes, this steel just adds some strength to the system. When things get very bad, however, these rods perform another function. As the movement of the earth tears the column apart, the steel catches the chunks of concrete and keeps them from falling. When the ground stabilizes again, the column is nothing more than rubble, but it still holds up the road. As one engineer told me, "Up to an earthquake of 7 (on the Richter scale), we design to protect property. After that, we design to protect lives."

Keep that thought in mind next time you're on a freeway in earthquake country!

THE LITTLE THINGS

Many buildings have disappeared over the course of human history, but only a relative handful have been destroyed by spectacular causes like earthquakes, high winds, or simple collapse. Most of them have simply been abandoned, and the forces of nature—the unspectacular but steady processes of weathering—have obliterated them. To close this chapter on the forces that tear down what humans build, I'd like you to consider a simple question: What would happen to (insert your favorite building here) if people simply walked away from it?

You have only to look at a derelict building to predict the first stages of decay. The building's weakest parts—the windows and roof—go first. Either because of vandalism or through the action of wind and weather, the protective outer shell will be pierced and the interior will be exposed to the elements.

Initially, the building will serve as a shelter to all sorts of wildlife—birds nesting in the rafters, raccoons and squirrels denning in the ceilings. As windblown dirt accumulates in odd corners, grass and a few hardy trees will take root. Just as grass grows up in the cracks of sidewalks, plants will start to move into the abandoned building, their roots wedging away at the integrity of the materials there.

With a mainly wood structure, the process of decay moves quickly because biological agents can go to work right away. What gives wood its strength is cellulose, a material made from long chains of glucose molecules strung together end to end. Glucose is the universal energy source for living cells, and even though humans cannot digest cellulose, there are plenty of living things that can. Termites will set up shop, and bacteria ("rot") will start to take back the energy that was produced by photosynthesis in the tree from which the wood came. Eventually, wooden beams will have been so weakened that an unusual event—a heavy snowfall or a hurricane, for example—will precipitate the collapse of the entire structure.

If the building is a new one, made of steel and concrete, the process takes longer. There's nothing in either material that can be eaten, so we have to look to physical and chemical processes (rather than biological ones) to bring the building down. For the decay of concrete, the best analogy is the weathering of rocks, a process that goes on in nature all the time. Water seeps into cracks in concrete and, through repeated cycles of freezing and thawing, breaks it up. You can see this kind of weathering in roads and sidewalks, and old concrete—stuff poured 50 years ago—has a worn and battered appearance because of it. There are many examples of the freeze-thaw cycle breaking concrete beams apart in exposed bridges, and the same forces would eventually break up the stairwells and walls of a high-rise building, although the process could take many centuries to run its course.

Steel skeletons are actually a lot more vulnerable to weathering than you might think at first. This is because they will rust and corrode unless they are protected, and a beam or column has to rust through only at one point to bring about a collapse.

This point was brought home to me very forcefully a few years ago when I heard a talk by an engineer who had been involved in the design of the World Trade Center in New York. Asked about the building's weak points, he thought for a while and then told us that the entire weight of the building was supported by the steel columns that make up the outer envelope. These columns come through the various basements and subbasements of the building, in areas that would almost surely be flooded were the building to be abandoned. His scenario: After several decades of flooding, the effects of the water at their base would have weakened the support columns considerably. After this, the first big storm would generate wind forces big enough to snap the columns off, toppling the building in the process.

No matter how big, how imposing a building may be, there is a force of nature that, given enough time, is capable of destroying it.

6

Of Snails and Subways

THE URBAN
INFRASTRUCTURE

*Isn't it wonderful that God put rivers right in the middle of cities, so that
we could have these beautiful bridges?*

—*Nineteenth-century American tourist in Europe*

Cities are complicated. Look at what's underneath a city street
(see Figure 5) if you don't believe me. There's a lot more to a
modern city than tall buildings, and there is a fascinating story
associated with every part of it.

One seldom-explored aspect of the science of cities is the long
road that has to be traveled from the inception of a potentially
important concept to the actual working out of that concept in
the real world. There is nothing mysterious about the science or
engineering that goes into building bridges, for example, but
building a bridge is always surrounded by politics, human interest, and unexpected accidents, as well as technological challenge.

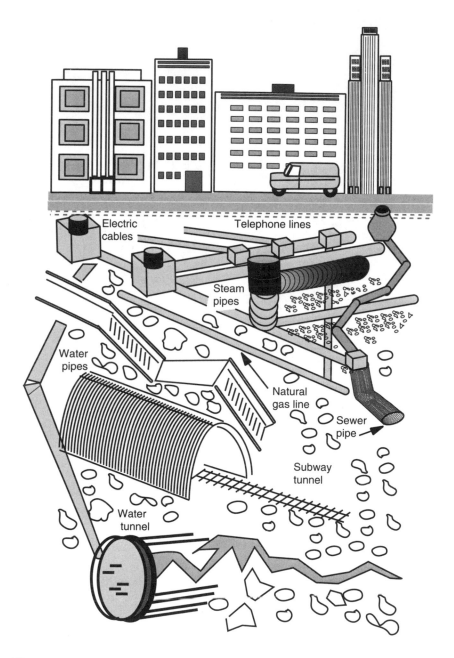

Figure 5. Beneath a city street

Before we leave our discussion of city structures, let's look at a couple of examples that illustrate this point.

BRIDGES

Chances are that you've already crossed several bridges today, most likely without even noticing them. Automobiles and railroads—or oxcarts, for that matter—work best on smooth and level roads, and nature seldom obliges us by supplying perfectly flat local topography at the same places we want to build our cities. Confronted with the essential unevenness of the land on which cities are built, modern engineers respond in the same way their predecessors did 5000 years ago: they smooth the road out by building a bridge.

From a scientific point of view, the problem of designing a bridge is simple, although the actual building of it, as we shall see, can get quite complex. The goal is to put something between two support points in such a way that it can hold up not only its own weight but the weight of whatever is likely to be crossing it. The easiest way to think about this problem is sketched in Figure 6. A beam laid across two support points will be distorted and bent down, as shown—think of a bookshelf loaded with books. And although the deflection will be greater if there is an extra weight on the beam, it will be there in some measure just because the beam itself weighs something.

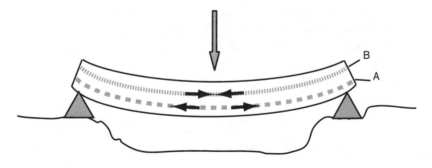

Figure 6. Distortion of a beam

Think of the forces holding the atoms in the beam together as tiny springs stretching from one atom to the next. The net effect of the deflection of the beam along a line like the one labeled "A" is to stretch those interatomic springs, while the effect along line "B" is to compress them. As with any other spring, when the interatomic springs are stretched, they pull back; and when they are compressed, they try to push back. Thus, the effect on the beam's deflection is to generate forces between atoms that resist further deflection.

This way of looking at how materials deform when they are carrying a weight explains a common observation at construction sites—the fact that steel beams always have an I-shaped cross section (the so-called I beams). The interatomic springs on the two outer surfaces of the beam are stretched (or compressed) more than those between other atoms, thus exerting a greater force than that associated with atoms in the beam's interior. It makes sense, therefore, to put more steel on the outer edges, where the atoms work to maximum effect, than to put it on the inside.

Different materials have different-strength interatomic springs and will therefore be able to support different weights. Thus, a material like steel that can stretch and flex will be a better bridge material than stone, whose interatomic springs are relatively stiff and inflexible.

Thinking about materials under stress in terms of their inter-atomic springs can get you to all sorts of unexpected places. For example, a flagpole or tree, as shown in Figure 7, is just a beam turned on its side and clamped at one end. As with a bridge, springs along some lines will be compressed, while those along others will be stretched. The ability of a tree to come back to an upright position after it has bent depends on the ability of those springs to exert enough force to overcome the downward pull of its weight. If the tree gets too tall, the extra weight overcomes the springs and the tree is permanently bent. Thus, the strength of the interatomic springs sets a limit on a tree's height. For a pine tree a foot across, for example, that limit is about 100 feet. I know of no better way to illustrate the essential unity of nature than to note that the amount of traffic the Golden Gate can support and the height reached by the tree outside your window are governed by the same law.

How long a bridge can be—how big a space it can span—depends on the kinds of materials in it. The earliest bridges were

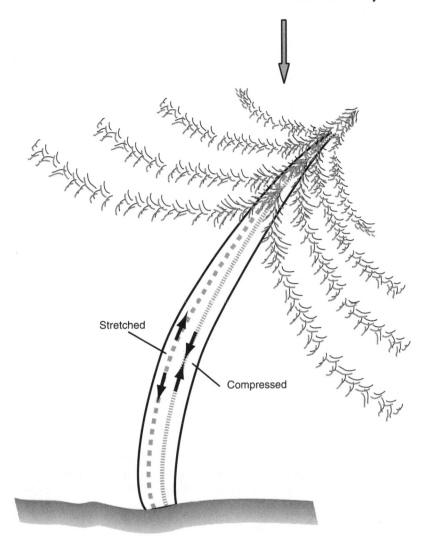

Figure 7. The interatomic springs of a tree

undoubtedly tree trunks laid over streams. (Indeed, I regularly use this sort of bridge during my summer hikes in the mountains, courtesy of the Department of the Interior.) More advanced versions of this sort of bridge can still be found, although in the United States they tend to be preserved for their artistic or historic value and are little used; the covered bridges of New

England are a good example of what I mean. Wood simply isn't a strong enough material to carry heavy weights or span long distances, and long wooden bridges usually need supports every 20 feet or so to keep the beams from sagging.

Stone arches have also been used for bridges from time immemorial. The arch is a wonderful design. In the word of one engineer, "It's almost impossible to build an arch that will fall down" (although, to be sure, a few individuals have accomplished this feat). In its simplest form, a bridge built on an arch will be a half circle, with the gravitational cascade directed to the sides, as we discussed in Chapter 5. These sorts of humpbacked stone bridges can be seen all over Europe, though they tend to be valued now more for their ability to draw tourists than anything else.

The problem with the arch is one of simple geometry. The bigger the space you want to span, the bigger the radius of the arch has to be—hence, the higher the hump in the middle of the bridge. One way to get around this difficulty is to span a large space by building several arches in a row. The old Roman aqueducts were built this way, as were the stone bridges that spanned rivers in medieval cities.

My own favorite multiarched bridge is the Karlův Most (King Karel's Bridge) that crosses the Vltava River in the Old Town of Prague. Built in the 1300s, it has guard towers at each end and intricate stone statues of saints every 20 feet or so along each side. It is no longer used for traffic but has become a kind of open-air mall, with street vendors and artists setting up shop against the parapets. During the Velvet Revolution of 1989, it served as a staging point for the demonstrations that brought an end to the Communist government.

Stories about the bridge abound. My own favorite concerns the fact that the builders strengthened the mortar by mixing in raw eggs (it's unconventional, I know, but on the other hand the bridge is still there 700 years later). Every village was given a quota of eggs to be delivered to the bridge, a fact that caused a certain amount of grumbling. One village decided to do something about the tax, and hard-boiled their eggs before they sent them. The official histories say that the king thought it was a great joke and exempted that village from having to deliver any more eggs.

It was the advent of railroads in the nineteenth century that really stimulated the building of bridges. The reason is simple: it's hard to get a locomotive to go up a hill. A river valley with broad, sloping sides presents no particular problem to someone on foot or horseback. The only bridge the traveler needs is the one over the river itself. A train, on the other hand, may need a bridge running across the whole valley so that it has a level run from one side to the other.

At first, railroad bridges (mostly in England) were extensions of the past—long rows of brick arches that are still part of the national transportation system. But as cheap steel became available, there was a revolution in bridge building—the same sort that permitted the construction of skyscrapers. New vistas opened, new dreams were dreamt, and the seemingly impossible was accomplished.

The most spectacular vehicle for change was an adaptation of an old invention, the suspension bridge. In such a bridge, long cables—rope, perhaps, or steel—are strung over the chasm to be bridged, and then the roadway is hung (suspended) from the cables (see Figure 8). Before the nineteenth century, suspension bridges were usually rickety things limited to pedestrian traffic—the kind you see in photos of people trekking in the Himalayas today. The first modern suspension bridge was built in 1825 in England, using wrought-iron chains to hold the roadway.

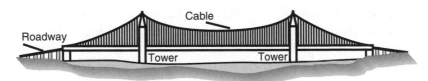

Figure 8. Suspension bridge

THE BROOKLYN BRIDGE AND THE GOLDEN GATE

We Americans are fortunate because we have two of the world's most beautiful suspension bridges, one on each coast. The Brooklyn Bridge in New York and the Golden Gate Bridge in San Francisco remain the most admired (and most photographed) bridges anywhere, though the latter is no longer the world's longest. It's no accident, of course, that our two most spectacular bridges are located in two of our most spectacular harbors, since the spanning of large stretches of open water is one of the most difficult engineering challenges there is.

Construction on the Brooklyn Bridge, linking the island of Manhattan to the suburb of Brooklyn, started in 1870. The most difficult problem the engineers faced was putting up the two towers that hold the cables, because the bases of the towers had to stand in the middle of the East River, under almost 80 feet of water.

To get down to a solid foundation under the river mud, the engineers used a large steel box called a caisson. Think of it as an inverted cup pushed down into the water so that its edges rest on the river bottom. Air was pumped into the caisson to keep the water out, and men went down through a shaft and started digging. As they cleared the mud away from near the caisson's edges, it sank down farther and farther into the river bottom.

As the caisson sank, other men on the surface laid stonework on its top. As the digging went on, the caisson would sink lower into the bottom and the stonework would go up to keep pace and stay above water level. Eventually, the "sandhogs" in the caisson got to a solid footing, at which point the caisson was filled with concrete and the tower built up from the stonework.

As you can probably guess, this sort of operation is pretty dangerous. For one thing, once the caisson is below 30 feet of water or so, the pressure of the air has to be kept so high that large amounts of nitrogen dissolve into the bloodstream of the men breathing it. Unless the men return to normal pressure slowly, so that their bodies can adjust, this nitrogen comes out of the blood in bubbles. The same sort of thing sometimes happens when a carbonated drink is opened: bubbles of carbon dioxide cause the drink to fizz up. In the case of nitrogen in the blood, the bubbles can cause anything from severe pain to paralysis to death.

This condition, known colloquially as the bends (because abdominal pain causes the sufferer to double up), was first understood by a physician working in a caisson under the bridge across the Mississippi at St. Louis. It struck repeatedly at the Brooklyn Bridge, and the chief engineer, Washington Roebling, suffered permanent paralysis from the waist down because of it. Happily, we now understand the condition and know how to decompress those who work in high-pressure environments.

Despite the casualties, the caissons moved down (to rock on the Brooklyn side, hard sand in Manhattan) and the towers moved up. The first wires were ferried across the river and then hauled into place at the top of the towers. To my knowledge, the first person who actually crossed the bridge was one E. F. Farrington, the chief mechanic, who rode a boatswain's chair from one tower to the other soon after the wires were up. Eventually, more than 20,000 steel wires were woven together to make the bridge's cables.

Actually, the builders were fortunate in getting a wire from one side of the bridge to the other so easily. A few years before, the chief engineer building a bridge over the river near Niagara Falls, faced with a similar problem, had sponsored a contest (with a $5.00 prize) to find a boy who could fly a kite across the river. Once the kite was across, successively heavier ropes were pulled back and forth until the steel wires themselves could make the trip.

A half century after the Brooklyn Bridge, and a continent away, another group of engineers faced an even more daunting problem when they began building a bridge across the Golden Gate—the gap in the coastal mountain range that serves as the entrance to San Francisco Bay. Not only did they set out to span a larger space (over a mile of open water), but they had to contend with some of the worst working conditions in the world. Don't be misled by those beautiful photos of the bridge showing a placid red sun setting over a peaceful bay. When the ocean tides are up, the water funneling through the gap produces currents of unparalleled treacherousness. The winter storms that build up their strength over thousands of miles of empty Pacific create winds and waves capable of snapping steel I beams like matchsticks. In this environment, the engineers proposed to build the world's (then) longest suspension bridge.

In one way, at least, the builders of the Golden Gate had an easier job than their predecessors in New York. Only one of the towers had to be built in the water; the other could rest right at the Marin County shoreline. Originally, the engineers planned to build a large enclosure to shield the site of the south tower from the worst of the ocean storms, then install a caisson to get the foundation down to solid rock more or less as had been done in New York. In October 1934, the caisson was towed from its construction site in Oakland out to the south tower site. It was a huge thing, made of 10,000 tons of steel and standing as tall as a four-story building. The night it was moored into place, however, another storm sent swells surging into the bay. The 2-inch steel cables holding the caisson in place snapped, allowing it to bang against the walls of the enclosure so forcefully that the engineers were afraid the caisson would start to leak and sink wherever it happened to be at the moment. Luckily, the storm abated, but with more storms on the horizon, it was decided to tow the caisson back to Oakland and build the foundation without it. The engineers strengthened the walls of the enclosure and pumped the water out; and for several months, while they poured in cement for the tower's base, there was a man-made hole out in the middle of San Francisco Bay.

As with any large construction project, there was a good deal of political maneuvering connected with the Golden Gate Bridge. The whole project was strongly (and skillfully) opposed by the Southern Pacific Company, for example, primarily because it would destroy their profitable ferry business. As a scientist, I was particularly interested in one aspect of the opposition. In 1934, Willis Bailey, an emeritus professor at Stanford University, launched an attack on the bridge from an entirely unexpected quarter. He claimed that the rock on which the towers were to be built was incapable of supporting their weight and was susceptible to landslides. The stone, he argued, would be turned into a kind of "pudding stone," causing a catastrophic collapse of the entire structure. He was the precursor of what has, unfortunately, become a fixture in modern life—the scientific Cassandra.

Always available to the press, always ready with what we would call a good sound bite, he became a major public presence in San Francisco. Each time one of his scientific arguments was demolished (he appears, for example, to have had the wrong location for the tower and thought that there was sandstone under it instead of the much harder stuff that was actually there), he blithely abandoned that charge and went on to make another. He claimed that using a caisson was an attempt to provide a "literal cover-up" for the engineers' mistakes, even though the plans for the caisson allowed for permanent inspection chambers. When the caisson was abandoned and the engineers invited Bailey to come down with them and "stick his nose in the rocks" at the bottom, he simply declined and kept up the drumbeat of accusations. Eventually, of course, the construction of the bridge (including frequent inspections of the rock from chambers left at the bottom for that purpose) provided the final refutation of Professor Bailey's allegations.

The problem with this sort of episode—and with its present-day counterparts—is that there really isn't any way to prove that some disaster *won't* happen. Nor do official reassurances necessarily help, since they can often be interpreted as (and sometimes actually are) simply attempts at a cover-up. In the 1990s, when Americans are once again wallowing in conspiracy theories, it's a good idea to remember that accusations of incompetence or cover-up don't necessarily mean that either is really there. Think about that next time you see a photo of the Golden Gate Bridge, still standing on the "pudding stone" over half a century after it was built.

There are all sorts of stories about the actual building of the bridge. My own favorite was recorded in the words of a laborer named Frenchy Gales:

> I worked on a night [cement] pour [on the Marin County tower foundation]. There were guys down in the cement. You'd walk on it to level it off. They took a count and we were short one guy. Everybody started stabbing around in the [wet] cement. We couldn't find the guy. We had to notify his family. The timekeeper asked me if I'd come with him. It was 1:30 in the morning. We went to his home. Knocked on the door. The guy answered in his pajamas. The timekeeper nearly fainted. The guy said, "I got tired. I went home and went to bed." That was the end of him on the bridge.

I suspect there are stories like this associated with almost every large structure in American cities. What a shame that most of them are lost!

SUBWAYS

Subways are so much a part of our cities today that we seldom think about the technological skills that had to be acquired before they could be built. What do you have to know, for example, to drive a tunnel for long distances under the earth?

Tunneling is actually a very old technology. Miners in the ancient Middle East followed seams of metals into the earth, building tunnels as they went. In 2160 B.C., Babylonian engineers diverted the Euphrates River long enough to build a brick-lined tunnel underneath it. The great Egyptian temple at Abu Simbel, built about 1250 B.C. and saved from the flooding caused by the Aswan High Dam in this century, had tunnels going back several hundred feet into solid sandstone. Through the Middle Ages, tunneling had important military applications. Someone laying siege to a castle or walled town would have his engineers tunnel under the ramparts, holding the roof of the tunnel up with wooden beams. The beams would then be set afire, the tunnel would collapse, and the wall, its foundations gone, would come down. (It has been suggested that the famous incident of Joshua and the Walls of Jericho was a precursor of this sort of strategy, with the trumpets serving as signals to the engineers to start the fires.)

This bit of medieval lore actually serves as a good introduction into the basic science involved in tunneling. The central problem can be stated simply: How can you dig a hole in the earth and not have the ceiling fall in?

Under normal circumstances, the forces on every chunk of underground dirt or rock are balanced. The downward force associated with the weight of the overlying burden is balanced by the upward force of the interatomic springs that have been compressed in the material below. In essence, this is the same kind of balance of forces that keeps you from falling through the floor as you read this. The downward pull of gravity on you is counteracted by the upward push of the atoms in the floor (a force you can feel in the soles of your feet). Dig a tunnel, though, and you remove one of the countervailing forces that keep the material in the new ceiling in place. The question, of course, is, what will replace it?

One technique, honored in history, is to shore up the ceiling with timbers—in effect, to replace the interatomic springs in the material that has been removed by the interatomic springs in wooden beams. The concrete tubes through which modern subways run are a direct descendent of this old technique.

In some cases, particularly in tunnels driven through rock, this sort of buttressing isn't necessary. The ceiling of the tunnel will deform, but the interatomic springs are strong enough to hold up the weight.

Having said this, I should add that there are some aspects of so-called hard-rock mining that would make me very nervous. While it is true that the interatomic springs in the rock may hold, they may do so only after some mutual shifting around. I remember a mining engineer's story of a new tunnel driven into solid rock. Each day, the miners would come back and find that the walls, ceiling, and floor of the tunnel, under the influence of the pressure in the surrounding rock, had moved in a few feet from where they had been the night before. They would remove the intrusions each day, only to have to repeat the whole operation the next day. Eventually, the rock stabilized, but I don't think I would have wanted to work in that area afterward!

The beginning of modern tunneling technology can be dated pretty exactly. One afternoon in the fall of 1816, a French émigré engineer by the name of Marc Isambard Brunel was looking at a worm-eaten piece of keel in the London shipyard where he worked. He happened to see a common shipworm, an animal that has probably sunk more ships than all the world's navies combined. Brunel watched as the creature, with a hard, horny shield on its head for cutting through the wood, secreted a material that hardened to coat the tunnel it left behind. The worm then braced itself against this new surface to gain leverage so that it could push its head farther into the wood.

In Brunel's hands, that lowly worm became the key to unlocking the space under the earth for human transportation. He patented a design for a tunneling machine that, in essence, is still in use today. Brunel's basic idea: pressed up against the working face of the tunnel would be a shield through which material would be removed. Behind the shield, an iron box would protect the workers and—here's the important part—horizontal jacks would be wedged between the box and the shield, providing a constant pressure to push the shield forward. Behind the box and shield, masons would construct the walls of the tunnel, so that the whole operation would be undertaken at once and the tunnel would be finished as it was dug. In Brunel's original design, the shield was made of planks that could be removed, one at a time, so that workmen could excavate material at the tunnel face. Today, the digging is done by huge drills, but the basic design of tunneling machines is still that of the humble ship-worm: you use the completed part of the tunnel to give yourself leverage to push the cutting tools forward.

When he wasn't tied up with his engineering, Brunel led a pretty eventful life. Fleeing from the French Revolution, he entered the United States on a forged passport (he did the forging himself) and is supposed to have met the future King Louis-Phillipe while hiding out in the North Woods. Between the time he got his patent for the tunneling machine and the time he got to put it into use, he spent time in jail (for debt) and had to be bailed out by his friends. By 1825, however, he had taken on one of the premier engineering tasks of his generation: running a tunnel underneath the Thames River in central London.

Now, the Thames isn't a very wide river as these things go— the proposed tunnel was only 400 yards long. But no one had ever run a tunnel under a river before, and the Thames, flowing through the muddy alluvial deposits of the English coastal plain, was a particularly nasty place to start. There were all sorts of problems: Water, sometimes in droplets, sometimes in cascades, came through the roof of the protective box and had to be pumped out. The solid clay Brunel expected to find under the river wasn't always there, and when one of his workers started to probe the bottom of the tunnel with a crowbar, it slipped out of his hand and disappeared completely into the swampy sand under the shield. And then there were the financial exigencies that, at one point, delayed construction for a seven-year stretch and, at another, drove the board of directors to sell admission to spectators who wanted to watch the work going on. The project went on for so long that some London papers began calling it the Great Bore.

It was quite an event, then, when the tunnel was completed and opened to the public in 1843—18 years after Brunel began it. There was a ceremony, complete with a speech by the Lord Mayor and a band playing a specially composed "Tunnel Waltz." However, by the time the tunnel was finished, no one really knew what to do with it. The original idea had been to use it as a freight tunnel for goods coming into the city from the south, but that was no longer economical. Instead, the tunnel served as a pedestrian mall where, by paying a toll, one could walk from one side of the river to the other without having to contend with traffic or the weather. Eventually, little shops and food stands were established between the arches holding up the roof. Nathaniel Hawthorne described it this way:

> By day the great tunnel was filled with stallholders, like an underground street market, and . . . the homeward journey was enlivened by exhibitions of paintings or a fancy fair with games of chance.

Sounds like the world's first indoor shopping mall! (The original tunnel is still in use as part of the London tube [subway] system.)

About this time, London was beginning to be the hub of England's rail system. Rail lines were coming into the city from all directions, but no lines actually crossed the city. A traveler from the west would come into one station, then have to go across town to get a train to the north. Given the incredible congestion of the surface streets, the problem of finding an efficient way to move people between the main railroad stations became a pressing one, not only for the city but for the nation. The solution, guided in no small part by the success of the Thames Tunnel: an underground train system connecting the stations.

Learning from Brunel's mistakes, the development of the London subway lines went ahead quickly, with the first station opening in 1863. To be sure, not everyone accepted the new technology without reservation. The British Prime Minister, Lord Palmerston, for example, declined to attend the opening run of the new system on the grounds that he wanted "to stay above ground as long as he could."

But the riders on those first London subways had something worse to contend with than vague fears of being underground. The engines that drew their trains were coal-fired, and despite efforts at ventilation, the air in the tunnels quickly grew foul. In the words of one journalist: "The sensation [of riding the train] altogether was much like the inhalation of gas preparatory to having a tooth drawn." The companies tried to counter the impression that their tunnels were unhealthy by getting doctors to testify that the air underground was good for asthma and other respiratory diseases. In 1890, however, the lines were electrified and the ventilation problem was laid to rest. (The sudden open cuts through which some London trains still run are a reminder of the engineering attempts to get more fresh air into the tunnels.)

London's subway system, or tube, as it is known to Londoners, showed that it was possible to provide quick underground transportation in cities, and other major cities began to plan their own systems. When they did, some fascinating debates took place. One of the most interesting was about whether intraurban trains should run in subways or on elevated tracks.

The debate got particularly virulent in Paris in the 1880s. Here's one argument against the subway:

> The subsoil is the repository of centuries of filth—the stinking inheritance of past generations. What mephitic exhalations will be released [by the tunneling]? Who can foresee what consequences may lie mucking about in this putrefying earth?

And here's another, couched in somewhat more nationalistic terms:

> What difference does it make to an inhabitant of London if he is surrounded by vapor, darkness and smoke. Parisians, however, love gaiety, color, light; they don't want some form of transport that is a foretaste of the tomb.

In America, on the other hand, it was the proposal of elevated railroads in New York that drew people's wrath. A document circulated containing the signatures of no fewer than 150 doctors, advising the public that riding the El would induce "mental and moral perversion, cerebral exhaustion, insomnia, mania, hysteria, paralysis, meningitis, and decay of nutrition." (There was some subsequent evidence for the "moral perversion" charge, anyway: apparently, prostitutes started renting second-floor apartments along the line in hopes of soliciting business from passengers.)

By the late 1880s, in fact, there were elevated railways running up many of the wide avenues in Manhattan. In effect, they turned the streets themselves into tunnels, darkening the lives of thousands of people. For the fact is that there can be only one upper level in any city. If that level is used for transportation, then the area under it will be dark and (usually) unpleasant. This, more than anything else, drove the move to subways. (It is an interesting footnote to history that the scrap metal from the dismantling of the Sixth Avenue El in 1938 was sold to Japan, while that from the Second Avenue line was used for ammunition in 1942 by the U.S. government. Thus, you could say the New York El fought on both sides in World War II.)

The first modern subway in North America was in Boston, where the Park Street station opened in 1897. It is a little-known fact, however, that a very unusual subway was operating in New York as early as 1870. It was a pneumatic train (a *real* tube) in which a large fan, located near where Nathan Hale's statue now stands outside City Hall, alternately pushed and pulled a car through a tunnel 312 feet long to a station on Broadway. The waiting room for this subway was about a third as long as the tunnel and contained, among other adornments, a grandfather clock, a large decorative fountain, and a grand piano!

Since these first tentative probings underneath the earth, subways have become a way of life all around the globe. In Washington, D.C., where I now live, the original Metro project is almost completed, and already the air is thick with proposals to extend and enhance the system. And with modern times have come modern tunneling machines. In the Washington Metro, for example, there are machines with drill heads 18 feet across for going through rock, some that have a large scoop for going through mud, and still others that operate at high air pressure to keep water and mud out of the work area. All, however, use the same basic shield-plus-jack design that Brunel thought of that day in 1816.

Megaprojects like the tunnel connecting England and France under the English Channel make use of the same sorts of monstrous drilling rigs and advanced techniques needed to build a modern subway system. And if the Superconducting Supercollider—the world's greatest atom smasher—is ever built in Texas, engineers will be called upon to drill a circular tunnel over 50 miles in circumference to house it. There seems to be almost no limit to how or where you can build a tunnel these days.

And to think that we owe it all to a single shipworm!

7

Moving Energy

GETTING THINGS DONE

What good is this device? Mr. Prime Minister, someday you will be able to tax it.

—*Physicist* MICHAEL FARADAY, *on the first electrical generator*

There aren't many times in the life of a physicist when he finds himself in demand at dinner parties and receptions. The last such occasion was in the spring of 1989, when two chemists in Utah announced that they had found a way to produce unlimited energy through what they called cold fusion. For a month (or, as one of my colleagues put it, "one moon"), everyone wanted to know if this was it—the final breakthrough to a future of unlimited cheap energy. Everywhere I went, I was surrounded by people wanting to talk about this new phenomenon. Then, too soon, it was over. The bubble burst, cold fusion was debunked, and life for physicists resumed its normal pace. *Sic transit gloria mundi.*

I guess it's no accident that energy is a subject that captures people's attention. Think of all the ways you use it in a typical day. You get up when your alarm clock (run by electric current or a battery) calls. The house is warm because it's heated (most likely by gas or oil). You cook breakfast on a gas or electric stove. And you get to work in a car or bus (burning gasoline) or a train or subway (using electricity). I could go on, but I think you get the point. There is precious little in the life of the modern city that doesn't involve the use of energy in one form or another.

Every city is a nexus of energy flows. Oil is pumped from the ground in Texas, Saudi Arabia, or some other oil field; refined into heating oil or gasoline; and brought into the city by pipeline and tanker. Natural gas from those same oil fields comes in through pipelines, to be distributed through the city network. Coal is mined throughout the country and hauled in mile-long freight trains to huge generating plants, capable of dumping a billion kilowatts into high-voltage transmission lines. All of this energy pours into the city, where it does whatever it's supposed to do and then leaves as waste heat in the atmosphere. A copious flow of energy is as much a part of the city as the bricks in its buildings and the pavements on its streets.

Now, we have to be a little careful with words here. "Energy" is a word with many meanings. We speak, for example, of the "energy" of a painting or performance. For a physicist, the term has a precise and narrow meaning, having to do with the ability to push something and make it move—to exert a force over a distance. When you lifted this book up to start reading, you were expending energy in this sense. Everything from human muscles to a jet engine expends energy.

There are other, less obvious sources of energy in the world. When something is heated up, its atoms and molecules move faster. This, too, is a form of energy—a form we call heat. One of the great milestones in the history of science was the realization that a fire is just as capable of producing energy as muscles.

There are two things you need to know about energy. First, it can't be created or destroyed but only shifted from one form to another; and second, it always moves from more useful to less useful forms. These two statements are called, respectively, the first law and the second law of thermodynamics. When you burn gasoline in your car, for example, you take chemical energy stored in molecules and convert it to heat. The machinery in your car converts this heat energy into the energy of motion that propels you along. Ultimately, that energy winds up as waste heat in the environment and is radiated into space. The energy changes form, as the first law dictates, and goes from a useful form (gasoline) to a less useful one (waste heat), according to the second law. We use it on the fly, as it were, as it moves from high-grade forms to unusable waste heat radiating out into space.

Throughout most of recorded history, virtually all the energy used by human beings (in cities and elsewhere) came from a single source: the muscles of animals. The main fuel that powers muscles in living things is carbohydrates, particularly a sugar known as glucose. Made in plants by photosynthesis, glucose molecules store energy from the sun in their structure. When the sugar combines with oxygen (burns) in the cells, that energy is released. The muscles in every animal, including humans, run on stored energy from the sun.

In ancient Egypt, for example, the sun shone down, pouring energy onto the earth below. Some of this energy was used to build glucose molecules in plants, and some of those molecules eventually found their way into human stomachs and human muscles. In some of those muscles, the sugar was burned, liberating some of that original sunlight and allowing a worker to help pull a stone up into the Great Pyramid. From a physicist's point of view, then, you could say that the Egyptian pyramids were built by solar energy.

I have always been amazed at just how much machinery can be run by human muscle power. I have on my wall, for example, a copy of a medieval drawing showing the construction of a cathedral. There is a huge crane in front of the construction site—it must be 50 feet high—with all sorts of pulleys and ropes to make it work. But if you look down into the corner of the machine, you see a wooden squirrel cage (the sort of thing we let hamsters exercise in). In the cage are three rather unhappy-looking men, walking endlessly and supplying all the energy needed to lift large stone blocks up to the cathedral walls.

Before the Industrial Revolution, there were only two exceptions to the general rule that all energy was generated by the use of muscles. One involved the direct generation of heat by burning things like wood. The other was the rudimentary, but very ancient, ability to tap the energy in moving water or in wind.

Although they have been around for a long time, waterwheels and windmills have never supplied a whole lot of energy, at least by modern standards. In 1085, for example, about two decades after the Norman Conquest of England, William the Conqueror commissioned a survey of his new lands, probably with an eye toward seeing what there was to be exploited. This first national survey was recorded in a publication called the *Domesday Book.* (The word comes into modern English as "doomsday," and it reflects the medieval belief that the Second Coming of Christ and the end of the world were near.) In that book, we find that England possessed no fewer than 5624 waterwheels. Figuring each wheel at about 2 horsepower, this would correspond (in modern terms) to a generating capacity of about a million watts—one megawatt. This would be enough to supply electricity to a smallish town today, and represents about one thousandth of the capacity of a normal large modern nuclear or coal-fired generating plant. Everything else needed to run the country came from burning glucose in the cells of animals.

One way of looking at the Industrial Revolution is to say that in the late 1700s, people learned how to tap the solar energy stored in fossil fuels—first coal, then oil and natural gas—instead of the solar energy stored in plant and animal tissues.

The story of fossil fuels isn't so very different from the story of glucose: Energy from the sun drives photosynthesis and is stored in plant fibers. When the plant dies, it and its cargo of energy are buried, perhaps in a swamp or bog, and over millions of years are converted into a fossil fuel. We human beings have mechanisms built into our cells to tap the solar energy stored in plant and animal tissues, but we need to build some sort of machine to get at the energy stored in fossil fuels. The Industrial Revolution had to wait until the first of these machines—the steam engine—came along.

THE STEAM ENGINE

That the steam engine was invented by James Watt is one of those things that everyone knows to be true but is nonetheless false. The first steam engine in the modern age was built in England in 1712 by a man named Thomas Newcomen. It was a pretty simple system. Coal was used to boil water to make steam, which was injected into a cylinder with a piston in it. The expansion of the steam drove the piston up, and when the piston got to the top, cold water was squirted into the cylinder to condense the steam. This created a vacuum in the cylinder, and the pressure of the outside air pushed the piston back down so that the whole cycle could start again.

The Newcomen engine was a cumbersome, inefficient affair. It sometimes required several minutes for the piston to go up and down, and the cylinder had to be heated and cooled on each stroke. Nevertheless, it was an immediate commercial success in coal mines, where there was a constant need to pump water from the tunnels and where the engine began replacing the horses that had been used up to that time. (Our habit of rating engines in horsepower traces its ancestry back to this particular episode of technology replacement.)

Watt's contribution to the steam engine came in a whole series of improvements to the original design—a separate chamber to condense the steam, a gear system that converted the up-and-down motion of the piston into the rotary motion of a shaft, and so on. His steam engine was the basis upon which the modern city was built, although, to be honest, the engine's potential wasn't universally recognized at first. In fact, the first spinning machine installed in Watt's native Scotland after his invention came on the market was powered by two Newfoundland dogs on a treadmill!

By modern standards, Watt's machine, even with all the improvements, was still incredibly inefficient. An engine capable of generating as much power as a modern lawn mower, for example, filled a two-story building. But for engineers in the eighteenth century, such a comparison was meaningless. For the first time, they didn't have to search for space near running water or keep a stable full of horses to run their machines. Instead, they could pick the site where they wanted power, shovel in some coal, and let 'er rip.

Over the years, the steam engine developed into many forms. It drove the railroads that carried goods and people into the growing cities; it carried ships across oceans regardless of the wind; and most important, it powered the factories that filled those ships with goods and those cities with workers.

For all its success, however, the steam engine has proved to have a fundamental drawback. Once you pare away the fancy additions, all the bells and whistles, all steam engines share one central property—they deliver energy mechanically, by making a shaft move or a wheel spin. This is a serious limitation on the steam engine's usefulness, because it means that the power must be developed close to the place where it will be used. Whatever is to be moved by the engine has to be connected to it. The great puffs of smoke issuing from a steam locomotive are a reminder of the fact that you have to carry both the coal and the engine along with you if you expect the wheels to turn. You can see the same thing in photos and etchings of turn-of-the-century factories, where long lines of lathes or other machines are run by belts connected to rotating overhead shafts near the factory ceiling. This meant that when the great manufacturing cities of the nineteenth century were built, every factory with power-driven machinery had to have its own steam engine (or engines) and supply of coal. A little over a century after Watt first started marketing his engine, a solution to this problem began to emerge from basic research in an odd field of science—the study of electricity.

THE ELECTRIFICATION OF CITIES

Electricity is different from other kinds of energy. When you turn on a light or use an electric tool, you don't need the source of the energy in the same building. In fact, the energy that drives the lights that allow you to read this book was probably generated some tens (if not hundreds) of miles from where you are sitting. Electricity provides a way of separating the generation of energy from its use.

Our modern electrically driven society owes its existence to an English scientist named Michael Faraday. Born in 1791 into the family of a poor blacksmith, he was apprenticed to a bookbinder to learn a trade. Surrounded by books, he began to educate himself by reading. Eventually, he became interested in science, and when a customer gave him tickets to a series of lectures by Humphry Davy (a well-known chemist and lecturer), he went. After taking copious notes in a neat hand, he bound the papers in leather and used them as a calling card to introduce himself to Davy. The result: a job as an assistant and an eventual career as Victorian England's best-known scientist.

In a series of experiments in 1831, he discovered that when a magnet is moved, an electric current will flow in wires near it. This discovery, part of Faraday's basic research into the nature of electricity, made it possible to build machines that could convert the energy stored in coal into electric energy carried in wires.

A simple generator—the device that carries out this conversion —is sketched in Figure 9. A loop of wires is spun around between the poles of a magnet. From the point of view of someone on the loop, the magnet is always moving, so a current will always flow —first one way, then the other. This so-called alternating current (AC) can be run through wires to the place where it is to be used. To get the electricity from a power plant to your house may require that it travel through many miles of wire, from huge power lines on pylons to the smaller wires that bring it into your home to the little cord that runs from the wall to your lamp.

So long as you have an energy source that can make a shaft spin, you can use that energy to produce electricity. The most common technique is to boil water to make high-pressure steam and then squirt that steam against curved blades attached to the spinning shaft (a device like this is called a steam turbine). It makes no difference how you make the steam—it can be (and is) done routinely by burning coal, oil, or gas, or by extracting heat from a nuclear reactor. You can also turn the shaft by damming a river and then letting water fall from a great height onto the turbine blades.

Today, the advantages of electricity for supplying a city's energy are so obvious that there would seem little point in arguing about them. When electricity was first produced commercially in the late nineteenth century, however, it was far from clear that it would prevail over its competitors. The first use of electricity was for lighting, one of the landmarks of urban electrification occurring in Chicago on April 25, 1878, when a jury-rigged system of batteries and lamps lit up Michigan Avenue for the first time. The demonstration showed up both the strengths and weaknesses of the new technology. The lights used weren't the steady incandescent lights we're accustomed to today but, rather, the

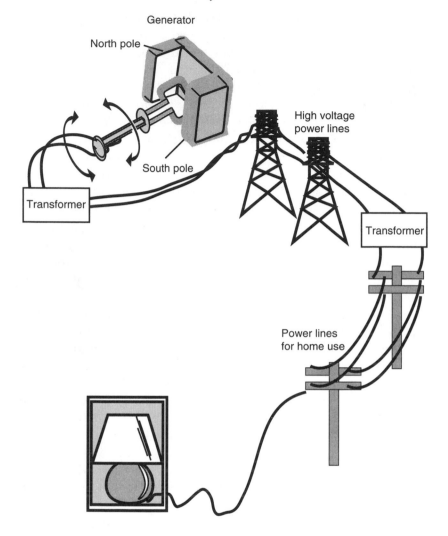

Figure 9. A simple AC generator

kind of carbon arc lights now used only for searchlights and stage lighting. They produce light by passing an electric spark between two cone-shaped carbon rods. In the Chicago demonstration, the result was an intense light: the two electric lamps produced an illumination equivalent to over 600 gas lamps. But they required constant adjustment as the carbon rods burned down. In addition, electrical systems in those days were unreliable in the extreme. The night after that first successful illumination in Chicago, for example, the whole system burned out, and it was months before another demonstration could take place.

The first people to use electrical power in a big way were stores and hotels in downtown business districts. At this stage of development, the main question was whether electricity would be generated locally, by each user, or whether there would be a central utility selling electricity to customers. Many businesses (Wanamaker's store in Philadelphia and the Palmer House hotel in Chicago, for example) installed their own generators. The first central power station was built by Charles Brush in San Francisco in 1879, but at that time the price of copper wire was so high that it was only economical to deliver electricity about half a mile—8 city blocks.

You can't imagine a city with generating plants every 16 blocks. Before our modern system could emerge, with its far-flung power plants and long transmission lines, a huge number of engineering advances had to take place. There's no single thing you can point to and say, "Here's the invention that made it all happen." Instead, there was a steady progression of nickel-and-dime developments that made it possible to generate electricity in large amounts and send it out over long distances—a better valve on a generator here, a better switch on a transmission line there. In the end, such developments wound up not only beating out gas lamps but giving our cities an entirely new shape.

There is no question that electricity is the energy form of choice for urban America. The energy history of our cities over the past century has seen the constant displacement of direct burning of fuels by electricity. The gas lamps were the first to go, except in "olde townes," where they are kept for their historical associations. They were followed by steam-powered factories and steam locomotives, and it probably won't be long, as we'll see in Chapter 12, before the gasoline-powered automobile joins the list. Let's face it: there's something very attractive about having energy available when you want it, while someone else has to deal with the pollution and other social costs of its generation.

THE URBAN ENERGY BUDGET

If you think of a city as a nexus of energy flow, then it is natural to do an energy balance sheet—to ask where a city's energy comes from and where it goes. This sort of data is somewhat difficult to gather for individual urban areas, but for the United States as a whole it is shown below:

Energy In and Energy Out

SOURCES OF ENERGY		USES OF ENERGY	
SOURCE	PERCENT	USE	PERCENT
Coal	23.3	Residential	17.8
Oil	41.6	Commercial	12.1
Natural gas	25.6	Industrial	39.3
Other*	9.5	Transportation	30.8

Note: About 35 percent of the primary energy is converted into electricity. About 71 percent of this 35 percent is lost as waste heat in generation and transmission; the remainder is spread among the different end uses.

*Includes hydroelectric power, nuclear power, and renewable energy sources.

A glance at the table shows the extent to which the great replacement of glucose by fossil fuels dominates modern society. Fully 90 percent of our energy comes from coal, oil, and natural gas. The simple fact is that virtually all of our energy comes from the same reserves opened up by James Watt over 200 years ago.

This is actually a rather surprising statement. We like to think of our time as one of rapid technological change, but as far as energy is concerned, that just isn't so. If Rip Van Winkle had fallen asleep in 1950 and woken up today, he'd see very little in the energy sphere to astonish him. To be sure, we use a bit more electricity these days, we no longer burn much coal for direct heat, and about 20 percent of our electricity now comes from nuclear reactors. But the basic outlines of our energy system wouldn't have changed much. The overwhelming percentage of the energy in 1950 came from fossil fuels, as it does today. Private gasoline-powered cars shaped urban growth then, and they still do so today.

If you contrasted the Rip Van Winkle who wakes up today to

one who fell asleep in 1900 and woke up in 1950, the difference would be amazing. The earlier Rip Van Winkle would have fallen asleep when steam engines ran factories and railroads and when most transportation in towns was still driven by animal muscles. Automobiles, diesel engines, and airplanes—the great fruition of the fossil fuel revolution—would all be new to him 50 years later. The first half of this century saw the fossil fuel–based infrastructure put into place, while the last half simply saw the details worked out.

From a purely economic point of view, there's nothing particularly wrong with running an economy on fossil fuels. They're cheap, they store a lot of energy, and they're easy to use. For Americans, the main inconvenience is that much of our transportation system depends on oil—and that our domestic oil reserves are not sufficient to keep us going. There is no energy shortage in America or even a shortage of fossil fuels. We possess over a quarter of the world's coal, which is enough stored energy to keep us going for centuries.

But there are larger problems with fossil fuel economies like ours—problems we can already see in our cities. The fact of the matter is that you cannot burn any fossil fuel without dumping harmful materials into the atmosphere. It seems obvious to me that our century-old love affair with fossil fuels is about to come to an end, not because of shortages of oil but because of our increasing unwillingness to add pollutants to the atmosphere. The first intimation of this trend can already be seen in the Los Angeles Basin, where automobile-produced smog has led to regulations that will, in effect, mandate a move away from the internal combustion engine for personal transportation.

HOW DO ENERGY SOURCES CHANGE?

Running out of a favorite fuel is not something new in America. Let me make this point by telling you about our first great "energy crisis."

Because urban civilization here began as a series of coastal cities perched at the edge of a huge forest, the first fuel of choice for Americans was wood. Virtually all the heat in Colonial cities was supplied by firewood brought in from the surrounding woodlands. As one traveler in Virginia put it in 1705:

In their Country Plantations, the wood grows at every Man's Door so fast that after it has been cut down, it will in seven Years time grow up again from seed to substantial Fire Wood.

But as cities grew in size, the woodlands were stripped, and by the mid-1700s wood was being brought into cities like Boston, New York, and Philadelphia by boat. In a scenario that will be familiar to anyone who lived through the oil crunch of the 1970s, the price of wood rose astronomically. In the winter of 1741, for example, the price in New York rose to 50 shillings a cord—over four times what it had been only a few years earlier. (A cord is a stack of wood 8 feet long, 4 feet high, and 4 feet deep.)

The response to this energy crisis was typical of the way people respond when a fuel of choice starts to get scarce. First, there was an effort to use the resource more efficiently, to get the same job done with smaller amounts of fuel. It was, after all, in 1744 that Benjamin Franklin announced the development of his Pennsylvania Fire-Place—what we now call the Franklin stove. The second response was to find another fuel. For eastern cities, this often meant burning coal imported from England or, when the internal transportation system had improved, burning coal mined in Pennsylvania and Virginia.

The quest for improved efficiency is important because it reminds us of one central fact about energy: in the end, what matters is that the job gets done, not the amount of fuel produced. We don't take oil out of the ground to put it into barrels, and we don't cut down firewood to stack it into cords. We refine oil into gasoline to run our cars so that we can get from one place to another. If we build a better car so that we can get from point A to point B with half the gasoline, then the technology has, in effect, doubled the supply of oil. In the same way, the Franklin stove increased the amount of heat delivered to homes by using less wood—in effect, it increased the forests around American cities without the growth of a single tree.

But improving efficiency doesn't produce radical changes in the structure of a society. It just allows people to go on doing what they've been doing all along. It is in the second prong of the response—the development of new ways of producing energy—that the real potential for change lies. And this ability, in turn, depends critically on technology. The invention of the steam engine made coal an important fuel, and the invention of the internal combustion engine did the same for petroleum. In fact, you can think of energy use in America as going through cycles. First, it was wood that dominated the economy, then coal, then oil; later on, as technology and the resource base changed, they sank (or will sink) into positions of relative unimportance (see Figure 10). Note that it has always taken people about 30 years to make all the adjustments needed to put a new energy source in place.

WHAT'S NEXT?

There is a whole laundry list of candidates for the next energy source, the one that will replace fossil fuels. The most prominent are the so-called renewable energy sources, which depend on ongoing astronomical or geological processes for their energy. Some of these, like wind or hydroelectric power, will undoubtedly play a role in our future, but only one renewable resource—solar energy—has the capability of supplying enough energy to run a modern urban civilization. (From a strictly technological point of view, I should add nuclear energy to this list, but given the political climate in America these days, I have little hope that it will figure prominently in our energy future.)

This is a very interesting development. Throughout history, human beings have always used solar energy at several removes: as glucose produced from photosynthesis or as fossil fuels. The move to solar energy, either in direct form (as in hot-water heaters) or as a generator of electric current, takes us back toward the ultimate energy source. In effect, it removes the middle man and allows us to use energy from the sun in undiluted form.

From the point of view of the engineer, however, there are two discouraging facts about alternate energy sources: (1) they are diffuse, and (2) they are sporadic.

By sporadic, I mean that they're not there all the time—the wind doesn't always blow, the sun doesn't shine at night and may be muffled by clouds during the day. This means that if we want to use these energy sources, we have to build both the original generating plant and some sort of storage system so that the energy can be used when it's wanted.

By diffuse, I mean that the energy of sun and wind is spread

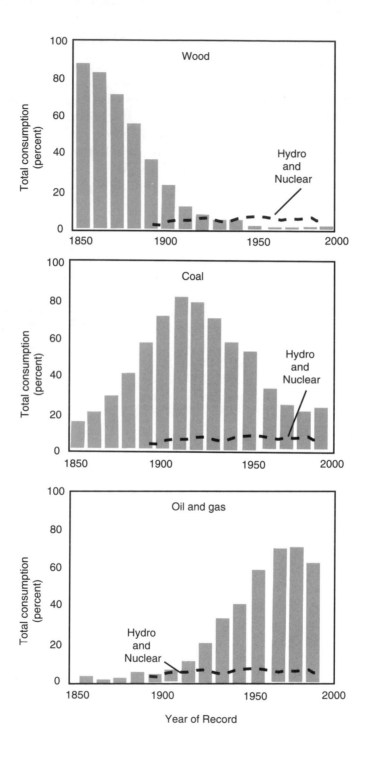

Figure 10. United States energy use

thinly. The average energy in sunlight (day and night) in the United States is about 177 watts per square meter. This means that to power a single 100-watt bulb, you'd need a square 6 feet on a side of the best solar collectors now on the market. You would need to cover enormous areas with collectors to generate a significant fraction of America's electricity directly from solar energy.

Let me give you an example of an alternate energy source from my own experience: firewood (although today it is given the trendier name "biomass"). This is a form of solar energy in which the trees act as both the collectors and the storage system. In the hardwood forests of the northeastern United States, you can expect an acre of land to generate about a cord of deadwood each year. A moderately well-insulated house will need about 5 cords to get through a winter, so you can say that each house needs about 5 acres of woodland to keep it operating on a renewable basis. I know this is about right, because I maintained 15 acres of woodland and heated a home in the Blue Ridge Mountains for over ten years. I almost never cut down a live tree, and when I left, there was more wood on the ground than when I came.

So how much land would you need to grow firewood for a 30-story apartment building? Even allowing for the fact that most units have internal walls that don't lose heat to the outside, it's hard to imagine getting by on less than 600 acres—almost a square mile.

Even if we switch to renewable energy sources, then, we can still expect to have a system in which energy is generated outside the city and shipped in.

A POSSIBLE SCENARIO

If we take the long view, there is little doubt that we're going to have to find something to replace fossil fuels as the source of our energy. Right now there is a great deal of ferment as people try to develop the appropriate new technologies. If you look at transportation, for example, you will find all sorts of prototype cars powered by things other than gasoline—solar panels, batteries, hydrogen, and fuel cells, to name a few. The situation is similar to that which accompanied the development of electricity at the end of the last century. Sooner or later, we can expect some of these technologies to win, push the others aside, and become the driving force in a new round of urban development. For what it's worth, here's my guess about how the process will play itself out.

The technology for building solar collectors (the kind that turn sunlight directly into electricity) will develop to the point where the electricity produced will be only a bit more expensive than that produced by coal. A largish area (perhaps a square mile or so) in the southwestern desert will be covered with collectors, which will feed power into the national electrical grid while the sun is shining. Other generators (coal, perhaps, or nuclear) will provide the basic generating capacity, but at crucial times (for example, on hot days when demand for air-conditioning peaks), the solar electricity will make up the difference. As we get better and better at making electricity through the direct use of solar energy, more of these installations will be built and the use of the stored solar energy in fossil fuels will decline.

The first big switch (already prefigured by the Los Angeles Basin situation) will be to replace gasoline with electricity as the main energy source for the transportation system, probably through the widespread use of battery-powered cars. After that, the main technological frontier will be storage systems that can take energy generated during the day and store it for use at night. This isn't a pie-in-the-sky idea, either. I recently had a chance to look at plans for batteries the size of a small building designed to do just that.

If this scenario plays out, we will have made, in the scientific sense, a change in energy generation as profound as that which followed the steam engine.

However, I must add that this great energy turnover will likely have almost no effect on the daily life of the average individual. Granted, the electric bill will be a little higher (what else is new?); but when you turn a switch, the light will go on, your TV will work, and your home will be cool in summer and warm in winter. Does it matter much whether the electricity comes from burning coal or a solar collector? You will plug in your car at night instead of stopping at the gas station, but you will still drive

around pretty much as you do now. This is all pretty mundane—
hardly the stuff of revolution.

My guess is that, as far as energy is concerned, the city of 2100
will not look all that different from the city of 2000. It will still be
a nexus of energy supply lines, and only the form of the energy
in those lines and the way it is generated will change.

8

Transportation

HOW ENERGY SHAPES A CITY

Any girl can be gay in a classy coupe
In a taxicab all can be jolly
But the girl worth your while
Is the girl who can smile
When you're taking her home on the trolley.

—Anonymous

The form of energy we use shapes our lives and our cities. A city powered by steam engines is different in shape and character from one powered by gasoline and electricity, and both are different from one powered by chemical reactions in animal muscles. The great transition from muscles to fossil fuels that marked the onset of the Industrial Revolution changed the face of our cities in many ways, but probably nowhere so radically as in the area of transportation.

Look at it this way: Napoleon couldn't move his armies in

1812 any faster than Hannibal had almost two millennia earlier. Julius Caesar got around in Rome pretty much the same way that the young Queen Victoria got around London. All of these famous figures had only one way to move from one point to another—they had to use muscles, either their own or those of some animal.

As a physicist, I know that it takes energy to make something go—energy to overcome friction where the wheel meets the road, energy to push the air aside as we move through it, energy to supply the force that gets us moving. My first question about a transportation system is "Where does that energy come from?"

The substitution of fossil fuels for muscles in transportation systems came in several stages, and each had a profound effect on both the size and the structure of cities. The railroad, which burned coal, made it possible for people to live at unprecedented distances from their place of work. The electrification of urban transportation, as exemplified in the development of the streetcar and trolley, produced a level of mobility within the city never seen before. Together, these developments shaped the expansion of the city in the late nineteenth and early twentieth centuries. The final energy transition, leading to the petroleum-powered automobile, has driven the continuation of that urban expansion which is still going on around us today.

What I'd like to do is follow the process by which these changes in energy technology played themselves out in urban transportation systems. Not only is this a fascinating story, giving us insights into how our cities got to be the way they are, but it shows how understanding the basic principles of nature leads, through a complex sequence of events, to changes in the world we live in.

TRANSPORTATION AND CITY SIZE

In 1819, the year of Queen Victoria's birth, London had a population of about 800,000 people. There was no place in the city more than 3 miles (a 45-minute walk) from the center.

Today, London sprawls out 30 or 40 miles in every direction. People who commute to jobs in the central city take trains or drive cars, and on a normal day the average commute time is 45 minutes or less.

The size of a city is determined by the ease with which people can move around inside it. When I first started looking into the history of urban transportation, I discovered that there seemed to be a general rule: Cities grew until the distance from the center to the periphery took about an hour to negotiate. I have to admit I was really excited by this discovery, thinking it was original with me. I planned to discuss it and give it some modest title like "Trefil's Law of Urban Expansion." Imagine my chagrin, then, when I found out that every city planner and developer in the world knows about the "Rule of 45"—the rule that says that most people will not travel more than 45 minutes to work or shop. From Baghdad on the Euphrates to Baghdad on the Hudson, the 45-minute rule has determined the maximum size of our cities.

For most of human history, this wasn't an important consideration. Cities—even famous cities—just weren't very big by modern standards. In 1600, for example, Paris contained only about 250,000 people; London, 187,000; and Moscow, 80,000. It wasn't until the mid nineteenth century that the first two topped a million inhabitants. In such cities, people could walk everywhere in town in less than 45 minutes.

Like primitive villages, many of these cities "just growed," with little of what today we could call city planning. Their casual arrangement—what scholars call a walking city—worked quite well as long as cities were small, most people stayed in their own neighborhoods, and there weren't too many goods to be moved. Cities of this type tended to be compact affairs. Other things being equal, points on the periphery tended to be located equal distances from the center—an arrangement we will see repeated in modern urban areas. (There were exceptions: when the first settlements were built in North America, for example, Phillip II of Spain outlined how they were to be laid out—the size of the church, the plaza, the fort, and so on. St. Augustine, Florida, founded in 1565, was built according to such a plan.)

When cities grew, the number of people needing to move from one place to another grew as well, and this led to a problem familiar to modern city dwellers—traffic congestion, and government attempts to ameliorate it. When ancient Rome was at its zenith, with over a million inhabitants, things got so bad that an imperial decree forbade anything other than official vehicles from being on the streets during the day. In modern times, narrow lanes that had accommodated medieval pedestrians and the occasional wagon with ease became impossibly congested. Stories of traffic tie-ups that would make the most hardened American commuter blanch became common. For example, in the middle of the nineteenth century, there were documented cases of merchants entering one end of London Bridge with a cartload of farm produce, then getting stuck in such a monumental traffic jam that their goods had spoiled before they reached the other side! In this sort of situation, people simply had to think about the consequences of the growth of cities.

A GEOMETRICAL DIGRESSION

There are some things about urban growth so obvious that I feel almost apologetic about bringing them up. They are so easy to overlook, however, that I want to make sure they're firmly in mind before we start looking at the history of urban transportation systems.

Let's take the simple example of a city whose diameter increases from 1 mile to 2 miles. In this expansion, elementary geometry tells us that the following things happen:

1. The periphery (the length of the "city wall") doubles.
2. The distance from periphery to center (the "longest commute") doubles.
3. The area (and hence, presumably, the population) quadruples.

The number of new inhabitants, in other words, is likely to increase much faster than the dimensions of the city. The effect of this growth depends on how that extra population lives. There is no general rule on this point. Indeed, as we shall see in Chapter 10, even computer predictions dealing with this question require what are, in essence, arbitrary assumptions.

We can, nonetheless, make some general statements. The key number we need to know is the number of people in the new periphery who travel often to the city center. This number could, in principle, be zero—everyone could simply stay in his or her own neighborhood. In this case, the city would just be a set of contiguous villages that were not in contact with each other.

Some postmedieval cities did, indeed, have a structure much like this.

It is more reasonable to assume, however, that there will be some connections between the old and new parts of the city. To see the point I'm driving at, let's work through the numbers on a simple example.

Assume that before the expansion 10,000 inhabitants of the original city used its roads and bridges to get to work. If the population quadruples during this growth, then the number of inhabitants after expansion will be:

$4 \times 10,000 = 40,000$

and the population of the new urban ring will be:

$\quad$ 40,000 (total inhabitants after expansion)
$\underline{- \ 10,000}$ (original inhabitants)
$\quad$ 30,000

Now let's assume for the sake of argument that one third of the new inhabitants actually use the roads in the old central city regularly, either by commuting to work there or by simply traversing it on their way to another destination. In this case, the number of new travelers on the city's central road system will be:

$^{1}/_{3} \times 30,000 = 10,000$

while the number of people using the (presumably) new road system in the suburbs will be:

$^{2}/_{3} \times 30,000 = 20,000$

Therefore, the total number of people using the roads in the old city will be the original inhabitants plus a fraction of the new ones, or, as in this example:

$\quad$ 10,000 (original inhabitants)
$\underline{+ \ 10,000}$ (new inhabitants)
$\quad$ 20,000

Roads will have to be built in the new parts of the city to accommodate 20,000 people—the part of the new population that will live and work there. You would probably expect something like this.

But look at what's happened to the central city. It now has twice as many people crowding into it *even though most of the new inhabitants don't work there.* As the story about London Bridge shows, most large cities in the industrial world began to run into this simple fact of life soon after the start of the Industrial Revolution. And it remains a central fact of life in today's megalopolis, where, despite the fact that most suburbanites do not commute into the central city, most central transportation hubs are being strained to the limit.

MASS TRANSPORTATION IN THE AGE OF MUSCLE POWER

Cities grow. This is the clear message of several centuries of experience. So what can be done to deal with the transportation problems that growth brings? One approach, exemplified by the broad boulevards of Paris and modern eight-lane freeways, is to build bigger roads and more bridges. Another approach is to make the movement of traffic more efficient by grouping travelers together in one vehicle. Bus lines, trams, and trains are examples of this approach. Finally, we can finesse the geometrical constraints completely by moving traffic to a plane different from the city surface. Elevated railways (like Chicago's El) lift traffic above the ground; subways move it below. A recent variation on this theme is found in many cities today: keep vehicular traffic on the ground and build a new "surface" of walkways, parks, and buildings above it. Except for mass transportation, all of these methods of dealing with congestion have obvious limits. There is, after all, only so much space in a central city that can be used for freeways and tunnels.

But mass transportation needn't necessarily wait for breakthroughs in energy technology. In fact, in the nineteenth century, cities developed their first systems based on the use of one of mankind's oldest suppliers of energy: the horse.

As far as I can tell, the first public mass transit system in the world was inaugurated by a man named Henri Baudry in Nantes, France, in 1826. A retired army officer who owned a resort outside of town, he thought he could help business by running a short, regularly scheduled stagecoach line from town to his establishment. The stages left from a location in front of a hatmaker named Omnes, so it quickly acquired the name "omnibus."

Baudry noticed that most of his passengers seemed to be getting off before they got to his place. He must have been a good businessman, because instead of getting upset and trying to restrict the use of his stage, he realized that this represented an opportunity and began running stages all over town. His fleet of omnibuses was so successful that it was quickly copied in Paris, London, and New York, which by 1853 had over 600 licensed coaches.

But just putting people in horse-drawn wagons didn't improve transportation all that much. For one thing, the roads were full of potholes and puddles, so the rides tended to be on the bumpy side. For another, there was already so much congestion in the streets that travel was slow—in most places, it was quicker to walk than to ride. The combination of uncomfortable ride and slow progress was probably what the *New York Herald* had in mind when it commented in 1864 that "modern martyrdom may be succinctly described as riding in a New York omnibus."

The development of the horsecar in the mid nineteenth century eased this burden somewhat. Also called the street railway, the horsecar ran on metal wheels over tracks laid in the street—think of it as a horse-drawn trolley. The ride was smoother and the progress a little more rapid than was possible with an omnibus; horsecars typically moved at speeds of 6 to 8 miles per hour, or about as fast as a jogger. They caught on quickly, particularly in American cities, where they provided transportation to what were then outlying suburbs. In New York, for example, lines on Second and Sixth avenues reached to what is now Central Park, and well-to-do people could commute downtown to work in less than 45 minutes. In the words of one Philadelphian in 1859:

> These passenger cars, which are street railroads with horse power, are a great convenience. Though little more than a year old, they have almost displaced the heavy, jolting, slow and uncomfortable omnibus. . . . They are roomy, their motion smooth and easy, they are clean, well cushioned and handsome, low to the ground so that it is convenient to get on and off, and are driven at a rapid pace. They offer great facility for traversing the city, now grown so large that the distances are very considerable from place to place.

Nor were horsecars confined to large cities on the East Coast. I was very surprised to learn from my father-in-law, for example, that the town of Billings, Montana—hardly a major metropolis—had a horsecar line connecting the downtown to the railroad yards. He can remember the tracks still being in the street when he was a boy (although the cars no longer ran at that time). Many scholars credit the horsecar with beginning the explosive dispersion of American cities by making it possible for people to live far from their place of work.

The organization of mass transportation systems was an important step forward in urban social organization, but it hardly marked a major breakthrough in technology. Horses, after all, had been used to pull wagons from time immemorial. Aside from the rather mundane development that saw rails put in city streets, there was very little to distinguish the early-nineteenth-century transportation engineer from his Roman (or even Sumerian) counterpart.

MASS TRANSPORTATION IN THE AGE OF STEAM

We usually think of the steam engine as the great driver of change in transportation systems. The first steam railroads were built at mineheads in England in the early nineteenth century. (Some of these early freight lines also offered a passenger service —using, oddly enough, horse-drawn cars.) The first railroad line in the United States, the beginning of the Baltimore & Ohio Railroad, opened in Baltimore in 1830. Long before this time, improvements in the steam engine had made it small enough to be portable and powerful enough to run not only railroads but ships as well.

In fact, that quintessentially American phenomenon, the flight to the suburbs, began in 1814, when the first steam ferry started operating between New York (what we would call Manhattan today) and the small farm town of Brooklyn across the East River. By 1860, the population of the town had grown from less than 5000 to 250,000 as people who worked in New York sought quiet, tree-shaded homes for their families. No less a personage than Walt Whitman, writing for the *Brooklyn Eagle,* talked of "Brooklyn the Beautiful," where "men of moderate means may find homes of moderate rent, whereas in New York City there is no median between a palatial mansion and a dilapidated hovel." He also cast a sardonic eye on the behavior of passengers when the ferry docked. His description will seem familiar to anyone who has ever negotiated a subway during rush hour:

> It is highly edifying to see the phrenzy exhibited by certain portions of the younger gentlemen when the bell (signifying the arrival of the ferry) strikes. They rush forward as if for dear life, and woe to the fat woman or unwieldy person of any kind, who stands in their way.

But it was the steam railroad that really shaped American urban areas. Its effect on cities was governed by one simple fact: a steam locomotive takes a mile or more to get up to its running speed. This means that the most efficient way for a railroad-driven transportation system to operate is to have towns strung every few miles along the railroad track. In this kind of situation, people in the "railroad suburbs" walk or ride to the station, then take the train into town. A typical string of such suburbs are towns along the Main Line near Philadelphia.

Not everyone was happy with the growth of suburbs. In 1849, the *New York Tribune* sounded a complaint that can still be heard in American cities today when it said:

> Property is continually tending from our city to escape the oppressiveness of our taxation. . . . While every suburb of New York is rapidly growing, and villages twenty and thirty miles distant are sustained by incomes earned here and expended there, our City has no equivalent rapidity of growth, and unimproved property here is often unsalable at a nominal price.

When the first urban transportation systems were built—London's Underground and New York's Elevated, for example—they used steam locomotives because there wasn't anything else available. But this form of steam technology just didn't fit naturally into city life and was quickly dropped. Some way had to be found to harness the power of steam in a form where energy was generated in a fixed spot, then sent out to be used on the streets.

For a brief period in the 1880s and '90s, cable car networks were built in a number of American cities. Today, we associate them with San Francisco, but Chicago, New York, and Philadelphia all used them at one time or another. A cable car works like this: A steam engine is used to turn a large cylinder that, in turn, pulls a long cable through a groove between tracks in a city street. The operator of the car pulls a lever that causes a pair of grippers under the car to grab the cable, and the car then moves along.

In San Francisco, such a system has obvious advantages. You don't have to lift the motor to get the car over a hill. On flat stretches of land such as are found in most eastern and midwestern cities, however, the cable system has proved remarkably inefficient. Up to 90 percent of the energy generated by the steam engine may go to pulling the cable, and only 10 percent to the cars themselves. Obviously, there has to be a better way to get the job done.

MASS TRANSPORTATION
IN THE AGE OF ELECTRICITY

That "better way" was demonstrated by a man named Frank Sprague in 1887. Working in Richmond, Virginia, he built the first electrically operated street railroad system—the first trolley. In this system, steam turbines generated electricity at a central location, and the electricity was run out to the cars through wires above the streets. A flexibly mounted pole on top of the car maintained contact with these wires and fed the electricity to the car's motor. (The word "trolley" is a corruption of "troller," the technical word for a little wheel at the end of the pole.)

Sprague installed some 12 miles of track in the Richmond system, but he never really cleared a profit on it. His demonstration was such a technical success, however, that cities all over the country began buying his equipment and taking out licenses on his patents. By 1893, there were no fewer than 250 electric railway companies in the United States; by 1903, there were some 30,000 miles of electrified street railways. Even in our own age of rapid change, when new subdivisions seem to spring up overnight, it's a little hard to envision such a massive revolution in transportation taking place in just 15 years.

The streetcars accelerated the explosion of American cities. "Streetcar suburbs" grew up around every major city, connected to the city by steel tracks and overhead wires. There were even interurban trolleys; for example, you could go from New York to Philadelphia on the streetcar. The "interurbans" also ran to small farm towns outside of cities. I can recall my grandfather talking about how he used to ride them out from Chicago to buy farm produce. Many of what are now established city neighborhoods and close suburbs got their start from the streetcars.

Like the steam railroad, streetcars produced a characteristic pattern of city growth. If a typical ride downtown is 20 minutes, then the Rule of 45 tells us that most people will live within a 25-minute walk (a mile or so) of the track. In this situation, growth will be along a series of fingers spreading away from the city center. This pattern will, in fact, be typical of any system that depends on public transportation built around a central city hub.

MASS TRANSPORTATION IN THE AGE OF PETROLEUM

It was the development of the automobile that filled in the spaces between the urban fingers created by trolleys. It is a product of the most recent change of energy source, from coal to petroleum products. The internal combustion engine, which burns gasoline and uses the resulting energy to turn a shaft that runs wheels, is ubiquitous today. It runs cars, trucks, and buses, of course, but we hear its high-pitched drone on summer afternoons when people are cutting their lawns; in the woods, where chain saws cut down trees; and at construction sites, where a variety of machines are used to excavate and shape the land. The first vehicle powered by an internal combustion engine was built in Germany in 1885 by Karl Benz (whose name survives on one of that country's more upscale products). In 1903, Henry Ford formed the company that bears his name and soon began producing the Model T.

The great advantage of the internal combustion engine was its use of energy derived directly from burning fossil fuels. Thus, all the messy apparatus connected with the use of steam could be eliminated. Both the engine and the fuel in the automobile were compact, so that it was economical to build a vehicle that would carry only a few people at a time.

The "automobilization" of America is a story too well known and too well told to be repeated here. Suffice it to say that it didn't take long for Americans to adopt the automobile. Not long after World War II, there was one car per family in this country; and in the 1970s, one car per worker. By 1985, the number of cars in the United States actually exceeded the number of registered drivers, and it now hovers at about 20 percent more than that number. (I didn't believe this figure, but experts I talked to pointed out that many cars are owned by corporations and rental companies, and many families own seldom-used machines like recreational vehicles in addition to their working cars.)

With the growth of car ownership—with almost all individuals now having a vehicle at their disposal—a new pattern of city growth has developed. Cities now grow in rings, with all the land a given distance from the city center being used before land farther out is built up. This is, of course, the familiar pattern of "urban sprawl." As we pointed out earlier, cities took this shape when individuals controlled their own travel by walking. It's not surprising to find it repeated today, when we control our own travel by driving.

At first, this kind of uniform concentric growth produced a metropolitan area that consisted of a central city full of jobs, surrounded by bedroom suburbs full of commuting workers. Books like *The Lonely Crowd* and *The Organization Man* decried the spiritual aridity of the suburbs and helped create a stereotype of the suburbs that persists to this day.

But whether such sociological views are valid or not, from a technological standpoint there is no question that the modern suburb owes its existence and its organization to the internal combustion engine. This engine has one important use, however, that tends to get overlooked in the story of suburban growth: it can drive trucks as well as automobiles. This means that, like automobiles, trucks can "fill in the blanks" between rail lines in the urban growth ring. Consequently, almost as soon as people started migrating to the suburbs, factories and warehouses started migrating with them. From the very beginnings of urban expansion, there were jobs available in the suburbs.

THE MODERN AUTOMOBILE SUBURB

With the advent of businesses based on processing information instead of materials (see Chapter 9), the movement of jobs to the suburbs has intensified. In fact, when you look at how people travel to their jobs today, you find that the traditional suburb-to-city commute plays a much less important role than our folklore suggests. As the following table shows, today most American workers live in the suburbs and commute to jobs in the suburbs. The next largest category of workers are those who live inside the central city and commute to jobs there. The number of people who undertake a reverse commute (from city to suburb), or who commute from one metropolitan area to another, is almost as big as the number making the stereotypical commute from bedroom suburb to city.

Commuting Patterns of American Workers in a Metropolitan Area*

From	To	Percent of Commutes Nationwide
Suburb	Suburb	37
City	City	31
Suburb	City	19
City and suburb	Neighboring metropolis	7
City	Suburb	6

*Does not include people living outside the metropolitan area and commuting into it.

In a sense, then, the bedroom suburb filled with people who worked in the central city was a transitory phase in the automobile-driven expansion of American cities. Within a few decades of the time that workers began moving to the suburbs, the jobs moved to be near them. City planners and intellectuals still haven't grasped this fact, nor has the reality of what's going on on the outskirts of American cities penetrated the national consciousness. The central feature of what Joel Garreau calls Edge Cities is that a combination of personal mobility (supplied by the automobile) and a new kind of industry (based on information technology and the microchip) has spawned a metropolis characterized by a network of work centers, or nodes, of which the central city is only one. In such a system, people live in developments between the nodes and commute to work in them, not necessarily into the central city.

The emergence of the city as a network of centers rather than as a single center surrounded by residential areas poses critical problems for the people responsible for transportation planning. As we saw earlier, the movement of jobs to the suburbs doesn't necessarily provide any relief on the streets in the central city—especially if, as is usually the case, the central city remains an important node in the network. As far as the new urban rings are concerned, it is almost impossible to imagine a public transportation system that could move people efficiently from their highly dispersed homes to their highly dispersed jobsites. Having made our bargain with our automotive devil, we may now be stuck with it.

9

Moving Information

BITS AND PIXELS

I can state that I am personally responsible for making the American people the only people in the world who will interrupt sex to answer the telephone.

—*Bell Telephone advertising manager (1919)*

What hath God wrought?

—SAMUEL MORSE, *first telegraph message*

Plato thought that no city should have more than 5000 citizens. His reason: this is the size of crowd that can listen to the words of a single orator. Even the ancient Greeks, it seems, recognized a connection between the ability of people to communicate with one another and the kinds of settlements they end up constructing.

For cities are more than just buildings, more than just systems to move people and energy around. They are places where actions have to be coordinated, places where knowing what is going on in one area is crucial in deciding what to do in another. And this means that cities are places where information has to be transmitted from one person to another. Our ability to move information shapes our cities just as surely as our ability to move people and goods.

We're used to thinking of things like weather reports, police broadcasts, and various government pronouncements as parts of a city's communications web, but there's a lot more to it than that. A large organization like a city can't operate without a huge flow of information back and forth. Even so mundane an occurrence as a food store running out of canned peas requires information transfer: the store manager has to contact the wholesaler, the wholesaler has to contact the delivery man, and so on. If you think about complex operations like running a transportation system or a bank, you realize that the flow of information is the lifeblood of the modern city. Indeed, it's not an exaggeration to say that the information system in a city plays a role analogous to that of the nervous system in the human body: it keeps all the subsystems in touch with one another and ensures that the entire system works.

A city's information system places severe limits on the sorts of things you can do in an urban environment. If, for example, you are limited to spoken and written messages, then information cannot travel around a city any faster than a person can, and the entire pace of urban existence has to slow down. It is no accident that the modern spurt in urban growth has been accompanied by the development of more and more rapid means of communication.

Although we tend to think of the telegraph as an interurban communications device, it was first used to link fire and police stations within a single city to allow quick responses to emergencies. You can see this same effect operating in cities today, where the fax machine—capable of reaching any spot on the globe—is used to order lunch at the corner deli.

Since the invention of the telegraph and the telephone in the last century, we have been living in an absolute deluge of information, and it's hard to imagine a city operating without it. We read newspapers, books, and magazines; talk to each other on the telephone; write to each other by electronic mail; watch news and drama on television; listen to the radio; look at pictures on bill-boards. Even our computers talk to one another electronically. It's too bad that the term "information age" has become a cliché, because there's no better description of the time we live in.

Scientists who think about information have come to understand that there are two fundamental facts that shape the whole field of communications. The first is that, in some sense, all communications—pictures, words, sounds, even touch—are equivalent and can be compared to one another in terms of the amount of information they convey. The second is that all information can be put into electrical or electronic form, so that it can be transmitted long distances in a short time. If we can come to an understanding of these two facts, we can gain a new appreciation of the web of communications in the modern city.

INFORMATION

Give a mathematician a concept and he or she will find a way to turn it into a number. To an information theorist, there is no essential difference between a written sentence and a song, between a spoken word and a picture. They can all be represented by cold, hard numbers. I know that this sort of urge toward quantification bothers many people. I have gotten violent reaction from friends when I suggest that the *Mona Lisa* or Beethoven's Fifth Symphony can be thought of as a series of numbers fed into a computer. So before I start, let me say that I am not in any way suggesting that because works of art can be regarded as collections of information in the mathematical sense, that they are *only* collections of information. What I mean is that the experience of seeing a painting or hearing a symphony—the actual sensory input involved—can be represented in this way. The emotional experience associated with such input is something about which scientists, at the moment, have very little to say.

The most fundamental unit of electronic information is called the bit (the word is a contraction of "binary digit"). A bit tells you one thing about a physical system, answers one question with a yes or no. Whether a light bulb is on or off, whether a valve or switch is open or closed, and whether a bit of magnetic material is aligned up or down are all examples of questions whose answers convey one bit of information.

Suppose you have two light bulbs side by side. Each bulb can transmit one bit of information ("on" or "off"), and the two bulbs taken together can transmit two bits. There are, however, four different configurations the bulbs could have—both on, both off, only the right-hand bulb on, and only the left-hand bulb on. If you wanted to, you could put together a little code for these two lights, perhaps making them correspond to numbers as follows:

Information Content

Right-hand Light	Left-hand Light	Number
On	On	3
On	Off	2
Off	On	1
Off	Off	0

Because each light can be in one of two possible states, the code involved in the example is called binary. Most modern electronic systems—the computer is the most obvious example—use binary codes in their operation. The usual way of representing a binary code is to write it as a string of 1's and 0's. In our example, the "1" might represent "on," and the "0" might represent "off."

This simple example shows that with a binary code, the number of things that can be communicated is much greater than the number of bits needed to do the communicating. The two light bulbs in the example can send two bits of information, but they can transmit a choice of four numbers. With more light bulbs, there are more possible combinations, and hence more numbers that can be sent. For reference, here is the number of off-on combinations you can get with different numbers of bits:

Information Content

Number of Bits	How Many Numbers
2	4
3	8
4	16
5	32
6	64
7	128

8	256
9	512
10	1024

We can use the simple idea of sending information by turning light bulbs on and off to find the number of bits in any written message, from a single letter to a book. To see this, imagine that you had a bank of six light bulbs. You could then arrange a particular off-on pattern (e.g., off-off-on-off-on-on), flash the lights, arrange another pattern, flash again, and so on. Each flash of the bulbs would then send six bits of information to someone watching you. There are 64 possible on-off combinations of six bulbs, and with a proper code, this is all you need to send any written message.

Look at it this way: you could begin your code by designating letters—"on-on-on-on-on-on" = a, "on-on-on-on-on-off" = b, and so on. This would use 26 of the available 64 combinations. Then you'd need 10 more for numbers, another bunch for punctuation marks, spaces, ends of lines, and so on. It's not hard to see that you could put together a code in which each of the 64 combinations of "on" and "off" stood for an important piece of a written message. Thus, it requires six bits of information to designate one letter of the alphabet or one punctuation mark. One character = six bits.

With this knowledge, we can work out the information content of any written message. For example, a single six-letter word would require $6 \times 6 = 36$ bits of information (you would have to flash the six light bulb bank six times to spell the word out). A printed page, which typically contains 500 words, would then require $36 \times 500 = 18,000$ bits, plus a few for spacing and margins. For the sake of argument, say a printed page contains 20,000 bits of information. Then a 300-page book would contain 6 million bits, or six megabits. You could convey the information in the book to a distant observer by flashing the bank of lights 6 million times.

You can follow this chain of thought further. A large research library might have a million books. The information content of the library is then about 6 trillion (6 million × 1 million) bits. A complete set of the Encyclopaedia Britannica (1800 words per page, 1000 pages per volume, 28 volumes) is about 2 billion bits.

The point of this sort of exercise isn't that anyone would actually try to send a message with light bulbs. The bulbs are simply a pedagogical technique that allows us to state precisely how many bits of information have to be transmitted to produce a written message. Once you know this number, you can use it to analyze information contained in any form whatever. Instead of light bulbs, for example, you might talk about the orientation (up or down) of tiny pieces of magnetized material in a cassette tape, or about the modulations on radio waves, or about an analogous quantity in any one of a number of other media. No matter what is used to store or transmit the information, the *amount* of information, as measured in bits, is the same.

Consider the spoken word—perhaps the oldest form of human communication. When you speak, your vocal cords cause molecules in the air to move back and forth, creating a continuous change in air pressure, as shown in Figure 11. Your ear picks up this change and interprets it as sound.

You can convert this continuous variation in air pressure into a string of numbers by measuring the pressure repeatedly as the sound wave goes by. Each measurement yields a number, and that number can be represented by a string of 0's and 1's. Thus, any sound, no matter how complex, can be represented by a string of bits of information.

Let's look at your telephone as another example. When you make a telephone call, the receiver transforms the waveform created by your voice into an electric current. This current is then measured 8000 times each second. The number of bits needed to record each measurement depends on the accuracy with which we want to record the sound. In ordinary phone systems, measurements are reported as 8 bit numbers. From the table above, you can see that there are 256 different numbers that can be represented by 8 bits, which means that each sound measurement is recorded as an intensity on a scale from 1 to 256. This is the level of accuracy that will give you the quality of reproduction you hear on the telephone every day. More bits would yield more differentiation and better reproduction, but would be more expensive.

A telephone conversation, then, transfers information at the rate of 8 bits per sampling × 8000 samplings per second = 64,000 bits per second. A written message of the same second of speech

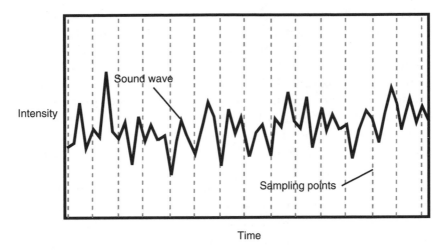

Time

Figure 11. Digital sound

probably wouldn't contain more than a few words, or a few hundred bits. What these numbers tell you is that the human voice carries a lot more information than the mere content of the words. All the things that we include in terms like "tone of voice" or "inflection" carry information not discernible from the script alone. If you don't believe that, ask yourself if there are really only 120 bits of information in the sentence "Of course I love you."

To get the higher fidelity associated with something like a compact disc recording, you have to extract more of the information contained in the original sound. Typically, you would sample the sound 44,100 times each second and represent each measurement by a 16-bit number. In this case, you would be able to distinguish between almost 65,000 grades of intensity, rather than the 512 in the telephone. In a CD, the digital information is stored as a series of pits in the disc surface. Light from a small laser is reflected from the disc, and depending on whether or not it encounters a pit, the light will or will not be reflected into a detector. Thus, the detector gives a string of 1-bit (yes-no, pit–no pit) signals that the CD player uses to reconstruct the original sound wave. A CD processes about 700,000 ($16 \times 44,100$) bits per second.

It's not only written and spoken messages that can be reduced to their basic information content by counting bits. It's possible to think about pictures in the same way. The basic idea is to divide any visual image into small square pieces by a series of horizontal and vertical lines. Each little square is called a picture element, or pixel. If the squares are small enough, your eye won't be able to distinguish them, and for all practical purposes, each can be thought of as a colored dot. Your eye will blend the pixels together, and you will see the smooth grading of colors characteristic of a visual image. At the end of the nineteenth century, in fact, a school of painting called Pointillism grew up around this notion. Images were produced by artists using only the tip of the brush to make a series of colored dots, with the expectation that the viewer's eye would assemble the dots into a picture. The most famous of these paintings is Georges Seurat's *La Grande Jatte* (also known as *Sunday Afternoon in the Park*).

From the point of view of information theory, the amount of information you need to reproduce the experience of looking at a picture is the sum of the information required to specify each individual pixel. A TV screen is a good example of this fact. The inside of the screen is coated with materials that give off light when they are struck by an electron. In the back end of the tube, electrons are boiled off of a heated wire and steered toward the screen by a series of magnets. When a stream of electrons strikes the screen, a brightly colored dot appears. Since every color can be made from a specified mix of the primary colors (red, green, and blue), color TV sets have three parallel systems like this, and the final color in a pixel depends on the mix of the three.

In North America, there are 525 lines each way, making a total of about 275,000 pixels on the screen. In high-definition TV (HDTV), the number of lines runs up to 1125, giving about 1.25 million pixels. In both cases, your eye produces the smooth picture from the collection of colored dots—the more pixels, the cleaner and sharper the picture looks.

How much information does it take to specify one pixel? We need to specify the intensity of each of the primary colors, and, as with sound reproduction, the accuracy you want in the final color determines the number of bits you need to specify each color intensity.

Suppose we want to specify each intensity on a scale from 1 to

1000. From the table, we see that we need 10 bits to do this. Thus, to specify the intensity of all three colors, we will need 30 bits. This is the information needed to specify a single dot in the picture. In a standard TV screen, with 275,000 pixels, the total information content is somewhat over 8 megabits—a little more information than is contained in all the letters in this book. A TV picture changes 30 times each second. For the kind of color accuracy we're talking about here, that means that information is flowing into your TV set at the rate of 240 megabits each second. (In point of fact, technical tricks reduce this information flow in standard commercial TV to about 200 megabits per second.)

So the old saying is true. A picture *is* worth a thousand words —in fact, by our calculations, if a word is worth 36 bits, a picture is worth 222,222 words.

Once you understand that every message can be analyzed in terms of its information content, you can apply the idea to all sorts of unexpected things. Human DNA, for example, is the genetic "message" that parents pass on to their children. The genetic code is contained in a sequence of molecules along the double helix of the DNA molecule. Each position can display one of four molecules, so each position represents two bits of information. There are 3 billion positions, so the total information content of human DNA is about 6 billion bits—three sets of the Encyclopaedia Britannica.

People involved in the search for extraterrestrial intelligence (SETI) have thought about the number of bits it would take to convey the content of a civilization. Although we haven't had much experience carrying out this sort of project between the stars, we have had a good deal of experience communicating through time. You could argue, for example, that what we know of ancient Greek civilization is contained in the information in a few hundred books and pictures. SETI people define a unit called the Hellas—the amount of information needed to convey a civilization—to be about a billion bits.

COMMUNICATING

Once you have information, there are only two things you can do with it. You can store it for future use, or you can transfer it to someone (or something) else. The oldest transfer and storage technology among humans is the oral tradition, with information transferred by speech from one person to another, stored in the brain of the listener, and then transferred again (perhaps in modified form) at some future date.

The driving force behind the development of modern communications technology was military necessity. From ancient times, military people used flags, trumpets, flashing mirrors, and even smoke signals to convey information quickly from one point to another. After the French Revolution, the new Republic (and later the Empire) found itself surrounded by hostile states and in need of a quick method of internal communication. The solution to the problem: the "optical telegraph."

This was the brainchild of a man by the name of Claude Chappe, who conceived of a series of towers, each equipped with a good telescope and a couple of movable hinged arms (see Figure 12). Each different position of the arms corresponded to a letter, and successive movements would spell out words. As soon as the men in the first tower started their signal, the men in the second would read it through a telescope and repeat it on their apparatus, thus sending it down the line. After some setbacks (some of his apparatus was burned when revolutionaries suspected that he was trying to communicate with the imprisoned Louis XVI), Chappe sent the first telegram on August 15, 1794. Eventually, there were lines all over France, with the tall towers waving their arms like something out of *Don Quixote*.

For half a century, a network of these towers connected French cities, and in 1852, when they were finally replaced by the electrical telegraph, there were some 556 stations in lines covering over 3000 miles. And although this system may seem crude, it was capable of amazing speed. When the English built a similar system in 1795, a message was sent from the Admiralty in London to the town of Deal on the English Channel and an acknowledgment received in under two minutes, despite the fact that the round trip covered over a hundred miles! Nevertheless, the rate of information transfer in the optical telescope was probably quite low. It's hard to imagine being able to send more than 10 to 20 letters (3 to 4 words) per minute through this system, which means that it transmitted information at about 100 bits per minute. Even a beginning typist can transmit information at a much faster rate than this.

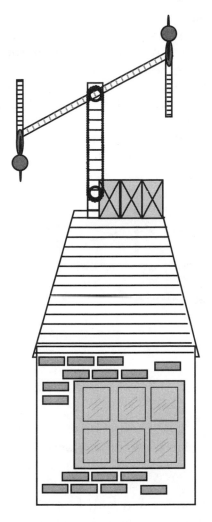

Figure 12. A Chappe telegraph tower

Despite its slowness, the Chappe system was so successful that by the 1830s Congress was contemplating construction of a Washington–New Orleans line. About this time, a well-known artist and art professor, Samuel Morse, realized that there was a better way to do the job. Using the new understanding of electricity that was emerging at the time, he designed a device that eventually evolved into something like the apparatus sketched below in Figure 13. Someone wanting to send a signal would push down on a key. This closed a switch and allowed electrical current to flow in the wire. At the other end, the current energized a magnet, which pulled down on another key, producing an audible *click*. Depending on how long the key was held down, the sender could cause a "dot" or a "dash" to be heard at the other end. Morse's code, which he designed so that his telegraph could send written messages, assigned different sequences of dots and dashes to different letters—"dot-dash" for *a*, "dash-dot-dot-dot" for *b*, and so on through all the letters of the alphabet.

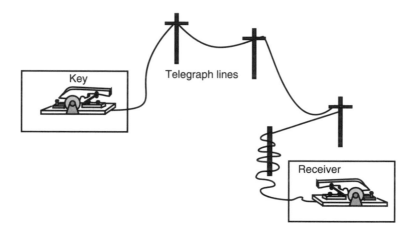

Figure 13. Samuel Morse's electric telegraph

Congress was so impressed with Morse's device that it authorized the then princely sum of $30,000 to have a line constructed between Baltimore and Washington, a distance of about 40 miles. The first message was sent on May 24, 1844.

No sooner had telegraph lines been spread around the world in the late 1800s than what analysts call a killer technology came on the scene. A killer technology is one that completely replaces (kills) an old way of doing things, as cars replaced horse-drawn coaches and transistors replaced vacuum tubes. In this case, the killer technology was the telephone.

Alexander Graham Bell was a professor of elocution at Boston University, and like many academics then and now, he supplemented his income with outside work. While trying to put together a device that would turn audible speech into writing (he was particularly interested in helping the deaf), he became fascinated by the working of the tiny bones in the human ear. He wondered whether a device built like the ear could produce and receive electrical signals that could be sent out over telegraph wires. The result of his work: the first working telephone, a device that he patented in 1876.

A simplified telephone system is sketched in Figure 14. When you speak, sound waves go out from your vocal cords and make a diaphragm in the telephone mouthpiece vibrate. In one of Bell's original working models, the diaphragm was made from the intestine of an ox, but today special plastics are used. The diaphragm is located near a metal plate, and the two together form part of a small electrical circuit. (The two plates form what is known as a capacitor.) When the diaphragm moves in response to the sound, its distance from the plate changes, and this shifts the small electrical current flowing there. The resulting current mimics your voice, and it is this current (suitably amplified) that goes into the telephone system.

At the other end of the line, the current goes into a telephone receiver, where it is used to run a small magnet; this, in turn, pulls on another metal diaphragm. The sound waves produced by this diaphragm are what you hear when you listen to the telephone.

The first commercial telephone system was installed in Charlestown, Massachusetts, in 1876. In this system, you rented a phone and a wire that connected you to only one other phone —a development that led some editorial writers to worry about the day when the streets of cities would be dark because of all the overhead lines. This system was quickly replaced by the present one, where calls go into a central exchange and are then routed out to a destination. Originally, the switching was done by hand, by banks of women (they went by the name "call girls" at that time) plugging wires into switchboards. Today, the switching is done by computer.

Both the telegraph and the telephone operate by taking information in one form (writing or speech) and converting it into electrical signals. Since they were developed, we have learned that once you have taken information from its primitive form

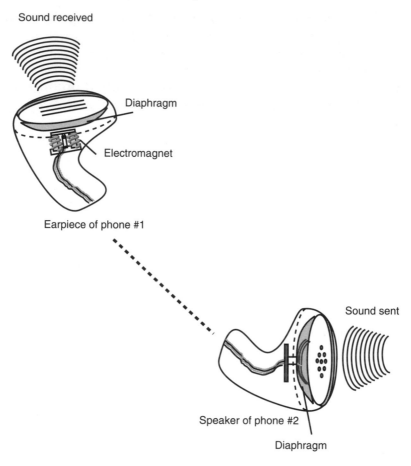

Figure 14. A simple telephone system

and translated it into an electronic format, there's virtually no limit to what you can do with it.

THE MODERN WEB

Stand on any street corner and, whether you can sense it or not, you are right in the middle of a shifting, changing flow of information. Under your feet—in copper cables or glass fibers— phone conversations, fax messages, and computer communications flow by the thousands. On the top of some tall buildings, you see radio and TV towers; on others, you see satellite antennas and microwave dishes. The information traffic to and from these devices is literally passing through your body as you look at them. The information content of all of these electronic messages swamps the more conventional messages you receive—people talking, traffic lights changing color, signs in store windows.

ANALOGUE AND DIGITAL

There are two major categories of electronic information transfer. When someone talked into one of Bell's telephones, the sound was converted into an electrical signal analogous to his or her original voice patterns. This is an example of *analogue information transfer*—transfer in which the medium of transfer is distorted in some way that is analogous to the original information source. The compact disc, on the other hand, is an example of *digital information transfer*—transfer in which information is converted to a string of 1's and 0's, transmitted in that form, and then reconstructed electronically. Here's a list of some familiar devices of both kinds:

List of Communications Devices

ANALOGUE	DIGITAL
Stereo record, Tape cassette	Compact disc
Xerox	Fax
Photograph	TV camera
AM or FM radio	Satellite phone call

A Xerox machine, for example, works by allowing light to hit a polished plate of silicon. Electrical charges leak off where the light hits, creating an electrical analogue of the original pattern of light and dark. Tiny bits of black powder then cling to these charged regions and, when heated, fuse there permanently. The result: an analogue reproduction of the original pattern.

A fax machine, on the other hand, breaks a page down into pixels—typically, 1800 across and 1100 down. Each pixel is considered to be light or dark, and represented by a 0 or 1. Thus, each page is represented by about 2 million bits of information.

After some recoding (e.g., defining the margin by giving the position where a line starts rather than a long string of zeros), this information can be sent in binary form over ordinary phone lines. Thus, despite the popular mythology, a fax machine is *not* a Xerox machine whose input and output are separated. (Here's a piece of trivia that you may find useful at a boring party. The world's first commercial fax system, which transmitted messages over telegraph lines, was inaugurated in Paris in 1865 [the "8" is not a misprint!].)

For most of this century, almost all communications devices were analogue. The big story today is that we are engaged in a massive, yet almost invisible, overhaul of the way we communicate with one another. As you read this, every aspect of our communications world—from telephones to TV to recorded music—is in the process of converting to digital transmission and storage of information. This process is inextricably linked to the availability of a single device: the computer.

THE DIGITAL COMPUTER

When you make a transatlantic phone call these days, the chances are about fifty-fifty that the information in your voice will be coded into a string of 1's and 0's, beamed to a satellite orbiting above the earth, then beamed back down to its destination. There the binary information will be reassembled into the voice pattern.

What makes this sort of operation possible—what has made the whole information explosion possible, in fact—is the availability of cheap digital computers. In one form or another, these machines are in constant contact with our lives. Sometimes they make our life easier (when we make airplane reservations, for example); sometimes they are a pain in the neck (when "the computer" sends repeated notices of bills that have already been paid). But they are always present.

A digital computer is a device that stores and manipulates information in digital form. (There are analogue computers that operate on information in analogue form, but they play a very small role in modern information systems.) There is a simple analogy that will give you a sense of how a computer works and how it manipulates information. Think of the faucets in an old-fashioned sink, the kind where there are a separate handle and spout for hot and cold water. These faucets could serve to carry information; for example, we could designate a faucet with water running as "1," and a faucet with no water running as "0." From the example on page 128, the two faucets would allow us to specify four different numbers.

Suppose now that we wanted to use these faucets to store and transmit some information. Let's say we wanted to set a meeting time. We could let one setting ("off-off") stand for noon, the next ("off-on") for one o'clock, and so on. One person could come into the room and set the faucets to the appropriate time. Anyone who came into the room after that could just look at the faucets and know the time of the meeting. In this case, the faucets would simply be used to store information, which could be read by anyone.

We could do more. We could send someone into the room with instructions to look at the faucets and then write a note that everyone could read. In this case, we would be storing information and printing (or, in computer jargon, "outputting") the results. We could even change the time of the meeting by sending someone in with instructions to turn the faucets on and off in a specific way. In this case, we would be manipulating the information we had stored, and the instructions we gave to the person going in and turning the taps would be a "program," or "code."

To be sure, two faucets are a trivial example of information storage and manipulation. But suppose we now expanded the room so that instead of two faucets, we had millions. Suppose we had enough faucets to store information about the names, addresses, credit card numbers, and seat assignments for all the passengers on all the flights of a major airline for next Thursday. Suppose further that we had the capability to go in and change the faucets as fast as reservations were made and changed. This would obviously be an enormously useful machine.

You may recognize the machine I have just described. If you substitute the flow of electrons (electric current) for the flow of water in the faucets, an electronic off-on switch for the faucets themselves, and a magnetic device for the place where information is stored, you have, in essence, a digital computer. Its basic working part—the switch that records the "on" and "off" and takes the place of the faucets in our analogy—is the transistor.

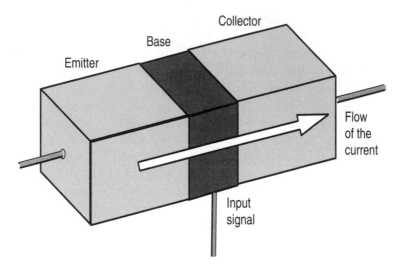

Figure 15. A transistor

A common type of transistor is a sandwich made of three pieces of modified silicon (see Figure 15). The "bread" consists of two pieces of identical material called the collector and emitter, while the "meat" is a piece of different material called the base. An electric current must get through the base to flow from the emitter to the collector. A small charge on the base can repel the electrons trying to get through and shut off the current, much as a faucet can shut off a flow of water. Just as a small amount of energy applied to a valve can turn a large flow of water on and off, small amounts of charge moving on and off the base of a transistor can turn an electric current on and off. The on or off state of the transistor, of course, represents a single bit of information, just as the flow or no-flow state of the faucets did in our analogy.

The microchip that is the heart of your computer or calculator contains thousands (or even millions) of transistors that can be switched on and off. It is the ultimate digital machine, for it can deal only with information expressed in the form of bits. Typically, information will be manipulated in the microchip and then stored in the form of the alignment of magnetic grains in a hard drive or floppy disk.

It is transistors in microchips that keep track of your credit card bills, your airline reservations, and (alas!) your tax returns. As you read this, billions of bits of information are flying around the world, transferring our money, keeping our transportation systems going, running our industry. But each of these transactions, as complex as it may be, ultimately can be broken down to the manipulation of bits of information, processed one by one in a transistor somewhere.

WHEN WILL IT END?

The communications revolution started with the discovery that information could be stored and transmitted electrically. Our ability to handle information has gone up from a few hundred bits per minute with the telegraph to hundreds of megabits and more today. The flood of information has us already inundated and shows no signs of stopping. While there may well be limits to the amount of material goods we can consume, there seem to be no limits in sight to the amount of information we can use, at least as far as people in information technology are concerned.

A few months ago, I had a glimpse into the "more is better, even more is best" mentality that dominates communications engineers. I was attending a seminar at NASA's Goddard Space Flight Center in Greenbelt, Maryland, and the speaker was discussing the use of compact disc technology to store huge amounts of information on optical discs—dinner-plate-sized versions of the ordinary CD. The talk was heavily attended by NASA scientists engaged in handling the flood of information being beamed down by our nation's fleet of space vehicles. After talking about the huge amounts of information the new technology would allow us to store, the speaker paused, sighed, and made a comment to the effect that at some point we would be able to store all the information we needed, and progress in information storage technology could be allowed to grind to a halt. From the back of the room came an anguished cry:

"Never!"

PART TWO

The City of the Future

10

Predicting the Future

Leave us reminisce about tomorrow night's fight.

—Boxing manager

The shape, the fabric, the very essence of a city depends on the technologies that its builders bring to their task. Looking at our cities today, we can see how the three technological threads we have traced—the ability to manipulate atoms, to extract energy from nature, and to process information—have made them what they are. The obvious question, of course, is whether we can use this understanding to predict the shape of cities of the future.

This is a particularly interesting question because each of these technologies is at a different stage of development. The ability to manipulate atoms to make new and useful materials is a mature branch of science, but in spite of this, exciting things are happening in the field. Will they have a profound effect on the cities of the future, or will they just let us do what we're doing more easily? Energy production is also a mature field, even though we are on the brink of yet another shift in our main energy supply, this time from fossil fuels to renewable energy sources. What effect will this have on the mobility that is so much a part of modern urban life? As for the third thread—information processing—we are just at the birth of this new technology. What kind of cities will develop around it?

Anyone foolhardy enough to make predictions must be wary of the pitfalls inherent in extrapolating from current trends to future "realities"—in particular, the faults hidden in that ubiquitous modern phenomenon, the computer study.

PREDICTIONS: THE COMPUTER MADE ME DO IT

We all make predictions every day, whether we realize it or not. We expect our car to start when we turn on the ignition, we expect water to come out of the tap when we turn on the faucet. We expect these things to happen, and order our lives accordingly, because they usually do. But we are also aware that there is no inevitability to such predictions. If your car has no battery, for example, it won't start—no matter how often you turn the ignition key.

These simple examples illustrate two important features of all predictions. They depend on our having some familiarity with the way things have behaved in the past, but they also depend on our having some sense of how the system works so that we can know under what circumstances to expect change.

So long as we really do understand how the system works, everything is fine. But if the system is complex (as a city certainly is), we may not know all the details we need in order to make predictions. We may not know where the battery is, in effect, or be really sure what it does. In this case, we make assumptions and use them in place of certain knowledge. All too often, I'm afraid, this simple fact gets lost, especially in large-scale studies.

In Chapter 8, we looked at the example of a city that grows by doubling its diameter. Let's use this to illustrate the point I'm trying to make. Imagine that you are on the city planning staff and you have to decide whether or not to start a very expensive engineering project, such as widening a bridge or highway in the old part of town, to deal with the expected growth. This decision depends on how much increased traffic you anticipate for the new bridge. This prediction, in turn, depends on where you think all those new residents will be driving.

As I pointed out earlier, there are many possible kinds of cities within the overall framework of growth. You could have a city where everyone lived and worked in his or her own neighborhood, in which case there would be no new traffic in the city center and no need to widen the bridge. Alternatively, you could have a situation in which all the new territory was composed of bedroom suburbs and every new worker commuted downtown, in which case you not only might have to widen the bridge but might have to build new ones as well.

Most likely, of course, you'd have something between the two extremes. Only some of the new residents would probably wind up using streets in the old city. In Chapter 8, we picked a fraction (one third) at random to make our point about traffic patterns in growing cities. In a real-world situation, you wouldn't be so arbitrary. You would look at the expected influx of factories and offices, the demographics of the expected new residents, and a host of other factors to determine this number. No matter how complex the calculation became, however, somewhere in each of these considerations you would have to make assumptions—from the type and size of factories the city would attract to the availability of federal funds for new highway construction.

The more complex the analysis becomes, the more the assumptions get buried. By the time you put together all the numbers that go into the final answer, it's easy to forget the assumptions that underlie the projections. This is particularly true if the analysis is done on a computer.

A computer simply follows instructions—instructions fed into it in the form of commands. For example, the exercise we did in Chapter 8 would be reduced to a series of commands like this:

1. Multiply the present population by 4.
2. Take 75 percent of the result. This is the new population.
3. Take $1/3$ of the new population.
4. Add this result to the current population. This is the number of people who will be traveling in the city center.

Stated this way, of course, it is clear that the assumption that a third of the new inhabitants will travel on the old roads is just that—an arbitrary assumption. It is also obvious that running the assumption through a computer doesn't change this fact.

On the other hand, a more realistic set of commands might look more like this:

1. Take the number of factories in the new area and multiply by the average number of employees per factory.
2. Take the number of offices in the new area and multiply by the average number of workers per office.
3. Take the number of stores in the new area and multiply by the number of employees per store.
4. Add (1), (2), and (3). This is the number of new inhabitants who will work in the new area.
5. Subtract (4) from the number of workers in the new area. This is the number of people who will be driving in the central core.

Stated this way, it's not so obvious what assumptions have been made to arrive at the numbers (such as the number of new factories) that go into the final working out of the result. This is particularly true in situations in which different people are involved in writing different pieces of the program. Each, though well aware of the assumptions in his or her own work, tends to take the others' pieces at face value. For example, the guy who does the factory projections may not talk to the woman doing the analysis of retail stores, and both might be blissfully unaware of the assumptions involved in the office-worker calculation.

In the end, the computer spits out a prediction that has the ring of authenticity because it gives projected traffic flow to eight decimal places. All doubts and questions get buried in a flood of false certainty induced by the flow of numbers from the machine. The result: headlines that scream MILLIONS NEEDED FOR NEW BRIDGES.

The lesson is plain: If you're going to make predictions, either in words or in numbers, *you have to state your assumptions explicitly.* With this in mind, I'll now introduce the set of assumptions that will guide my thinking as we explore the future of cities.

THE FIVE FUTURES

One way of looking at the history of cities is to notice that at any given moment there are limits to what can be done. Invariably, these limits are partly economic, partly cultural, partly historical. There are, for example, only certain things that a society can afford to do and feels are appropriate in a given situation. But there have also always been technological limitations as well— things that couldn't be done no matter how much money was available.

Look at it this way. Napoleon was a man with no shortage of vision and with the resources of an empire at his disposal. He caused many large structures to be erected in Paris and else-where, but he could no more have built a 50-story office building than he could have flown to the moon. Even in the unlikely event that he had wanted to build such a structure, none of the materials available to his engineers could have supported a building that tall, regardless of how much money and manpower he could have put into the project. This is an example of a tech-nological limitation.

The history of our ability to control matter, energy, and infor-mation leads, it seems to me, to an interesting hypothesis: *There are no longer any technological limits on the kinds of cities we can build.*

There may be cultural and historical reasons why we don't do certain things in our cities. There are certainly economic factors that constrain us. But I am suggesting that, for the first time in history, there are no *technological* constraints. Virtually any city that can be imagined can be built, at least in principle. It's a whole new ballgame.

Having said this, let me hasten to add a few caveats. Just be-cause something can be built doesn't mean it will be. We will see later, for example, that the main problems in building supersky-scrapers—buildings virtually as tall as we care to make them—do not lie in developing materials and designs; these are already available. The problems are traffic, zoning, cost, and other nontechnological things.

Available technology alone doesn't determine the future of cit-ies, though it plays an important role. In fact, I think the case can be made that technology defines limits to what cities can be—

how big, how populous, how well organized, and so on. People can choose the kind of city they want, but only within those technologically determined limits. In the language of the engineer, technological limits set the "envelope" within which a city must develop. And that, in the end, is why the disappearance of technological limits is so important. We can now have whatever kind of city we are willing to build and pay for.

But you really can't talk about the urban future without dealing with human behavior, a subject about which scientists (and especially physical scientists) know very little. I will, in fact, make several assumptions about the long-term behavior of human beings—assumptions for which I can give no justification except that they seem to be reasonable and to describe the way humans have behaved in the past. Specifically, I will assume that (1) the human population will continue to grow, and (2) people will continue to concentrate themselves in cities. The first of these assumptions agrees with every population study I have seen. The second seems reasonable, given the fact that urbanization has been a major trend for a century and a half in every advanced country in the world. Sometime in the late 1990s, in fact, the human race will pass a milestone: over half of us will live in metropolitan areas. Since the upshot of these two assumptions is that cities will continue to grow, predictions of their future must necessarily deal with how to handle the increased population. This will be my central focus in what follows.

I am also going to concentrate on white-collar workers—those usually lumped into the "information technology" category—and ignore the manufacturing workforce. My reasoning for doing this is as follows: Had I been writing this book in the 1890s instead of the 1990s, I would have been writing at a time when a large fraction of Americans were still employed in agriculture, still raising food for people to eat. Yet it is now clear that had I wanted to see discerningly into the twentieth century, I would have been well advised to concentrate on manufacturing and ignore agriculture. By the same token, I would argue that today the future lies with information processing, not manufacturing, and that that is where we should look if we want to make predictions.

This is not to imply that I believe manufacturing will somehow become less important in the years ahead. Agriculture is, after all, still a crucial part of our economy. But advances in technology have allowed a few percent of our population to grow enough food to feed the rest of us, and I am assuming that a parallel process will reduce the number of people involved in manufacturing to a like fraction in the future.

Even with the aid of these rather minimal assumptions, I am not going to try to predict the detailed future development of American cities. Instead, I am going to take some current technologies and see the sorts of cities they might produce if they were the only agents of change operating. In this way, we can explore many possible futures without binding ourselves to any of them. The real future, of course, will surely involve some blend of the ones we do explore (and probably a few that we haven't thought of).

Having said all this, I would like to make one personal comment. I do not find most of the futures I talk about very inviting. I would not want to live in most of them. But people have adapted to, and come to love, stranger urban settings than any I've drawn, so there's no reason why they couldn't adapt to these as well.

So let's look into our crystal balls and see what lies ahead.

A Day in the High-Rise Future

Dick rolled out of bed when the alarm went off, picked up his coffee, and strolled over to the window. The sun was shining brightly, but it looked like there were clouds down around 110. Let's see—it was winter now, wasn't it? Or spring? He really had to make an effort to get outside more often.

He bolted breakfast and ran to catch the 8:32 elevator down to 125, walked across the enclosed bridge to Building 20, and caught the 8:53 local up to 137, walking into his office, as usual, at just about nine o'clock.

After work, a quick trip to the food stores on 100, dinner in his apartment, and a quick handball game and swim in the gym area on 95 rounded out his day. Maybe this weekend he'd go down to G and take a walk outside. . . .

11

The High-Rise Future

And it came to pass, as they journeyed from the east, that they found a plain in the land of Shinar, and they dwelt there.

And they said to one another, Go to, let us make brick, and burn them throughly. And they had brick for stone, and slime had they for mortar.

And they said, Go to, let us build us a city and a tower, whose top may reach unto heaven . . .

—Genesis 11:2–4

I'm sure the designers of the legendary Tower of Babel, whose story this is, used state-of-the-art materials for their work. We know, however, that a structure made of ordinary brick, with "slime" (tar) for mortar, would hardly have reached the heavens. On the contrary, it would probably have been a fairly modest structure, lost in any modern city skyline.

The availability of appropriate materials has limited the size of buildings throughout most of recorded history. As we saw in

Chapter 3, it was the development of cheap steel that sparked a skyward surge in this century. But since the completion of Chicago's Sears Tower in 1974, there has been no new "World's Tallest Building." Does this mean that the upward movement is over? Does a 1500-foot, 110 story building like the Sears Tower represent the limit of skyscraper technology?

Since the late 1980s, architects have given this question a good deal of thought. What has emerged is a rather striking consensus: as far as engineers are concerned, the sky is, quite literally, the limit. It is human beings, as building occupants and as members of governments, who now determine what city skylines will look like in the future.

Take elevators as an example of what I mean. The fastest elevators in modern skyscrapers travel at about 20 miles per hour—roughly three floors per second. It takes over a minute to get to the top of a place like the Sears Tower or New York's World Trade Center. There's no mechanical reason why elevators can't go faster, but if they do, passengers' ears start to hurt. The limit on elevator speed, then, is set by the design of the human ear, not by the design of the elevator.

And then there are more subtle human constraints. As buildings get taller, they get wider at the base—the base of the Sears Tower already takes up a whole city block, for example. Can you imagine going to a zoning board with a request to use several blocks for the base of a larger building? Can you imagine the protests that such a disruption of any city would generate? The very thought reminds me of a rueful joke told by engineers. God comes to Moses and says, "I have good news and bad news. The good news is that I will part the Red Sea, let the Children of Israel through, and then close it over Pharaoh's army." Moses asks, "What's the bad news?" God's reply: "You have to write the environmental impact statement." (My editor at Doubleday, who works in a high rise in Manhattan, pointed out another difficulty with superskyscrapers. "There would be," he says, "even fewer offices with windows for people to fight over.")

Despite the very real difficulties involved in putting up supertall buildings, however, my own guess is that sooner or later someone with a lot of ego, coupled with political and financial savvy, is going to want his or her name attached to the world's tallest building. And when this person comes along, the

engineers will be ready. For despite the fact that in 20 years no one has succeeded in clearing the financial and political hurdles attendant on the next jump in building height, architects and engineers have worked out the details of how to build a "super-skyscraper." A number of them have gone so far as to produce drawings and scale models, as well as perform engineering studies. The verdict from these studies is clear: there is no technical reason why a 3000-foot, 200-story building could not be put up today, and even taller ones in the future.

THE TECHNOLOGY OF SUPERTALL BUILDINGS

Before we talk about the problems people will run into when they build superskyscrapers, let's dispose of something that—despite what you might expect—*won't* be a concern. The weight of a superskyscraper will not crush the rock that holds it up.

As we saw in Chapter 3, the chemical bonds that hold materials like rock together are pretty strong, especially when they are called upon to counteract forces trying to compress them. Although skyscrapers may look massive, they are actually pretty light (they are, after all, almost completely empty space). Even today, it is not unheard of for the rock excavated to make room for underground garages and utility rooms to weigh more than the entire building that is put up later. In this case, the bedrock is actually supporting less of a load after construction than it was before! So, although there are engineering problems inherent in superskyscrapers, sheer weight —what engineers call gravity load —isn't one of them.

The real problem that would be encountered in erecting a superskyscraper can be summarized in one word: wind. The higher up you go, the stronger the wind force gets. They are 4 times as high at the 100th floor as at the 50th, and 16 times stronger at the 200th. The wind at the top of a 200-story building will be 4 times as strong as it is at the top of the Sears Tower. All of the problems we discussed in Chapter 5 about wind force and vortex shedding will be multiplied in supertall buildings.

Unlike the first skyscraper builders, the people involved in the next push skyward will not have to worry about whether their materials are strong enough to hold up their structures in the face of stormy blasts. The modern steels we talked about earlier are plenty strong enough to support the weight of any supersky-scraper, as well as to keep it from being pushed over by the wind. There is, however, an analogy that illustrates the true difficulty. Think of a superskyscraper as being like a 10-foot antenna on a speeding car. The antenna whips back and forth continuously as the car moves. It is strong enough not to break, but you wouldn't want to be riding on it!

In the same sense, it is theoretically possible to design a 200-story building that sways 50 feet from the vertical in each direction when it sheds vortices—this wouldn't even begin to test the strength of the materials in its skeleton. If you built a skyscraper this way, though, everyone on the upper floors would get seasick, and you'd have trouble renting office space to anyone but test pilots.

The real problem is to keep the sway within human tolerance. If it isn't, the results can be disastrous. When Boston's John Hancock Tower was built, for example, the top quickly moved over a foot each way whenever the wind blew. Doors opened and closed by themselves and water sloshed in the toilet bowls, making the occupants quite nervous—understandably, I think.

Every building will sway—that's a fact of life. In a good-sized storm, the top of the Empire State Building will swing 2 feet from the vertical in each direction (although slowly enough that the motion will be largely imperceptible to the occupants). You can't eliminate sway, but you can keep it within acceptable limits. There are two ways to accomplish this: by making the building design stiff enough to resist the wind in the first place, and by incorporating active controls that take over once the building starts to sway. Both have been used in the past, and both will almost certainly be used in superskyscrapers.

In buildings of up to 30 or 40 stories, the ordinary steel frame of a skyscraper is stiff enough to resist wind force all by itself. But for a taller building, more has to be done. In Chicago's John Hancock Center (1,127 feet tall), huge braces crisscross the outside of the building, stiffening it against the wind. In New York's World Trade Center, the steel runs solidly up the outer walls; each of the twin towers is, in effect, a vertical tube of steel, and hence much harder for the wind to bend. Chicago's Sears Tower is built in the same way, except that it is made from nine such tubes, each of a different height.

These methods of wind control are passive—you make the building right in the first place and it won't sway too much thereafter. But there is another way of dealing with sway, one that you use unconsciously all the time. Think about the last time you were in a car or a plane (or on a bicycle). When the vehicle started to tilt going around a curve, you automatically leaned in the opposite direction. You've probably seen sailors do the same thing in a race as they lean far over the rail to keep their boat from tipping over when it turns.

The basic physical principle behind this common phenomenon is simple: Every object reacts to the sum of all the forces that act on it. The wind on the sails of a boat tends to make it rotate one way, while the force of gravity on the sailors as they lean over the rail tends to make it rotate the other. Thus, the force of gravity partly cancels the effect of the wind.

Engineers have learned to use this same natural law in controlling the effects of wind on tall buildings. In the Citicorp Center in New York, for example, there is a room near the top that houses a 400-ton block, attached to the building by springs and pistons and resting on a smooth concrete surface. When sensors indicate that the building is starting to sway in the wind, oil is pumped under the block, which is then free to slide on the concrete surface. As the building frame bends, the spring stretches, but inertia makes the block stand still. The system is designed so that the block doesn't start to move until the building itself has reached its maximum deflection and has started back. In this way, the block moves "out of sync" with the building—it moves to the left as the building moves to the right and vice versa. In effect, it plays the role of those sailors leaning over the side of the boat, supplying a force that opposes the one exerted by the wind. The result: the building's oscillations are damped. Mechanical dampers, some with slightly different design features, have been installed in many tall buildings, including the World Trade Center and Boston's John Hancock Tower.

Most designs for supertall buildings call for this sort of active response to wind force. The advantage of such designs is that they allow engineers to put up buildings with less steel than they would otherwise have to use. The disadvantage is that the designs are not fail-safe—they require that the control system be operating, or at least that someone be on the 200th floor during a storm to turn the system on. But they do give a sense of the sort of active, intelligent buildings we'll be living in during the next century.

Having discussed these various ways of dealing with wind, however, I have to point out that climate scientists are now saying that this problem may potentially be much worse than we think it is. People who examine climate records are starting to argue that the weather during the last century, and especially the last 50 years, has been unusually mild and that storms have been much less frequent than the historical average. This period, of course, coincides with the time during which we acquired our experience in putting up tall structures. In particular, the sorts of building codes that tell architects how to design for the "hundred-year storm" all assume that the sort of weather we've had throughout most of our lives will continue into the future. If this turns out not to be true, those codes will have to be toughened, and all the problems with wind will be just a little harder to solve.

SOME OTHER PROBLEMS

Any engineer will tell you that getting the building built and keeping it vertical are only part of the story in superskyscraper design. The real problems begin when you start to think about what the building's occupants will be doing. Before going on to look at the high-rise future, I'd like to talk about some of these problems and how they might be solved.

VERTICAL TRANSPORTATION

For starters, during working hours a superskyscraper might well contain 100,000 people—a population only slightly less than that of Peoria, Illinois. How do you get all those people to their jobs? This is what engineers refer to as the problem of vertical transportation.

The most basic question here is "Can you get people to the upper stories safely?" This question was answered definitively by Elisha Graves Otis of Yonkers in 1852. A sketch of his "safety elevator" is shown in Figure 16. Its key point? The cogs that are held away from the walls of the shaft as long as there is tension in the cable holding the elevator. If that cable breaks, the cogs automatically swing sideways and catch onto ratchets in the wall. The elevator simply stops where it is. It may be inconvenient to get stuck this way, but it isn't dangerous. In fact, there is a wonderful etching of Otis, doffing his top hat to an admiring crowd, as he demonstrates the safety of an open elevator by having a work-man cut the cable while he is suspended two stories above the ground.

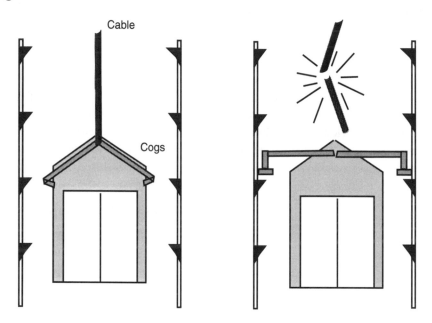

Figure 16. The Otis safety elevator

In a sense, it was Otis's invention that made the entire sky-scraper boom possible. After all, who would want to walk up 50 flights of stairs to get to an office?

The improvements in elevator design over the years have been largely invisible to the public. Today, elevators are driven by elec-tric motors that wind cables around a shaft or, in a few very advanced systems, by motors contained in the elevator's counter-weight. Safe, efficient elevators have become so much part of our lives that we hardly notice them.

The extra height of superskyscrapers poses no particular tech-nical problems per se. After all, gold mines use elevators that routinely lift quite heavy loads from 10,000 feet underground, and could easily do more. The fact that elevator technology sets no limits on the depth of mines or the height of buildings was brought home to me quite forcefully when I interviewed the chief engineer of the Homestake Gold Mine in Lead, South Dakota. I asked him how deep a mine he could dig if cost were no object. After a moment's thought, he gave me an answer that reveals a great deal about the realities of technical life in America today. "Boy," he said, "it would be hard to get the permits for that!"

So there is no difficulty in imagining elevators that could lift people 3000 feet into the air. The real problem in the superskyscraper is moving large numbers of people in short periods of time. Most of the solutions to this problem are already being tried out. In many buildings, there are express elevators to sky lobbies, where people can transfer to local elevators for the last part of the ride. With this system, you can actually have several elevators in each shaft (the Sears Tower, for example, has 87 elevators but only 40 elevator shafts).

Given the expertise of modern elevator designers, I can't imagine that vertical transportation will be a limiting technology for high-rise buildings.

Having said this, I should point out some of the novel situations that will face those designing elevators for superskyscrapers. One has to do with the effect of wind. If the sway gets too pronounced, a situation may develop where elevator cars are forced to stop because they get pinched by the sides of the elevator shafts.

Another problem, already evident in places like the Sears Tower, is called the stack effect. The air temperature and pressure at the top of a skyscraper are considerably lower than those at the bottom. This means that strong air currents will flow up each elevator shaft, so that the shafts will have to be sealed off and be virtually airtight. When revolving doors at the base of the Sears Tower broke recently, air blasted up the elevator shafts and was clocked at 70 miles per hour as it came out the doors of the observation platform. Obviously, some careful thought will have to be put into sealing off the elevator shafts in a superskyscraper.

If you flush a toilet on the top floor of a 200-story building, the water will be traveling at speeds exceeding 100 miles per hour when it hits the bottom. How do you build a plumbing system strong enough to withstand such a force? Even the ordinary force of water pressure could become enormous in very tall buildings. After all, the higher the location of a reservoir, the greater the pressure of water in the lines. This is why small towns go to the expense of putting their water supply in tall towers. In a superskyscraper, the water pressure on the ground floor could easily exceed 1000 pounds per square inch—more than seven times the maximum rating of standard plumbing fittings.

The most likely solution to such problems would be compartmentalization. From the plumbing point of view, a 200-story building would be seen as four 50-story buildings stacked end on end, with each smaller unit being totally self-contained in its water and waste systems.

CONTROL

How in the world will you keep track of everything going on in a 200-story building? Where are the elevators? Is the 157th floor warm enough? Is the water pressure on 183 high enough? If it does nothing else, the building of a superskyscraper will give systems-control people quite a workout.

It will be impossible to run a building like this without the help of computers, of course. And we already have a fair amount of experience with "smart" buildings, where sensors in each room keep a central computer apprised of the state of affairs and the computer responds by increasing or decreasing the temperature, light level, ventilation, and so on.

I have to admit that I remain a little skeptical about the notion of turning a huge building over to computers. I'm reminded of a friend who worked in a "smart" building. This building had automatic light switches: if motion sensors told the computer that no one was in the room, the lights were turned off; when someone came in, the lights went on automatically. The system worked beautifully until people in one office wanted to show some slides. They turned the lights off, all right, but as soon as someone moved, the computer turned the lights back on. For a while, they tried sitting stock still, but sooner or later someone had to scratch and the lights came back on. Finally, in what I regard as one of the great triumphs of the human spirit, the irate workers unscrewed all the light bulbs in the room and watched their slides.

Who knows how many little dramas like this await us on the 207th floor?

THE DESIGNS

This rundown of problems should give you some sense of the level of detail reached by engineers and architects who have concerned themselves with supertall buildings. Indeed, there is a long history of thought on this subject. The granddaddy of actual designs was done in 1956 by Frank Lloyd Wright. A mile high (528 stories) and topped by a 400-foot antenna, this building was intended to be the last word in skyscrapers (see Figure 17). It included such visionary features as atomic-powered elevators (design unspecified) and lower structures that extended almost as far below ground as the Empire State Building does above. As far as I can tell, no one took the design seriously, and it remains a footnote in books on architectural history. (The only mention of this building that I recall was a tongue-in-cheek article in the undergraduate humor magazine at the University of Illinois. *The College Tumor*—"An Outgrowth of the Student Body"—suggested that if Chicago didn't want Wright's design, he should build it in Champaign-Urbana. The city fathers were not amused.)

Today, there is an entire generation of more advanced (and more realistic) designs than Wright's. And what a collection they are! The 207-story "Erewhon Center" is a tube with external trusses. Its name ("Nowhere" spelled backward) is a joking response to the problem of finding a place on which to build it. The 210-story "World Trade Center" is proposed for a specific vacant site north of Chicago's Loop. It twists around as it rises, allowing diagonal steel girders 5 feet across to hold it down the way guy wires hold down radio and TV transmission towers. Other designs deal with wind in even more imaginative ways. In

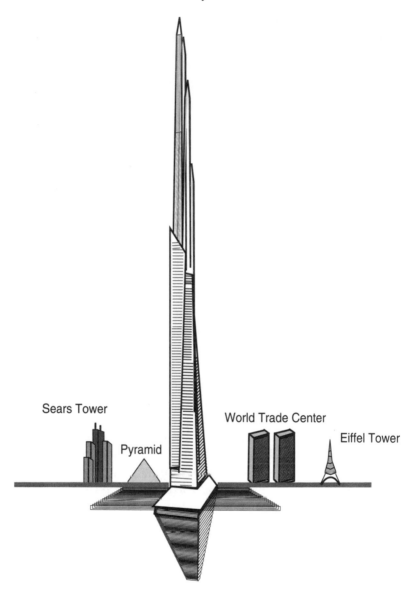

Figure 17. The Frank Lloyd Wright superskyscraper (with other buildings to scale)

some, large "sky windows"—holes a dozen stories high—just let the wind whistle through. In others, groups of superskyscrapers are connected near the top, so that each braces, and is braced by, the others. With all of the intellectual firepower that lies behind these designs, it would be truly amazing if at least one way to push up building height wasn't technically feasible.

THE HIGH-RISE FUTURE

Cities are concentrations of people, and as the concentrations get higher, space at the center becomes more valuable. When this happens, the enormous effort involved in building multistory structures begins to be economically worthwhile. Tall buildings mark the downtown regions of most major cities as more and more businesses are crammed into smaller and smaller areas. Suppose we take this trend to its limit and imagine a city in which high-rise technology has produced the ultimate concentration. What would such a city be like?

You'll probably be amazed at the levels of concentration that superskyscrapers can achieve—at least, I was when I first did the numbers. A 200-story building (3000 feet tall) would have about 20 million square feet of floor space. Allowing for elevator shafts, utilities, and some public space, and allowing each inhabitant 250 square feet of living space (about what you would have in a moderately upscale urban apartment today), there could be apartments for about 50,000 people in the building, or living and working space for about 30,000. The building would be only 300 feet on a side at the base and would therefore take up very little land area.

In fact, even allowing for space between buildings, you could easily put over 200 of these superskyscrapers (6 million people) on a square mile of land. The population of the entire New York metropolitan area could easily fit on Manhattan Island south of Greenwich Village. In effect, the area of New York could be taken back to its early-nineteenth-century size without any diminution in its population.

You can amuse yourself by figuring out how small your own hometown would be in a superskyscraper future. My adopted hometown of Red Lodge, Montana, for example, would fit easily into four floors of one building. The population of the entire Washington, D.C., metropolitan area could inhabit a series of buildings that would just about fit on the land now occupied by the monumental Mall (between the Capitol and the Lincoln Memorial).

In a sense, the high-rise future represents the ultimate ecological city. All the people would be contracted into a tiny space, leaving the rest of the earth largely free and "natural"—no urban sprawl, no shopping strips.

This is a little misleading, however. The high-rise city would still need energy, although probably somewhat less than a spread-out metropolis of equivalent population. Each tower block would probably require a couple of nuclear or coal-fired power plants, or perhaps a few square miles of solar collectors nearby to keep the elevators and air conditioners running. A small fraction of the population would have to live outside the towers to run these plants, to operate the farms needed to grow food, and to oversee the (presumably highly automated) factories. This pattern—most people living in metropolitan areas, with a small percentage taking care of things in the countryside —is a logical extension of the trend toward centralization that has already been going on in America.

What would life be like in a superskyscraper? We can get some hint just by thinking about the technical constraints on the building. To counteract the main structural problem—namely, wind force—it's likely that a set of towers would be connected to one another at the top for bracing. People could walk from one tower to another without going all the way down. Similar crosswalks every 20 or 30 floors among the towers would allow residents some horizontal (as well as vertical) mobility. You can imagine the city, then, as a kind of high-rise version of the Minneapolis Skyway, where it's possible to walk all over the downtown area one floor above the traffic, staying indoors the whole time.

There are already buildings in America that function in much the same way that a superskyscraper would. The tallest of these "mixed use" high-rise buildings is the John Hancock Center in Chicago. Standing over 1000 feet tall, the building includes 44 floors of luxury condominium apartments near the top, 23 floors of offices closer to street level, a 6-floor parking garage, and a 5-floor vertical shopping mall. Between the offices and the condominiums is a floor devoted to public space—gym, swimming pool, and grocery store (complete with delivery service). It is possible, at least in principle, for someone to move into the Hancock upon graduating from college and never leave the building until he or she retires.

People have already learned that there are some advantages to this sort of life. Joggers who usually run along the shores of Lake Michigan, for example, now run up the stairs for exercise on rainy days. On the other hand, knowing what to wear if you're going out can be a problem. It's not uncommon for the sun to be shining on the top floors at the same time that it's raining in the streets. The solution: residents phone the doorman to ask what it's like at street level.

I have to admit that this kind of future, where people are locked up inside huge buildings, doesn't really appeal to me very much. But some people have already chosen a life very similar to what they'd have in the high-rise future, and seem to enjoy it. In any case, the high-rise future is possible—we can build this sort of city if we want to.

A Day in the Edge City Future

Helen locked the townhouse door and walked down the stairs to her Buick Electric. She unplugged the charging wire, made sure its housing was locked, and got in. The car started noiselessly, and the trip to the nearest S-way entrance was mercifully short. As she approached, the on-board computer flashed her recognition code and queried for her destination. She punched in the number of the exit nearest her first meeting of the day and, after making sure that the central guidance system had taken control of the car, sat down to go through her notes. A fax was already coming in—her workday had started. It was going to be a busy one, and as she settled down, she hoped the central computer that ran the smart highways wouldn't screw up the way it had last week, when she had been stranded in the middle of the smart highway system for two hours. . . .

12

The Edge City Future

The unshakable observation [of the real estate developers] *was this: if they gave the people what they wanted, the people would give them money.*

—JOEL GARREAU, *Edge City*

When I first moved to the Virginia suburbs of Washington, D.C., in 1987, I assumed that they would be the same sort of place that the suburbs had been when I was growing up in Chicago—pleasant tree-lined bedroom communities for people who worked downtown. The early 1960s subdivision I moved into certainly did nothing to contradict this notion; my adult son, in fact, began referring to it as a "set from 'Leave It to Beaver.'"

But as I settled in, I began to notice things that didn't quite fit this image. I'd be driving down a street lined with small stores and gas stations, for example, when I'd suddenly encounter a multistory office building that looked as if it had been transported in from some science fiction movie. The flat suburban landscape was dotted with clusters of high-rise buildings—clusters usually associated with freeway interchanges and large indoor shopping malls. I became curious about what these decidedly nonsuburban agglomerations were doing in suburbia.

One such development near my home, for example, is called Tysons Corner. Thirty years ago, it was, quite literally, a country crossroad featuring a white clapboard general store, with a single gas pump in front, sitting in an expanse of woods and open fields. Today, there is more office space in Tysons Corner than there is in downtown Miami. The suburbs where I was living, in other words, were nothing like the suburbs I had in my mind. They were not there to provide living space for people who worked downtown. Instead, they were places where workplaces and homes seemed to be intermingled.

In fact, these suburbs reminded me of nothing so much as the parts of nineteenth-century industrial cities. There would be a few factories at one location, surrounded by workers' housing, then more factories, more housing, and so on. The idea was for every worker to live within a half hour's walk of his factory. The new suburbs, I realized, were designed the same way, except that distances were stretched out because people no longer walked but drove their own cars.

I also began to notice that the "factories" in this new kind of suburb weren't like the ones now standing vacant in many industrial cities. The modern glass office buildings were often topped with microwave antennas; and inside, workers stared at computer screens instead of assembly lines. In fact, almost all the new (and highly skilled) jobs being created around me had to do with the manipulation and processing of information rather than material. What I was seeing, I began to realize, was the birth of a new kind of economy, as well as a new kind of city structure. I began to feel, in fact, that I was living in the midst of a vast (though unnoticed) sociological experiment.

Once I knew what to look for, I began seeing the same thing happening in every city I visited. From the window of my favorite hotel in Chicago, for example, I could see the glass high-rise buildings around O'Hare International Airport—Chicago's version of the Virginia suburbs. And when I went to Boston, New York, Atlanta, Miami, San Francisco, and Houston, I had similar experiences.

I also realized that these developments on the edges of major cities were largely invisible to people living in the urban core, and especially to scholars at urban universities. At lunch with the president of a major Ivy League school, for example, I was astonished to find that he still thought of suburbs as simple dormitories for commuters who ultimately wound up in the city proper. When I spent some time at the University of Chicago, I noticed that people would drive through these new communities at the edge of the city without even noticing they were there.

Imagine my relief, then, when one of my favorite authors and observers of America, Joel Garreau of the *Washington Post,* took it upon himself to look at this whole phenomenon. In his book *Edge City* (Doubleday, 1991), he argued that the sort of information-based clusterings of office buildings and malls I had noticed were going up on the outskirts of every major city in the world. He gives them the name "Edge Cities," and because of them, he argues, the city of the future will be very different from that of the past. Instead of the classic city with its concentric ring of suburbs around a central core, the new city will be a network of coequal centers, with living space in between the nodes. In other words, each edge city reinforces, and is reinforced by, the others. The old central city remains a part of this network, of course, but may or may not be the most important part of it.

Garreau identifies some 265 edge cities (existing and developing) in America. Cities from London and Paris to Singapore, too, are sprouting information-based business centers on their peripheries. The numbers can be astonishing. In Houston, for example, almost 75 percent of the office space is outside the city limits, and even in a classic central city like London, that number is over 50 percent.

As a dyed-in-the-wool curmudgeon, I was quite taken with this new development. For years, intellectuals and urban planners— the sorts of people who seem to delight in telling other people how to live their lives—have been telling us that we weren't supposed to expand out into the exurban countryside, adding terms like "urban sprawl" and "soulless suburbs" to our vocabulary. And yet, in spite of all this preaching, people seem to have voted with their feet and created a new kind of city on the outskirts of metropolis. And, of course, as entrepreneurs read the trends correctly and became enormously wealthy, terms like "developer" and "land speculator" entered the planners' lexicon of demonology. Sometimes it's just fun to see people decide what they want and refuse to eat their spinach.

The new urban complex that has resulted from such growth resembles a kind of spiderweb connecting the old downtown area and the edge cities growing up on its periphery. Information and people flow along the strands of the web, making the entire structure into an integrated, coherent whole. The technological challenge of making this urban structure work isn't limited just to the flow of information—that problem, as discussed in Chapter 9, is pretty well under control these days. It's the movement of people that's the problem.

In a very real sense, the existence of today's edge cities, as well as the possibility of the edge city future, depends crucially on high levels of personal mobility. Not only must people be able to get into edge cities when they go to work, but they must be able to move around between edge cities during the working day. Salesmen and contractors have to visit their clients; executives have to get to the airport. Without this kind of mobility, edge cities simply could not function.

And this brings us to the problem of automobiles. Edge cities wouldn't be possible without them, but they are a true Achilles' heel. The central technological challenge to the edge city's future is whether automobiles will remain the principal mode of transportation for urban Americans in the next century.

ELECTRIC CARS AND SMART HIGHWAYS

There are two great hurdles to an urban future dominated by the construction of edge cities. One is the pollution associated with the widespread use of automobiles; the other is the congestion resulting from the need for constant traffic between nodes. Both these problems must be dealt with to make this sort of future possible.

The Los Angeles Basin contains a quintessential edge city system, and it should come as no surprise that the factors limiting the edge city's future were first seen there. As more and more people moved in and started driving from one edge city to another, the legendary Los Angeles smog—exacerbated by vehicle exhaust—got worse. As for traffic congestion, the fact is that you can put only so many cars on the road at a given time without producing traffic jams. There are now stretches of Los Angeles freeway where "rush-hour" traffic lasts all day.

Since California is where the air pollution problem first reared its head, it's only fitting that California has taken the lead in solving it. The legislature has mandated that by 1998, 2 percent of new cars in the state must emit no tailpipe pollution; by the year 2003, the fraction must increase to 10 percent. This is, in effect, a mandate for electric cars. Frankly, I see no way the automobile can survive as a mode of transportation without the widespread use of electric cars, and this means that the edge city's future is intimately tied to them as well.

I should make one point right at the start of this discussion. While electric cars emit no tailpipe pollution, it should be remembered that the energy that moves them has to come from somewhere. Electric cars run on batteries, and the energy that one day may be needed to keep those batteries charged will most likely be produced in an ordinary electrical generating plant. But even taking this fact into account, and assuming that we generate the electricity for the cars in the same way that we generate it for other purposes, electric cars are a boon. They produce 98 percent less carbon monoxide and nitrogen compounds, and 25 percent less carbon dioxide, than their gasoline-powered equivalents. It is, after all, easier to clean up the emissions from a few smokestacks than from a million tailpipes.

Actually, electric cars really aren't a new technology. Until the 1920s, they were as common on the streets as the legendary Stanley Steamer. Henry Ford's wife drove one even as her husband was churning out Model T's. But the electric car suffered then (and suffers now) from one fatal flaw: the energy stored in a battery, pound for pound, is a lot less than the energy stored in gasoline.

An ordinary car battery stores about half a kilowatt-hour of energy, enough to run a 100-watt bulb for five hours. It takes almost a half ton of state-of-the-art lead-acid batteries to store the energy equivalent of a gallon of gasoline. If you want an electric car to go 200 miles between rechargings, it has to have an equivalent fuel efficiency near 200 miles to the gallon—far beyond the efficiency of cars in the commercial gasoline-powered fleet. (Today, this fleet gets about 28 miles to the gallon.)

This, in a nutshell, is what makes it so hard for us to convert to electric cars: the weight of the batteries is so high in relation to the amount of energy they can store that most of that energy is used up in moving the batteries, with little left over for car and passengers. There will be no edge cities without electric cars, and no electric cars without batteries that pack in more kilowatt-hours per pound. It's as simple as that. As so often happens in the world of science and technology, matters of great moment (in this case, the future of our cities) depend on our ability to deal with grungy details like improving the storage battery.

Look at it this way: whenever you travel somewhere in a car (or any other vehicle), you're taking energy that was stored somewhere and converting it into energy of motion. A bicycle operates on energy from yesterday's dinner; a car, on ancient sunlight stored in petroleum; a subway train, on energy stored in coal or uranium nuclei. From the standpoint of a physicist, the only thing different about an electric car is that the energy is stored in the arrangement of atoms in a battery. It requires energy to charge a battery, and that energy is then available in the form of electric current when the battery is being used. Instead of taking petroleum from the ground and using its energy directly, the electric car employs a more subtle and circuitous strategy to get its energy.

You can get some sense of how this works by thinking about the battery you use most often—the lead-acid battery in your car. A simplified sketch is shown in Figure 18. Plates of lead (Pb) and lead dioxide (PbO_2) are immersed in a bath of dilute sulfuric acid (H_2SO_4). The lead plates are connected to the post marked with a minus sign on the battery, while the plates made of lead dioxide are connected to the post marked with a plus. If you connect the two posts (by turning your ignition on, for example), chemical reactions start to take place. At the lead plate, the sulfuric acid interacts to produce lead sulfate (the white crud that collects around old battery contacts) and some free electrons. These electrons run through the wire to the other plates, where they interact with the lead dioxide and sulfuric acid to make more lead sulfate and water.

In this system, we use the electrons as they move through the wire. In effect, we drain the stored chemical energy in the battery to create electric energy, then convert that energy into some-

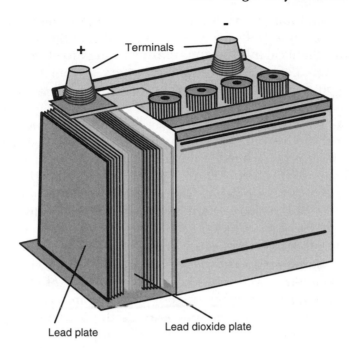

Figure 18. Lead-acid battery

thing useful (in a gasoline-powered car, the turning motion of the starting motor; or in an electric car, the motion of the car itself). The battery will continue to produce current until both plates have been turned into lead sulfate and the liquid has turned into water. At this point, no more energy can be taken out, and we say that the battery is drained (or, more colloquially, "dead").

If you run electric current from another source backward through a discharged battery, the chemical reactions will proceed in reverse. The lead sulfate plates will be transformed back into lead and lead dioxide, and the liquid will once again be sulfuric acid. At this point, we can once again get energy from the battery, and we say that it has been recharged. Whenever you run your car, the generator drains some energy from the engine and uses it to recharge the battery. Thus, your car battery is always maintained in a charged state by using some of the energy stored in the gasoline.

In a sense, a battery is like a rock perched on top of a hill. As soon as conditions are right, the rock gives up its energy by roll-ing down the hill. In the same way, the atoms in the battery "roll down the chemical hill," giving up their energy to electrons mov-ing through a wire. Recharging the battery in your car is analo-gous to putting the rock back up on top of the hill so that it can roll down again.

Not all batteries are rechargeable. The small alkaline cells you use to run your Walkman or flashlight typically have plates of zinc and manganese dioxide immersed in a gel of potassium hy-droxide. Once this sort of battery is discharged, running current backward doesn't reproduce the original configuration, so the battery can't be recharged and has to be replaced after it runs down.

All the electric cars built to date (including millions of golf carts) use some version of the lead-acid battery that you have in your gasoline-powered car. There are a number of other kinds of batteries now in various stages of development, all of them working in essentially the same way as the lead-acid type but using different chemicals to get more "oomph."

One of these has plates made of nickel and iron rather than of lead and lead oxide, and it develops about 50 percent more power per pound than an ordinary car battery. These batteries are supposed to become available by the mid-1990s; they store more energy than conventional batteries but cost more. There are even more advanced batteries on the horizon, such as those using sodium and sulfur, but they have to operate at tempera-tures of 600 degrees Fahrenheit or more, which makes me skep-tical they'll be used in private vehicles.

An electric car can be driven a certain distance (called its range) before its batteries are discharged, at which point the bat-teries have to be plugged in and recharged. You can refill your car with gasoline in a matter of a few minutes, but recharging a battery can take anywhere from 15 minutes to 8 hours, depend-ing on technical details. This is why most planners talk about making the range of electric cars big enough so that they can be driven all day, then recharged overnight.

Most electric cars built until quite recently tended to resemble golf carts—light, flimsy things that few of us would want to take out on the freeway. But they don't have to be this way. Using state-of-the-art lead-acid batteries, the Electric Power Research

Institute and an industry consortium have built an electric van that is now being marketed to selected companies around the country. Called the G-Van, this vehicle is powered by 36 lead-acid batteries, has a range of 60 miles, and can accelerate from 0 to 30 miles per hour in 13 seconds. The limited-production model costs about $50,000.

The choice of a van as the lead vehicle for an electric fleet is reasonable: service vans generally travel short distances and return to a central location where they can be recharged each night. But the G-Van typifies all the problems of electric cars: 60 miles is not much of a range (it wouldn't, for example, get you around the Washington Beltway), 13 seconds is a *long* time to get to 30 miles per hour, and $50,000 isn't just pocket change.

On the other hand, more advanced electric cars are on the drawing boards. In 1990, General Motors received a lot of publicity when it unveiled a sporty electric called the Impact. This two-passenger car is powered by 32 lead-acid batteries, has a range of 120 miles and a top speed of 110 miles per hour, and accelerates to 60 miles per hour in 8 seconds.

Although the Impact, a so-called concept car, is not intended for mass production, it shows what can be done using state-of-the-art technology and a lot of imagination. It carries 870 pounds of batteries but weighs only 2200 pounds total. It has an extremely light aluminum frame, tires that produce half the ordinary road friction, and an aerodynamic design that reduces wind resistance to a third of its normal value. Given the interest that the government has shown in bringing about change in the American auto fleet, it seems highly probable that by the end of the decade we will be well launched on a conversion to electrical vehicles, at least in major metropolitan areas. If this occurs in conjunction with the development of large nuclear or solar electrical generating plants, Americans will, for the first time, have the use of an almost nonpolluting form of personal transportation. Thus, the first great hurdle to an edge city future—the problem of air pollution from cars—can probably be overcome.

But once we control air pollution, we will still have to face the second hurdle: traffic congestion. It doesn't matter much that your car is pollution-free if it's barely moving. Today's average speed on Los Angeles freeways is only 35 miles per hour—far below the posted speed limits. If nothing is done, engineers estimate that by 2010 the average speed may drop to 11 miles per hour. On the national level, estimates run to some 2 billion wasted person-hours each year because of traffic delays, a number expected to increase to 11 billion by 2005.

Traffic delays have become so much a part of the urban scene, in fact, that they have spawned all sorts of new industries. Car phones, books on audiocassettes, and even car fax systems allow people to put the time they spend in their cars to productive use. General Motors is even developing the concept of a "car office." For myself, I wouldn't dream of attempting a major drive on the Washington Beltway without taking along a dictating machine and some overdue correspondence or memos, just in case I get stuck.

It seems to me that traffic congestion sets the ultimate limits on the future of edge cities. In fact, scientists have thought a lot about traffic flow, and some of their theories may give you something to muse about the next time you're in a traffic jam.

Each driver on the road has a clear destination, but from the standpoint of overall traffic flow, a crowded highway resembles nothing so much as the atoms in a gas or fluid. Each atom moves along independently, yet the overall motion of the fluid can be described quite simply. An expressway is like a big water supply line, and each branching off to secondary roads is analogous to water flowing into successively smaller pipes as it approaches its final destination. An accident is an obstruction in the pipe, around which a small stream "leaks" until the obstruction is removed. The computer systems that control traffic lights in many central cities use sophisticated versions of this sort of theory to set the green-red cycle times.

The fluid analogy for traffic flows also explains one of the most puzzling phenomena of modern driving: the traffic jam that seems to have no cause. If one driver on an expressway steps on the brakes, drivers in back, sensing trouble, step on their brakes as well. Because each driver slows down as soon as he or she sees the brake lights ahead, the effect is to create a wave of slower-moving vehicles moving backward and superimposed on the general forward surge of traffic. Under the right conditions, this backward-moving wave can grow until, somewhere back along the line, cars actually have to stop when it reaches them. When you enter this kind of jam, you figure there's an accident ahead, but suddenly traffic resumes speed for no apparent reason. Although individual cars obviously aren't molecules in a fluid, they sometimes behave as if they were.

Such theoretical understandings of traffic flow are all based on the notion that individual drivers will always retain control of their own cars. But, as the above examples show, there are limits to how much traffic can be moved on even the biggest conventional highways. This is why I think the essential technology for edge cities is likely to be the "smart highway."

The smart highway is a system that monitors traffic flow and uses the information gained to increase the efficiency of road use. Most systems being tested right now concentrate on getting information to drivers and then leaving the drivers free to react to it. More advanced systems, on the drawing boards today, would actually leave the response to central computers, in effect turning drivers into passengers on highways where all traffic is managed to obtain maximum efficiency of movement.

You've probably already seen some rudimentary kinds of smart highways in your own town—lighted signs that warn you of construction or traffic tie-ups ahead, for example, or traffic reports on the radio. All of these everyday systems have one goal: to convey information to the driver so that he or she can make decisions. The next step, which already exists in prototype form, would put a computer in your car so that a constant stream of such information would be available to you as you drove. Sensors buried in the highway concrete would keep track of passing cars. The sensors' findings, coupled to data relayed by the on-board computers themselves, would be processed in a delicate minuet of information flowing back and forth from individual automobiles to Computer Central.

If you think of the smart highway as a way of getting information to drivers, you realize that there are some interesting nontechnical questions that have to be addressed. There is, after all, a certain amount of game playing inherent in this sort of situation. For example, it may improve the overall traffic picture to have you take a side road, but at the same time, it may lengthen your own trip. What happens then? Do the engineers feed you false information to get you to do what they want? Do they tell you the truth and watch the system clog up? It will be interesting to see how this conflict between human nature and efficient technology plays itself out.

The ultimate smart highway would deal with this problem by taking the ability to choose away from the driver and investing it in a central planning system. With the computer knowing the position of every car on the highway as well as everyone's destination, it would be a straightforward (though complicated) operation to control the speed and steering of each car. In effect, the driver could put the vehicle on "automatic pilot" and read the morning paper while he or she was being driven to work.

THE EDGE CITY FUTURE

Presuppose, for the moment, the development of electric cars, powered by nonpolluting generating plants and guided around smart highways at maximum efficiency by computers. In this case, the growth of American metropolitan regions will take place with the expansion of edge cities into the countryside.

In this future, you would expect cities to grow outward in a kind of spiderweb pattern, with clusters of office complexes and shopping malls surrounded by residential areas running heavily to detached, single-family homes. People would commute to work in these edge cities, as outlined above, and daytime trips from one edge city to another would proceed in the same way. I suppose people would use their car time more or less as they use time in their offices right now—working and making phone calls.

But there are self-limiting features to edge city growth. At the moment, edge cities seem to be moving farther and farther into the countryside, with no end in sight. In Boston, the "old" edge cities around Route 128 have been supplemented by a new set of nascent edge cities around Route 495—more than 10 miles farther out. Given the importance of mobility in the formation of edge cities, it's hard to see how this trend can continue forever. The thicker the network around the center of a metropolitan area becomes, the more people will try to make their way from one node to another, and the more congested traffic will be, regardless of what improvements are made in highways. But will this stop the network when the outer limits are 20 miles away from downtown? Fifty? Ninety? Your guess is as good as mine.

Suppose, though, that the limits set by traffic congestion are sufficiently loose to allow all future population growth to be shunted out into an ever widening network of business centers. What would life in such a city be like? The standard criticism of edge cities is that, while they may make business sense, they are not good places to live. The various things that we lump together in the term "quality of life" just don't exist in an edge city. What are we to make of such an argument?

QUALITY OF LIFE

The fact that edge cities are primarily involved in the information economy means that the workers there tend to be highly skilled, highly educated, and well paid. A crucial ingredient of the edge city equation, then, is that life there be agreeable and pleasant. As Joel Garreau points out, edge city is largely about "nice." Will they remain "nice" enough to prosper in the future? This is a hard question, because it's not clear how edge cities are going to develop as places for human activity.

Right now, there is a certain raw flavor to most edge cities—a certain air of the frontier. A beautifully landscaped office park, complete with glass buildings and graveled walkways, may be located next door to a weed-choked auto graveyard. There are enclosed malls for strolling, as well as little specialty shops in shopping centers here and there, but to get to them you have to drive past rows of car dealerships and gas stations. Edge cities are not ambulatory environments like central cities, not places where you might stumble over an interesting shop or restaurant on your way to somewhere else. By and large, they are not yet real communities.

Will this change as they mature and develop? I suspect that most urban intellectuals would say no. As far as they are concerned, edge cities will always be undifferentiated urban sprawls, places to be driven through on the way to somewhere else. I'm not so sure that this prejudice is justified. Let me tell you about my own experiences in one edge city, and you decide for yourself.

There are many ways of measuring whether or not a given community is a "good place to live." If things like spacious housing, high-quality public education, good medical services, and lots of green space rank high on your list, then an edge city is for you. There is money in an edge city, and the residents normally don't mind spending it on such things. If cultural institutions and events rank high on your list, the picture isn't so clear. Obviously, the established cultural institutions—museums, symphony orchestras, newspapers—are centered in the old downtown areas. The cultural centers in edge cities tend to be large public arenas that book well-known musicians on tour, the road versions of Broadway hits, and the like. These places, I suspect, contribute something to the perception of the suburbs as cultural wastelands.

But my own experience in the edge cities of Washington, D.C., tells me that there's more than meets the eye on the cultural scene. Here and there (particularly at suburban universities), I find performing-artist programs as good as you'll find in any college town—that is, programs of sufficiently high quality that most people won't have time to take them all in. In the older suburbs, where things have had time to develop, I find reasonable experimental theater and all sorts of unusual musical groups. And, of course, in many cities professional sports activities have moved to the suburbs, where cheap land makes the construction of the facilities possible. For the kinds of things I like to do, there is at least as much going on in the suburbs as within the city limits.

Once the basics are taken care of, each of us has his or her own way of judging the value of a city. Personally, I tend to look at two areas: interesting restaurants and bookstores.

The edge cities I have known do pretty well when it comes to general bookstores. They are, after all, areas where education and the propensity to read are much higher than the American average. Sometimes they develop specialty bookstores. My own region, for example, with its high population of people connected to the Pentagon, boasts several bookstores specializing in military history. There are even a few that have reasonable coffee bars (a most atypical development for a town like Washington).

As far as restaurants go, the situation is better than you might think. There is never a problem finding expensive restaurants that serve good food. The real challenge is finding that obscure ethnic establishment where you can get a great meal for a fraction of the price—the kind of place where you may be the only person speaking English. In my youth, I spent many happy hours prowling the back streets of Chicago hunting these places down, and I felt an almost parental sense of satisfaction when some of them developed into fixtures on the Chicago restaurant scene. In all this, I had one unshakable rule: Never, if you can help it, eat at a restaurant in a shopping mall.

This won't work in an edge city. It's not that there are no ethnic communities. The availability of cheap land (the same factor that is so important in attracting office parks) also provides lots of low-rent nooks and crannies. The same economic forces that put those Chicago restaurants on obscure side streets put their modern equivalents in edge city shopping centers. My own current favorites—Salvadoran, Afghan, and Indian—are all located in little malls wedged in between the major nodes of the edge city network.

In fact, the evening before I wrote these words, I had what I consider to be a typical edge city experience. I drove to the outer ring of suburban development, where open fields alternate with modernistic glass towers and new townhouse subdivisions. In a small business park, rambling rows of one-story shops intermingled with parking lots. There, between a computer store and a consulting firm specializing in construction waterproofing, was a hole-in-the-wall Afghan restaurant. While papa cooked, mama ran the cash register and the daughters waited tables. My friends and I enjoyed a dinner of *aush* and *quabili pilow* while being entertained by two very talented belly dancers. One of the dancers was a systems analyst at the Department of Defense; the other, general counsel for an organization whose name you would recognize instantly if I were to embarrass her by naming it.

And if that doesn't give you some hope for the future of edge city as an interesting place to live, nothing will!

A Day in the New Suburban Future

Jason and Jennifer stood on the front steps of their frame house. It was a beautiful day—the sun was shining, the kids were off to school, and the leaves on the maple tree in the front yard were flame red. They'd probably have to get out the rakes by the weekend.

It took them ten minutes to walk downtown to the railroad station, and they arrived, as usual, a few minutes before the train arrived. It was a sleek, streamlined thing, made up of several small segments. They said good-bye on the platform, and each went into a different segment. As they sat down with the morning paper, the train moved forward and—responsive to invisible magnetic forces—lifted a few inches off the track. At 300 miles per hour, it literally flew through an open countryside dotted with small towns. Twenty minutes after leaving the station, it approached the city, where the different segments of the train split off, one carrying Jason to his job in an edge city high-rise development, another carrying Jennifer to her office downtown. Door-to-door time for both of them: 40 minutes. They'd both be home by six o'clock, in plenty of time to get ready for the barbecue. . . .

13

The New
Suburban Future

*Our property seems to me the most beautiful in the world. It is so close to
[downtown] that we enjoy all the advantages of the city, and yet when we
come home we are away from all the noise and dust.*

    —*Letter of the Persian ambassador to Babylon (539 B.C.)*

Let's face it: Americans just don't like to live in central cities.
They've been flocking to them for centuries, but as soon as they
make enough money, their first thought is to move to the suburbs or buy a home in the country. As the ambassador's letter
quoted above shows, this is not a new phenomenon. Everybody,
it seems, wants to have it all—the excitement and bustle of the
city and the peaceful quiet of the countryside.

    As we saw in Chapter 8, the development of the steam railroad
led to a great suburban boom in this country. It also produced
metropolitan areas with a distinctive configuration—railroad
suburbs strung out at intervals along tracks leading into the cen-

tral city. And believe it or not, technology now being developed
may very well lead American cities in that same direction again.

Remember the Rule of 45, which says that most people will not
live more than a 45-minute travel time from their place of work?
While Americans have been exploring the possibilities of a transportation system based on cars and airplanes, other countries
have been developing and building a whole new generation of
fast trains—trains that have as much in common with the old diesel locomotive as an Indianapolis 500 car does with a Model T.
Through the use of sophisticated technologies involving such
forefront scientific areas as superconductivity, the "railroad suburb" scenario may in fact be repeated, since the territory included inside the 45-minute radius of every large city may soon
be expanded dramatically.

It all depends on how fast you can make the trains go.

THE TECHNOLOGY OF FAST TRAINS

One of the more pleasant surprises I encountered when I moved
to the Washington, D.C., area a few years ago was the Met-

roliner. This train, one of the crown jewels of the Amtrak system, connects major cities on the eastern seaboard on hourly runs between Washington and New York. Let me take you along with me on a typical trip to visit my publisher in New York.

I get up early to drive downtown, beating the morning rush and pulling into Union Station at about 6:20 A.M. During most of the winter, it's still dark when I come in, and the lighted dome of the Capitol seems to float above the city, unattached to the earth. I stop to pick up a copy of the *Washington Post* and a cup of coffee, arriving at the gate at 6:40, when the train starts boarding. A short stroll along the platform and I get on, tossing my coat into the overhead rack and settling into a wide reclining seat. At 6:50, the train pulls out, stops for a minute at a suburban station to take on more passengers, then settles in for the express run to New York. I take a short nap to make up for the sleep I missed by getting up early, go through the *Post*, and read through the material I'll need for that day's meeting.

Meanwhile, the train is moving along at speeds of up to 125 miles per hour. Baltimore, Wilmington, and Philadelphia glide by outside the window. At about 9:15, the marshes of New Jersey disappear as the train descends into a tunnel, to emerge five minutes later at Penn Station in Manhattan. At 9:25, I walk onto the streets of New York, invariably marveling at the experience and remarking to myself, "What a civilized way to travel!"

The most amazing thing about the trip I've just described is that it's all done with what is basically 1950s technology. The Metroliner is a square, blocky electric train that runs on track that's only slightly improved over what it was a half century ago. As pleasant and convenient as it is, it represents the past, not the future.

As far as trains are concerned, the future began in 1964, when Japan Railways inaugurated their now famous Bullet Train, or Shinkansen. Traveling at speeds not too different from those of today's Metroliner, it made the 320-mile trip from Tokyo to Osaka in about four hours. Today, the descendants of that first Bullet Train carry about 400,000 passengers a day on some 1300 miles of track—enough to reach from New York to Kansas City. The trains travel at a top speed of 175 miles per hour and have been clocked on occasion at over 200. They are, in every sense of the word, high-speed transportation.

The Bullet Trains aren't the only high-speed trains in the world these days. The French have the TGV (Train à Grande Vitesse) and the Germans their ICE (Intercity Express). The TGV is, at the moment, the fastest train in the world, having exceeded 320 miles per hour on a stretch of track in western France in May of 1990. These trains have been operated with no serious accidents and an admirable record of punctuality—the Bullet Train, for example, is on schedule over 99 percent of the time. More important, they all make a profit, which explains why both Germany and Japan are spending money to develop the next generation of high-speed trains.

To understand how trains can be made to go so much faster than the Metroliner, you have to realize that every moving train represents a balance between forces: the engine turns the wheels, providing a force that tends to accelerate the train. At the same time, there are forces tending to slow it down. At cruising speeds, the forward and backward forces balance each other. This means that for a given size engine, the only way to reach higher speeds is to cut down on those opposing forces.

When a train goes by, the steel tracks flex and vibrate in response to the load. Air molecules are pushed aside to make way for the engine. After the train has passed, then, both the tracks and the air are slightly hotter than they were before, and that heat represents a gain of energy. That energy must come from somewhere, and in this case it has been drained from the train's energy of motion. Usually called friction and wind resistance, these drains are what set the speed limit for an ordinary train.

Wind resistance goes up rapidly with speed: a twofold increase in speed will produce at least a fourfold increase in resistance. Metroliner locomotives were not designed with this fact in mind; they have a square cross-section that creates lots of swirls and eddies as they push through the air. All of the fast trains, on the other hand, have streamlined locomotives that cut through the air easily.

The problem of friction is not so easy to overcome, but it's clear that if you want fast trains, you have to think about the track itself. One way to cut down on flexing is to weld the segments together so that the track is continuous. This eliminates the *clickety-clack* associated with the bounce as the wheels move from one segment to another. Another technique is to design the roadbed to cut down on track movement as the train goes by.

While the Metroliner's roadbed was converted from earlier freight and passenger lines, all the other fast trains started out with a new right-of-way specifically designed to accommodate them. This was no trivial undertaking—the first Bullet Train line, for example, required no fewer than 66 tunnels and 3100 bridges in addition to the track itself.

Keeping the special track level and straight for day-to-day operations is a time-consuming job. Every night, for example, some 3000 employees of Japan Railways must go out and adjust the Bullet Train tracks for the next day's traffic.

But conventional trains, and even the legendary Shinkansen, have one inherent characteristic that limits their ability to shape the future of cities—a characteristic so obvious that it's easy to overlook. Every conventional train must have a locomotive. It must carry its own engine, even if it derives its energy from elec tricity generated on the ground. This means that when the train stops, every car must stop, whether the passengers in it are getting off or not. In the case of the nineteenth-century railroad suburbs, this fact dictated that stations (and towns) be several miles apart. In today's city, it means that fast trains can move people quickly and efficiently from dispersed suburban locations to locations in the city center, but cannot efficiently drop them off at suburban business centers on the way in. For this reason, the historical role of conventional wheel-and-track trains has been to facilitate movement into and between city centers.

The real city-shaping technology will be a new wave of trains that operate on a principle called magnetic levitation, or "maglev." These trains (which have operated at the prototype level for more than a decade) overcome the basic limitations of wheel-and-track trains by using a totally new type of technology.

MAGLEV

There are three basic principles behind maglev. The first principle was discussed in Chapter 7: When the magnetic field near a piece of metal changes, electrons in the metal move and an electric current flows. The second principle involves another basic law of physics that was discovered early in the nineteenth century: When electric current flows in a wire or a piece of metal, it creates a magnetic field—in effect, the wire turns into a magnet. (The most striking example of this so-called electromagnetic effect is the huge magnet that moves wrecked cars around in a junkyard. When the magnet is brought down on a car, current is run through to energize it. The car is lifted up and moved over, held aloft by the magnetic attraction. When it is over the place where the operator wants to put it, the electric current is cut off, the magnetic field disappears, gravity takes over, and the car falls.) The third principle behind maglev is one familiar from grade school science: Magnets exert forces on each other. North poles of magnets repel each other, south poles do likewise, but north and south poles attract.

Maglev works like this: When a magnet is moved over a piece of metal, electrons in the metal see a changing magnetic field, so they start to move (principle one). These electrons move in a loop, so that they, in turn, produce a magnetic field of their own (principle two). The easiest way to visualize this process is shown in Figure 19; the moving magnet, in effect, conjures up an image magnet in the metal. The point is that the laws of physics tell us that the image magnet will be oriented so that it repels the original one. If the original magnet has its north pole down, in other words, the image magnet has its north pole up and vice versa.

Since like poles of magnets repel each other (principle three), the net effect of moving a magnet over a piece of metal is to produce a force that pushes up on the moving magnet. If the magnet is moving fast, this force can be big enough to overcome the downward force of gravity and literally lift (levitate) the moving magnet. It will float above the metal as it moves, kept aloft by the forces exerted by the movement of electrons that it itself induces. This process is called magnetic levitation.

It can be incorporated into a train, as shown on the right in Figure 20. If there are magnets in the floor of the train and if the train starts to move (on retractable pneumatic tires, for example), then there will be an upward force generated. At this moment, the train is like an airplane accelerating down a runway prior to takeoff. When the upward force is big enough, it lifts the vehicle off the ground so that it floats above the metal guiderail. In practice, the train is designed so that the cars are lifted between ³/₈ inch and 6 inches off the ground. The train starts to fly.

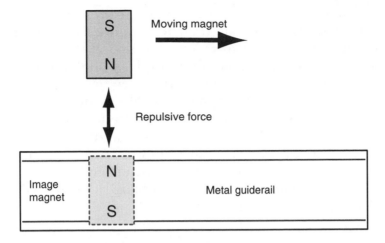

Figure 19. The principle of magnetic levitation

From this discussion, we can see the first great advantage of the maglev train. There is no energy loss due to friction between the wheels and the track for the simple reason that there are no wheels and no track. One great source of energy loss in conventional trains has been eliminated. The only thing limiting the speed of the train (in principle) is wind resistance.

The second great advantage of maglev trains becomes clear when we start to look at how the train moves. While it is true that the north pole of one magnet will repel the north pole of another (this is what produces levitation), it is also true that the north pole of one magnet will be attracted by the south pole of another. This is the principle used to move maglev trains forward.

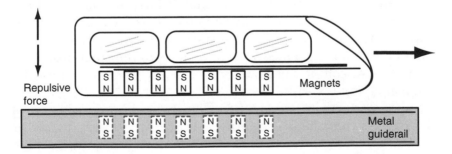

Figure 20. The maglev train

The system is shown in Figure 20. At the same time that electrons are moving under the train to produce the lifting force, current is run through wires along the side of the guiderail to create another set of magnets ahead of those on the train. These magnets, however, are arranged so that their *south* poles are near the *north* poles of the train's magnets. The train is then pulled forward by the attractive force, and the current along the side is adjusted so that the "pulling magnets" stay just ahead of the train. In effect, the train is engulfed in a kind of magnetic wave, or magnetic cocoon. You can think of the moving magnets along the side as producing a wave and the train as riding the wave like a surfer (see Figure 21).

SUPERCONDUCTING MAGNETS

The magnets in the train body itself are obviously a crucial feature of the maglev train. The problem of making them has largely been solved, although there will surely be improvements in the future. They will not be huge chunks of iron (analogous to the magnets that hold notes on your refrigerator); rather, they will be electromagnets, powered by electric current.

It is possible, as in the German system (called the TransRapid), to make the electromagnets from ordinary copper wire, drawing current from the same outside power source that moves the train. The maglevs of the future, however, are much more likely to use electromagnets made from superconducting wire, maintained at temperatures near absolute zero by being immersed in a bath of liquid helium (as in the current Japanese maglev prototype).

Superconductors are materials that behave normally at high temperature but undergo a sudden change as the temperature is lowered. In the superconducting state, they can conduct electric current with no loss. Once a current starts to flow in a superconducting wire coil, it will flow forever, even if the source of the original current is withdrawn.

Superconductivity, though first discovered in the early part of this century, remained a scientific oddity until the last decade or so. How a material becomes a superconductor is an interesting story.

In an ordinary copper wire, the moving electrons that consti-

tute the current collide often with atoms of copper. In the process, they lose energy and the copper atoms start to vibrate more
rapidly. The wire heats up as energy is drained from the current
—this is why the heating coils on your toaster glow red when it is
operating.

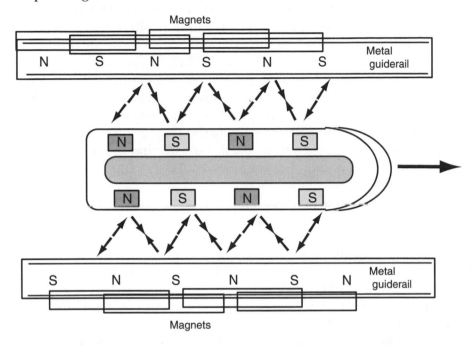

Figure 21. Magnetic waves around a maglev train

In a superconductor, this simple picture is replaced by something more complex. One electron moves quickly between some
metal ions, exerting a force on them that tends to pull them
toward itself. Because the electron is moving quickly, it is long
gone by the time ponderous atoms respond. As a result, the two
metal atoms find themselves close together when the first electron is far away. They attract another electron, though, which is
induced to follow in the path of the first. The two electrons going
through the metal are like two bike racers moving down a highway: the passage of the first makes the way easier for the second.

If the temperature is low enough so that ordinary vibrations
don't upset the delicate balance of this process, all the electrons
pair up. In addition, all the pairs intertwine and lock all the

electrons together. If you think of the two electrons as being the ends of a single strand of spaghetti, then all the electrons are like a bowl of spaghetti, with everything twisted together.

As a result, the electrons move roughshod through the metal. They cannot give up energy in collisions, because in order to scatter one electron, you have to scatter them all. The electrons just keep moving because there's nothing in the metal that can stop them. As long as the temperature stays low, so that the atoms don't vibrate too much, they will move forever.

You can make a superconducting magnet by connecting a loop of superconducting wire to a battery to get current flowing, then taking the battery away. The current will keep on flowing, producing its magnetic field, so long as the temperature is kept below the critical point. In practice, this means that the magnet has to be immersed in liquid helium, which has a temperature about 4 degrees above absolute zero.

Superconducting magnets may sound magical, but they have been in widespread use for many years. In medicine, for example, they are a vital part of the apparatus that does magnetic resonance imaging to form pictures of soft tissue inside the body. The technicians who maintain MRI machines say that the magnets are very easy to deal with—"We just pour a little more helium in once in a while" was a typical comment I received when I asked about them.

The same is true for superconducting magnets in a maglev train. Once they are immersed in their cold bath and turned on, the only thing needed to keep them going is an occasional topping up with liquid helium. And while this may sound like an exotic substance, it is easily available in the commercial marketplace. It costs about $5.00 per quart—a little less than an equal amount of cheap whiskey.

WHAT A MAGLEV SYSTEM WOULD LOOK LIKE

Maglev isn't a brand-new idea. It was conceived in the 1960s by American physicists Gordon Danby and James Powell, but disappeared from the American scene in 1975, when the federal government suspended all research on high-speed ground transportation. The first prototype maglev ran in Japan in 1971, and prototypes have been running in both Japan and Germany for

years. There was even a maglev train at an exhibition in Yoko-
hama in 1989—it carried a million and a half passengers before
the exhibition shut down.

This long experience has given engineers some confidence in
their ability to make maglev trains work, and can give us some
sense of what a maglev system would be like.

The problems of track maintenance that loom so large for conventional fast trains, for example, don't seem to be important for
maglev guiderails. The German prototype has used the same
track since 1982, with only occasional routine maintenance. We
should note that it is the German prototype that will be used in
the first commercial maglev system projected for the United
States—a line connecting Orlando International Airport and
Walt Disney World that may begin operation as early as 1995.

So how would maglevs be built and operated around American
cities? The most likely approach would be to build overhead
guiderails, perhaps as much as 40 feet off the ground. Most of the
prototype and demonstration systems have been constructed this
way, and they seem to have worked pretty well. One important
advantage of overhead lines is that they don't require new rights-
of-way. Maglev guiderails could easily be built on the edges of
interstate highways—wherever they go, maglevs could go.

The reason for this relates to another technical detail about
trains. If you look down next time you're in an airplane, you'll
notice that rail lines go across the country in fairly straight lines.
Trains aren't built to go around curves, particularly at high
speeds; they're too heavy, and there's too much danger of turning over. This is why the Bullet Train needed a new, ruler-
straight right-of-way when it was first built in Japan. Highways,
on the other hand, tend to twist around a lot more. Cars can
easily negotiate curves a mile or so in radius, even though conventional trains can't.

Maglev trains, however, can take curves easily because they
can bank. Some engineers, in fact, compare a maglev in its
guiderails to a bobsled in its chute. Thus a maglev train going
300 miles per hour could negotiate a turn in a highway that
would be beyond the capacity of a wheeled train going a third
that speed. This gives maglev trains the ability to worm their way
into all the corners of a city. It is one advantage they have over
conventional trains.

But by far the greatest advantage of maglev trains comes from the simple fact that they need no locomotive. All the motive force comes from the on-board magnets and the current in the wires. This fact is crucial (even though it generally gets overlooked in much that is written about maglev trains) because it gives maglev trains the potential to change the face of our cities. In effect, each car can be its own train and can move independently of the other cars.

This means that a maglev line entering a major city might look something like a major freeway. There could be express lanes for through traffic in the middle, with local lanes for slower-moving vehicles on the sides. As the train approached the city, it might split up, with each car (or small string of cars) shunting off to the local lanes at a different spot, to serve a handful of stops. Each passenger would be decelerated only a few times near his or her stop, and there would be no energy expended on repeated accelerations of passengers bound for distant destinations.

In other words, a maglev train could easily bring in a group of people from a distant destination and distribute them around the city—not, like a conventional train, depositing them in the downtown area only. Some visionaries even talk about "a maglev at every shopping center." And while this may be a bit optimistic, it is certainly true that a maglev system could easily distribute passengers to major work centers—whether downtown, in the city at large, or in the suburbs.

Looked at this way, a maglev system could function like a reverse funnel, speeding cars from widely scattered towns in the hinterlands toward the city at 300 miles per hour along interstate highways, then scattering them to diverse destinations within the city itself. The towns from which the passengers came would be a new generation of railroad suburbs.

Having drawn this picture of a possible technology, I should say a few words about safety. Any vehicle that travels near the ground at 300 miles per hour is potentially dangerous. A good deal of current research on the maglev is devoted, in one way or another, to this topic. How will the train behave in high winds? What if it gets off the center of the guiderails? What if something falls in front of it? What if there are snowdrifts? I've heard serious engineers discuss all of these questions and more.

Engineers, you know, are a gloomy lot, always dwelling on

what can go wrong with their systems. But they seem to have worked out the contingencies in this case. Snow? Send out a car with a plow and no people. Branches on the track? Design the cars with fronts like the old cowcatchers on steam engines. Stability? There are a host of electronic feedback systems to deal with it.

As a matter of fact, the maglev system is inherently protected against a lot of the hazards one encounters with conventional trains. Maglev trains, for example, cannot overtake each other and crash. Remember that each train is ensconced in a magnetic wave all its own. If two trains come near each other, the waves will interact to slow down the faster train until the two are moving along together. Automatically.

There is, however, one aspect of maglev travel that I don't think people have paid enough attention to, and that is the reaction of passengers to the peculiarities of travel on these vehicles. It's one thing to speak glibly of a maglev's ability to navigate a tight turn by banking around a curve at 45 degrees. It's quite another to imagine sitting in a train doing this at 300 miles per hour while suspended 40 feet above the ground. This fact hit home forcefully when I was returning by plane to Washington after attending a meeting on high-speed rail travel. As the plane approached National Airport, it went into a slow turn. It was one of those turns where, sitting in the window seat, you have the impression that you're looking almost straight down at the ground. There was an off-duty airline pilot sitting next to me, and I asked him what the angle of the plane had been. He said it had been 25 to 30 degrees. I then told him about the speakers at the meeting and their talk of building 45-degree banked turns into the maglev lines.

He laughed.

THE NEW SUBURBAN RING: BACK TO THE FUTURE

The very existence of trains like the Shinkansen and the TGV has triggered some thoughts about how they might affect American cities. Mary Hurley, the mayor of Springfield, Massachusetts, told a 1991 conference on high-speed trains, "This is an economic development the likes of which we haven't seen since the steam engine was invented." Her notion was that Springfield, some 80 miles from Boston, could become a new railroad suburb, a bedroom community for people commuting to work on a high-speed rail line between her town and the city. In this case, fast-train technology would produce a rerun of the turn-of-the-century development of bedroom suburbs spread out along the original railroad lines.

Actually, the development of a new ring of railroad suburbs may not wait for all the political and economic problems to be solved. In the summer of 1992, for example, rail service—using plain old garden-variety electric trains—was initiated between several towns in Virginia and Washington, D.C. Drawing passengers from 40 to 70 miles away—the outer reaches of suburbia—it was a clear portent of things to come on the railroad scene.

If rail technology really develops as we've outlined it here, it's easy to guess what the future shape of our metropolitan areas will be. All you have to do is go back to the last time railroads dominated patterns of urban growth.

Railroad cities are characterized by a concentrated central business district and small towns centered around train stations. Philadelphia and its Main Line, San Francisco and the towns stringing south along the Southern Pacific lines, and Chicago and its North Shore are all examples. The peculiar capabilities of the maglev make it unlikely that it will produce the linear arrangement characteristic of such established railroad cities. Instead, the central city will have a network of business centers like edge cities, all served by maglev lines bringing people in from distant locations.

Sometimes it's a little hard to picture the size of the commuting area that would be opened up by maglevs. A train with a cruising speed of 300 miles per hour would put places 100 to 150 miles distant from a city within the limit set by the Rule of 45. Take a map and draw a circle this size around your town—you'll be amazed at what's included. Below, I've listed a few towns that could be considered candidates for bedroom suburbs of some major cities:

Maglev Commuting Areas

CITY	POSSIBLE MAGLEV "SUBURB"
Los Angeles	Fresno, Calif.
	Needles, Calif.

San Francisco	Reno, Nev.
	Redding, Calif.
Chicago	Davenport, Iowa
	Fond du Lac, Wis.
New York	Harrisburg, Pa.
	Havre de Grace, Md.
	Schenectady, N.Y.
Washington, D.C.	Richmond, Va.
	Altoona, Pa.

The point isn't that Reno would become a suburb of San Francisco, but that all of the towns between these two cities would be within the Rule of 45 circle for maglev trains. A pure maglev future, then, would replace today's urban sprawl with a series of separated towns and villages built around train stations. The city would grow, but the population would be dispersed throughout a 150-mile radius. In effect, urban sprawl would be diluted to the point of nonexistence.

The typical commute for people living in the maglev suburbs would seem familiar to many Americans today—drive to the station early in the morning, board the train, ride for 30 to 40 minutes, get off and walk to work. The only difference would be the view from the train window. Instead of a string of suburbs and shopping centers, there would be open countryside, punctuated here and there by small towns.

I have always thought that the old railroad suburbs must have been pleasant places. For one thing, they were real towns, with real business districts of their own. Within a few blocks of the railroad station, you would find restaurants, the courthouse, offices, and stores. There was a center to each town, and a clear distinction between one town and the next.

Life in these towns was not rural, but it wasn't suburban either —or wasn't until they got swallowed up as the metropolitan area expanded. I suspect that many Americans who are bothered by the anonymity and lack of community in today's urban and suburban settings would enjoy the chance to live in maglev suburbs. Surrounded by open space, in a very real sense they would be participating in the rebirth of an old American dream.

A Day in the Virtual Future

It was dark by the time Carol went into her workroom. Her after-noon jog had been a little longer than usual, and she had lingered over dinner to watch the desert sunset—a particularly good one this time. Walking into the room and donning her control gloves, she asked for an office. Immediately, she was surrounded by leather-bound books stacked to the ceiling, with a desk in front of her. "Let's have the last month's sales figures," she said, and a series of numbers started scrolling over the top of the desk. Occa-sionally, she pointed at a particular figure to move it to another list.

After a few hours, a voice announced that her call to a colleague in Japan was ready. One end of the room dissolved and was replaced by a man sitting in bright sunlight at the side of a swim-ming pool. Together, they compared notes on their analyses and prepared for a conference call that would take place in a few hours.

The most interesting thing about this whole story is that nothing —the books, the desk, the pool, or even the sunlight—was really there.

14

The Virtual Future

I do not know whether I was then a man dreaming I was a butterfly, or whether I am now a butterfly dreaming I am a man.

—CHUANG-TZU, *"On the Leveling of All Things"*

The revolution isn't going to start with a manifesto or with people putting up barricades in the streets. It's going to start on a stalled freeway at 6:30 P.M. on a hot July evening, with cars stretching away to the Crack of Doom and heat waves shimmering on the horizon. It's going to start with someone watching his air conditioner die as his car overheats, realizing he'll never get home in time for his son's Little League game. It's going to start when that guy says, "To hell with it—I'm not doing this anymore."

And why should he? Back in the days when most workers stood on assembly lines and manipulated real physical objects, it made sense to think of the workplace as a place one went to, a place where people congregated in a central location to pool their efforts. But why should a worker who takes information into his or her computer, manipulates it, and then sends it out again have to be on the highways at all? Why can't he or she just as well work at home?

Look at it this way. You can do a lot of things with cars: run them on batteries, recharge them with solar energy, run them efficiently around smart highways. What you can't do, however, is make a car that takes up less than 40 to 50 square feet of space. There are only so many 50-square-foot areas on a highway, only so many parking spaces. Sooner or later, even if the system runs perfectly, there is going to be congestion. Episodes like the one described above are going to happen more and more frequently —you just can't avoid them if large numbers of people have to travel to and from their workplaces in cars.

Some people have already anticipated this congested future and have opted to work at home, either full- or part-time. With a phone, a fax machine, and a computer connected to the outside world through phone lines, these people can do almost any job at home that they could do at the office. They can set their own work hours, watch the kids, and avoid the daily commute. And of course, while they're working at home, they're not taking up 50-square-foot areas on their local highways. There are estimated to be about 3.7 million full-time "telecommuters" in the American workforce (3 percent of the total) and about ten times that number who spend at least part of their workweek at home.

This phenomenon is important enough to have attracted the attention of sociologists and government agencies and to have generated a couple of magazines devoted entirely to a readership of home office workers. On the San Francisco peninsula, county governments have contributed to the trend by requiring that some office workers stay home one day a week, "commuting" to work via telephone lines instead of cars. The Rocky Mountains seem to attract a disproportionate number of "lone eagles," who live in the mountains but plug themselves into the national information grid.

According to the conventional wisdom, there are limits to how far the home office movement can go. The argument goes like this: In the information era, the most important thing is for people to have new ideas, and the most fruitful way to generate

these ideas is for people to interact with each other informally—to brainstorm. For this to happen, people need to be in informal contact with each other. And it won't happen, the argument goes, if everyone's at home staring at a computer screen.

There is a superficial credibility to this sort of argument. I know I have gotten some of my best ideas over a cup of coffee or an informal lunch with colleagues. People who do most of their work at home tell me that they need to go to the office a couple of times a week just to feel connected to things. But is it actually necessary for everyone to go to a central location to interact in these informal ways? This may sound like a question for a psychologist, but I want to argue that it's actually a question about information transfer.

In Chapter 9, we saw that we could assign numbers to the information content of things like pictures and books and symphonies by counting the number of bits of information it would take to reproduce them. Why shouldn't we analyze a working experience in the same way? The conversation over the coffeepot has an information content—sounds come to your ear, pictures to your eye. What if it were possible to deliver that same information to you at home? Suppose you could see your colleagues in a lifelike three-dimensional visual field and hear their voices in high-fidelity reproduction. Would it matter if they were really there? Could you have a "day at the office" without ever leaving home?

Think about what happens when you walk into your office at the start of a day. The first thing that impinges on your consciousness is the sight of the things in it. What I'm asking is whether it would make any difference if the information in the light, instead of coming to you directly, was first converted into a string of electronic bits and sent halfway around the world, then reconverted to light waves and sent to your eye. If enough information was retained in this process—enough detail, enough color, enough three-dimensionality—I think there is a sense in which you could say that the transmitted image was just as real (to you, at least) as the original.

It's no good saying that in your office you could go and touch something like your desk, because the sense of touch involves just another information flow. A large human hand might measure 200 by 100 millimeters (a millimeter is about the thickness of a dime). Imagine wearing a glove that could exert a different pressure on each of the 20,000 square millimeters of your hand. From the table on pages 128–29, we know that we can distinguish 1028 different grades of pressure with 10 bits of information. We can argue that 1000 grades of pressure is more than adequate to describe the human sense of touch, in which case the information contained in a touch would be about 200,000 bits. If you imagine changing the pattern ten times a second (much more rapidly than your senses can follow), you can see that the sensation of touching something corresponds to an information flow of about 2 million bits per second—a hundred times less than the information flow in an ordinary TV signal. In the end, we can make the same argument about touch that we made about sight. Provided enough information is sent, the sensation of touching the desk and the sensation of wearing a glove that produces the same pressure on the sensors in your hand should be indistinguishable.

The visual cues you get from reading this book, in other words, could be reproduced by projecting an image into your eyes, perhaps through the use of specialized goggles. The sense of holding the book could be transmitted through a set of specialized gloves. Would there be a fundamental difference between the real and the transmitted experiences?

In some ways, this argument gets back to the old sophomore bull sessions about solipsism—to the question of whether the world is real or whether there are only sense impressions. I'm not trying to reopen all those questions about reality and appearance that we all agreed to ignore years ago when we walked out of our last philosophy classes. I'm just trying to point out that if we have a technology capable of processing and transmitting information fast enough, our definition of "going to work" may change radically, and with it our cities. At some time in the future, it might indeed be possible to have everything from an informal conference to a business lunch without any of the participants leaving home.

FIBER OPTICS AND VIRTUAL REALITY

The sort of thing I have been describing—the simulation of real-life experiences by information flow—is called virtual reality. The concept of virtual reality rests on the notions that any human experience depends on input from the senses and that any sensory input can be thought of as a flow of information—a flow that, ultimately, is interpreted by the brain. In the everyday world, this information comes directly from the external world. In a virtual world, the information comes from a computer. The question I would like to raise is this: When do virtual worlds become so real that people get as much out of staying at home as they do out of going to work? When, in other words, does virtual reality become so "real" that "reality" itself becomes unnecessary?

The home office today makes no pretense to this kind of realism. Telephone, fax, and modem transmit information over conventional phone lines at the rate of tens of thousands of bits per second—enough to keep someone in contact with the rest of the world, but hardly enough to provide the illusion of being there.

Nevertheless, you can see the glimmerings of the future in equipment that is already common in the information industry. The teleconference, for example, is a routine way for people at different offices to get together for meetings. In a teleconference, a group of people sit around a table at one location and see a large-screen TV image of a group of people sitting around a table someplace else. In a fancy system, things can even be set up so that you barely notice the break where your "real" table ends and their "virtual" table begins. Conversation flows around the real-plus-virtual table as if everyone were in the same place. In the conferences I've seen, everybody brought the same documents to the meeting, so people just referred to them, but it wouldn't be hard to imagine documents moving back and forth by fax as the conference proceeded.

A few years ago, I initiated a little experiment with this sort of technology at my home institution, George Mason University, which is located in the heart of the edge city region of the Washington, D.C., metropolitan area. Like many universities, we offer advanced courses to people employed in our area. Given the rush-hour traffic situation, however, there are problems with the conventional late-afternoon and evening adult classes. So long as we have to move people—either bring students to our campus or send faculty out into the community—we run up against the delay and frustration generated by local traffic.

There is already a well-established way of getting around this difficulty—it's called the telecourse. Someone lectures into a camera, and students around the region (or even around the world) watch and listen, talking to the instructor through microphones on their desks. The instructor can hear the questions but can't see the students.

The experience of giving a telecourse is a little like lecturing to an audience hiding behind a veil. It also has some weird consequences (for the instructor, at least). I gave such a course to most of the high school physics teachers in Virginia a few years ago, and to this day I am greeted like an old friend by people who know me (from having seen my image on the screen through all those lectures) but whom I have never met.

But no one would ever mistake the experience of being in a telecourse for the real thing. I did an experiment on this recently. I wanted to try something that actually mimicked what you might find in a virtual workplace. I split my advanced science writing seminar into two groups, putting each in a different building on campus. The two halves of the class were linked by both audio and video—that is, the people in each room could both see and hear those in the other.

At first, everyone was painfully aware of the TV cameras and lights—I found, for instance, that if there were fewer than three people in a room, students would betray their nervousness by mugging at the cameras. But as the experiment went on and everyone got used to the situation, there were more and more times when the cameras and screens became invisible. Even with the crude linking via standard TV screen and sound reproduction, you could actually forget that the people you were talking to were across campus and not in the same room. It felt as if everyone were together in a normal face-to-face classroom.

That experience made me receptive to the idea that work experiences can be reproduced by the rapid exchange of information. It also made me start reading about people who argue that *any* experience can be reproduced the same way.

Perhaps the ultimate theoretical limits of this idea were reached a few years ago by Thomas Furness of the University of Washington in Seattle. He calculated that to transmit a "completely satisfactory sexual experience," you would have to be able to send about 6 billion bits of information per second— roughly a million times more information than is now exchanged between personal computers when they're linked. Presumably, "infonauts" experimenting with this idea would use a full bodysuit to transmit the sense of touch. When technicians talk about "any experience," they really mean it!

The crux of the creation of virtual realities (at whatever level of verisimilitude) revolves around the question of how many bits can be moved from one place to another in a given length of time. The real breakthrough in information transmission took place back in the 1970s, and it's in the process of being put into place around the world even as you read this. Called fiber optics, it involves the use of light to send information from one point to another.

You can do a simple experiment to teach yourself the basic physics behind fiber optics. Put some water into a wineglass and go into a room in which only one floor or desk lamp is turned on. Hold the glass high above your head near the lamp and look at the underside of the water surface. You will see the color of the ceiling through it—the surface will be completely transparent. Now start to lower the glass toward you. At some point, as shown in Figure 22, the undersurface of the water will appear to change —you will see the color of the walls instead of the ceiling.

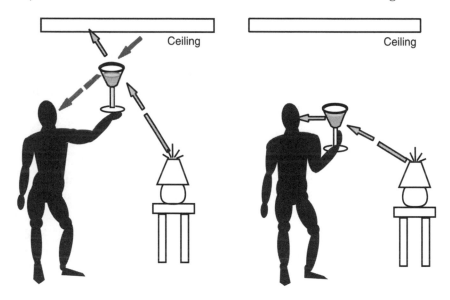

Figure 22. The wineglass experiment

What has happened is that at the upper position, light from the lamp and walls is hitting the surface of the water and going on through, as shown. You see the light from the ceiling coming through. At the lower position, light from the lamp and walls is being reflected back down into the water and, ultimately, your eye, completely blotting out the light from the ceiling. This phenomenon is called total internal reflection, and it can happen whenever light moves from a dense medium (like water) to a less dense medium (like air). And that sudden change of color you see may, someday, allow you to inhabit a virtual reality all your own.

The basic reason is this: if you have a glass tube, as shown in Figure 23, and shine light into it at the right angle, the light will be totally reflected every time it hits the edge of the tube. It will, in fact, be trapped in the tube, even if the tube is bent or, indeed, even if the tube is tied into a knot. Each time the light comes to the surface, it is reflected back in.

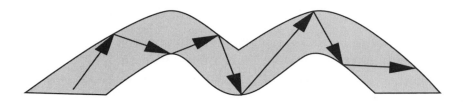

Figure 23. Reflection of light in a fiber optics tube

Fiber optics is the generic name given to systems that use this effect to carry light from one place to another. The basic science behind the optical fiber has to do with the way light moves through a transparent material. Like a traveler making a trans-continental flight by changing planes at several airports instead of flying directly from one coast to another, light moves through a material by being absorbed and reemitted by atoms along its path. Consequently, the overall speed of light—the time it takes a signal to get from one point to another—is less in a material than it would be in a vacuum.

When a light wave encounters a boundary (between air and glass, for example), the part of the wave in the new material will move at a different speed than the part in the old. As a result, the boundary causes the light wave to wheel around and move in a new direction. Many natural phenomena, from desert mirages to the apparent shortening of objects partially immersed in water, are caused by these changes of direction in light waves. In the case of waves moving from a dense medium to a less dense one, the change in direction can actually be great enough to bounce the wave back into the dense medium. This is the basis of the entire fiber optics industry.

One important use of fiber optics lies in the formation of images that allow people to see what's going on in places that would otherwise be inaccessible. In this situation, a bundle of fibers is placed near the object to be viewed, and light entering the end of each tube in the bundle is carried to the other end. Each tube constitutes a single pixel, and the collection of light and dark dots forms a picture, much like the one on a TV screen. In medicine, for example, fiber bundles are routinely inserted into the body (either through natural openings or through surgical incisions) so that physicians can examine organs in a nonintrusive way.

In communications, the great advantage of fiber optics is that a thin optical fiber can carry a lot more information than an ordinary copper wire. In copper, the signal is carried by small motions of electrons. Since electrons are material objects, it takes time to speed them up and slow them down. Because of this and other effects, there is a limit to how many times per second you can move an electron in copper—how many crests of a wave you can push past a certain point in a second. In practice, the waves that carry your phone conversation through a normal copper wire make the electrons move back and forth a few thousand times per second. Light waves, on the other hand, undulate hundreds of trillions of times in the same time interval.

All information can be thought of as composed of bits, and the simplest kind of bit for information sent down a wire is "on" or "off." The amount of information that can be carried in a wire, then, depends on how many times the wave can be turned on and off each second. And although the connection is actually a little more subtle than it may seem at first glance, it is nonetheless true that waves that go up and down rapidly can be turned on and off more quickly than those that go up and down more slowly.

Conventional copper phone lines can carry several hundred phone conversations at the same time by breaking each conversation into a series of chunks, then mixing chunks from many conversations and sending them down the wire and letting a computer at the other end sort things out. Commercially installed optical fibers, using the same general procedure, can carry tens of thousands of conversations, and there are prototype fibers that will be able to carry half a million. The sheer volume of information that can flow over a fiber is daunting. One estimate I've seen, for example, said that in principle a single optical fiber the size of a thread could carry the conversations that would ensue if every single American got on the phone to talk at the same time!

In the real world, however, optical fibers do not carry their bits of information with perfect fidelity. Glass always varies slightly in density from one point to another (see Chapter 4), so light waves hopping through it encounter different numbers of atoms in different places. This leads to distortion—the kind of thing you see when you look through old windowpanes. To carry light pulses over long distances, fibers have to have a uniform consistency and a freedom from impurities unknown to ordinary glassmakers. A half-mile-thick "window" made of typical fiber materials today, for example, would have about the same transparency as a normal pane of window glass.

But no matter how transparent the glass, sooner or later the signal will be degraded. Thus, long-range optical fibers usually have "repeaters" (devices that amplify the weakening signal) between stretches of fiber. In the next generation of fibers, these will probably be built into the glass structure itself, making the fibers even more capable of transmitting huge amounts of information over long distances. And there will soon be optical fibers capable of transmitting billions of bits of information per second halfway around the world.

Along with this increase in the ability to transmit information, engineers are trying to reduce the amount of information that has to be sent to do a given job—a technique called data compression.

When a wink is exchanged between a man and a woman, you could argue that only one bit of information has been transferred. Nevertheless, there are contexts in which an enormous amount of meaning can be carried by this small amount of information. In the same way, surrounding a small information flow with extra context can allow a computer to reconstruct the original material with much less information than it would need to do the job from scratch.

For example, if you want to send a TV picture pixel by pixel, you have to be able to process about 200 megabits each second into digital form, transmit them to a receiver, then process them again to reproduce the picture. But you can get the same effect with much less expenditure of effort if you send information only about pixels that change from one frame to the next, rather than sending each frame as if it were the first. This allows you to send the sequence of pictures with less actual information flow or, equivalently, to send more pictures at the same cost.

A somewhat more advanced technique I've seen demonstrated involves breaking the picture down into repeated mathematical forms known as fractals, then transmitting the formulas for the fractals and having a computer at the other end reconstruct the picture. (I have to confess that my favorable impression of this technique largely derives from the fact that the man who developed it chose to demonstrate his ability to transmit real-time images by showing the scene in *Casablanca* when Ingrid Bergman comes back to the café.)

STATE OF THE ART

As these examples of technical virtuosity show, bright people all around the world are working very hard to increase the rate at which information can be sent from one point to another. Some of the fruits of past efforts are all around us—computers that talk to each other, fax machines, and so on. They are what make it possible for people to work at home today.

But in a real sense, they are just the first drops in what is sure to be a major flood of new technology. Information now flows into your house through copper wires—phone lines and TV cables. If those copper wires were to be replaced by optical fibers, the amount of information coming in could be increased a thousandfold or more. It would be as if the 1-inch pipe that brings in your water were replaced by a pipe several feet across. Telephone companies are in the middle of a massive rewiring project that will, over a period of 10 or 20 years, replace almost all the copper wire in the country with optical fiber. Many companies already make it standard policy to replace copper with fiber whenever they carry out routine maintenance on their equipment.

The first commercial fiber optic cable was installed in downtown Chicago in 1977, and since then much of the long-distance phone traffic in the country has been transmitted in the form of light pulses. In the late 1980s, the first transoceanic cables were put into operation, spanning first the Atlantic Ocean, then the Pacific. But fiber isn't used just for business calls. Near where I live is a development called The Cascades. From the outside, it looks like any other edge city development, but there is one important difference: from the time the first shovel of dirt was turned over, phone and TV service was brought into the development on optical fibers. The lessons learned in this operation illustrate the problems that still have to be overcome before we can achieve a complete fiber system.

Signals are routinely sent through fiber in digital form, but the equipment now in your home—your telephone and TV set, for example—can deal only with analogue signals. This means that before the information can be turned back into sound or image, it has to be converted back from digital to analogue. This is easy to do, but it's a bit expensive. In order to keep the costs at The Cascades down, then, engineers installed one converter to serve several homes, with signals coming into the converter in the form of light pulses but leaving it as ordinary signals on copper wire. This is, in fact, the last bottleneck that will have to be eliminated before we can build a communications system that brings optical fiber, with its ability to carry enormous amounts of information, right into your house.

When it is eliminated, the possibilities for changing the nature of the workplace become endless. Right now, for example, in the virtual reality forefront, there is something called the head-mounted display—essentially small television screens over each eye that present a computer-driven visual image. Turn your head and the computer presents a new visual field appropriate to the new direction of view. It's easy to imagine this sort of technique being used to turn a room into another place, at least visually. There are even discussions about doing away with screens and eyepieces and having miniature lasers paint images directly onto the retina. (I admit to being a bit squeamish about this particular idea.)

Work in the area of touch is a bit less developed. There are a variety of "virtual gloves" on the market, but they are designed mainly to allow the wearer to control a computer by pointing or gesturing. One development that I find particularly intriguing is a combination eye-hand program in which one "sees" complex molecules and moves them around with a joystick. The program is designed so that you can "feel" the force between the molecules and, ultimately, find the orientation where they can pull each other in and bind together. This program, I imagine, is a great help to chemists trying to make new kinds of molecules.

These systems are primitive compared to the kinds of virtual reality systems I've been talking about, of course, but progress is being made. About the time this book went to press, for example, a prototype virtual reality full bodysuit became available. Can virtual sex be all that far behind?

The point is clear. Fiber optics bring us to the verge of being able to produce any visual or tactile sensation we want. What does that mean for the future of cities?

THE VIRTUAL FUTURE

The United States has a land area of about 3.5 million square miles and somewhat more than 70 million households. If every household were located on an equal parcel of land, we would need to have about 20 houses per square mile, with each house commanding a bit more than 30 acres. This is the maximum possible dispersion that could be achieved with the American population, the farthest apart we could be from each other. It corresponds to population densities like those found in far exurban areas of major cities. It is much lower than that found in suburbs but is actually higher than that of many rural areas.

It's unlikely, of course, that everyone will decide to leave the cities and light out for the territories, but this simple arithmetical exercise shows that even modern urban sprawl has come nowhere near exploiting the living space available to Americans. Using a combination of fiber optics (to send information) and virtual reality (to interpret it), nearly all everyday travel could be eliminated, and most people could live where they wanted (in principle, at least), regardless of what they did for a living.

Think for a moment about what a business meeting between two people might be like in this virtual future. You'd go into your office at home, dial your opposite number, perhaps don a helmet, and start talking. You'd see the other person sitting in his or her office. You could look around the other room or out the window because every time you moved your head, your computer would make the necessary adjustment to your field of vision. You could certainly pick up any nonverbal cues your colleague was sending, and if papers had to be exchanged, you could always use the fax. It seems reasonable to assume that such a meeting would accomplish as much as it would if one of you had fought traffic to come to the other person's office for a face-to-face encounter. This sort of exchange would probably be the paradigm of the virtual future.

Here's a brainteaser: Where did that meeting I just described take place? It certainly wasn't at your home or the home of your colleague. In fact, you could argue that it took place outside the normal three-dimensional world we live in—in a region people are starting to call cyberspace. Cyberspace is where interactions between people and things will take place in the information age. It may even be the place where the city of the future will be located.

With a little imagination, you can see that a meeting in cyberspace could be a lot of fun. After all, the information going out to your colleagues about your surroundings would be just a string of bits. Why should it be restricted to a string describing the mundane appearance of your office? It would be no trouble for your computer to manufacture another image—an image that existed only in cyberspace. You could then choose the backdrop against which you would appear—a book-lined library for conventional types like me, a tropical beach for the environmentally conscious, a moonlit birch forest for the romantic, the deck of a pirate ship for the adventurous. The choice of virtual background might someday become as much a part of your work image as your choice of clothes.

In fact, you might be able to shop for clothes much as you shop for them by catalogue today, with the added benefit that you could actually touch the items you wanted to purchase in cyberspace. An engineer whose work involved supervising robotic manufacturing could "see" his or her assembly lines, "feel" the working machinery, "handle" the output—all in cyberspace. When you think about it, there are very few occupations that actually require the physical presence of a human being. Most of us could easily do what we do in cyberspace rather than in real space.

You can amuse yourself by thinking about how almost any part of your day would look in cyberspace. For example, I recently renewed my driver's license. Assuming people still did such things in this future, how would that process work?

Instead of driving down to the motor vehicles department, I'd dial up the clerk, perhaps getting into an electronic queue. When he or she was ready, I'd get a signal back and we'd meet in cyberspace. The eye test and formalities would be handled electronically, perhaps by having me type answers to the form questions directly into the computer network. The photo for the license could be constructed directly from the flow of bits between me and the clerk, and instructions could easily be sent to my computer to print out a new license. Quick, easy, and no traveling by either of us. And there would be no need for the clerk to be at a central office either—he or she could just as well be at home.

This sort of example can be multiplied without end. In a city where everyone was connected by optical fibers, the only people needing to travel to work (or from one place to another) would be those, like plumbers, chefs, and surgeons, with essential services to perform—services that could not be performed easily by information transfer alone. And even in these cases, you can imagine a future with these sorts of jobs done by robots in each home, so that no one would ever have to leave his or her dwelling.

So if work in the future is done largely in cyberspace, will people continue to group themselves into the huge communities we call cities? Will the great American metropolis of the future be like the midwestern farm town today, burdened with a shrinking, aging population as young people go off to seek a better life elsewhere? Or will people, freed from the need to deal with the real world, spend more and more of their time in cyberspace, indifferent to their physical surroundings and more or less staying where they were when cyberspace first opened up to them?

In many ways, the virtual future is the most uncertain of the futures I've chosen to discuss because it presents human beings with choices and temptations that they have never faced in the past.

It is also, in some ways, the scariest of the futures. The writers of "Star Trek" recognized this when they imagined a planet where everyone could live inside their own fantasy world—their personal virtual reality. In the TV series, the Federation recognized the danger of such a place and placed the planet under its most severe quarantine. The problem, you see, was that people could go there and simply drop out of the real world. We've seen a mild version of this in our own time, when some particularly sensitive teenagers get so caught up in the imaginary world of Dungeons and Dragons that they have trouble coping with the rest of their lives.

Suppose our information-age computers and optical fiber networks could give us a virtual world so true to life that we would have difficulty distinguishing it from the real thing. Suppose we could make the virtual world perfect, with no suffering, no injustice, no ugliness. Would we have the strength of character to come out to face the real problems that surround us now?

I wonder.

A Day in the Future in Space

Dick rolled out of bed when the alarm went off, picked up his coffee, and strolled over to the balcony. He could see other balconies spreading out below him, down to the base of the tower 200 feet below, and the aluminum and glass ceiling curving away in the distance. The weather guys had made rain again last night—he could see the leaves on the trees in the park glistening—and now they were swinging the mirrors to let sunlight in. Why they bothered to keep up those old earth customs was beyond him. As he mused about this, a lone counterclockwise jogger passed by the path beneath him.

Later, a short walk brought him to an elevator that took him to the zero-gravity chamber at the center of the colony. Slipping into his excursion suit, checking the survival systems, and getting into his vehicle were all second nature to him by now, but he could remember when it had been a daily thrill. It turned out to be a good day at the construction site as he and Clair maneuvered their thin aluminum tubes into place and guided the robots that fastened them into the superstructure. Over sunward he could see another crew laying the solar collectors on the platform they'd finished last month. That made the fifth power station they'd finished this year—not a bad output record, if he said so himself.

He glanced back at the colony rotating slowly in space, with the blue globe of the earth behind it.

One human race, two homes.

15

The Future in Space

Silently we went round and round . . .

—OSCAR WILDE, *"The Ballad of Reading Gaol"*

The kinds of future cities I've talked about up to this point are all different from each other and from the cities we live in now. There is a sense, however, in which I have been very conservative. The technology needed to build each of these futures is not only available in the laboratory right now but, in many cases, already being deployed commercially. It really doesn't take much imagination to look at the electric car and the maglev train (to take two examples) and extrapolate futures in which their descendants have transformed the kinds of cities we live in. It's more difficult to look at capabilities that may be, for the moment, little more than gleams in the eyes of their creators and imagine what effect they may have on the cities of the future.

Nevertheless, before we leave the subject of the future of our cities, we ought to look at something more adventurous, ask a question that doesn't have an obvious answer. My own favorite question in this category was first posed by the late Gerard O'Neill, an experimental physicist at Princeton University. It is this: Is the surface of a planet really the right place for an expanding technological civilization?

What's intriguing about this question is this: it exposes an assumption we often make when we think about cities. Aside from a few visionaries, most people assume that cities built in the future will develop more or less like those of the past, at places where the natural terrain provides an economic rationale for building—around harbors, rivers, and crossroads.

There have always been writers who imagine cities unlike those they live in—cities at the bottom of the ocean, for example, or on the moon or floating in the clouds. But all such writers share a common basis. They all pick a location and accept the environment they find there, then build their city to suit it. Inhabitants of the imaginary lunar city, for example, weigh only one sixth of what they do on earth. The citizens of cloudland still breathe earthly air and drink earthly water. The city always exists, to some extent, as an adaptation to a natural setting that predates it.

What O'Neill and his class realized was that the newly dawned space age offered a possibility never before available to human beings. For the first time, they argued, we can build an entirely new kind of habitat, one in which nothing need be taken as given, where everything can be adjusted or built to our needs. They proposed the construction in space of the ultimate architectural dream—completely man-made cities in a completely man-made environment. The kinds of cities they described (which have since come to be known as O'Neill colonies) would be creatures of space, cut off from their mother planet. They would get their energy from the sun and their atoms (even those in their air and water) from the surface of the moon and the asteroid belt. They would even produce their own gravity. In a sense, they would represent the ultimate technological city—a city in which the last ties to terrestrial nature would be severed.

DESIGNING THE O'NEILL COLONIES

We can start thinking about human colonies in space by thinking about some of the most basic things needed by the human body to survive. In particular, we can start by thinking about something so much a part of our lives that we never notice it: gravity. From the moment of our birth, we are surrounded by the earth's gravitational field. Our species evolved in this environment, so we shouldn't be surprised that the human body doesn't seem to do very well in weightlessness. Astronauts returning from extended periods of weightlessness in orbit, for example, are usually found to have sustained serious loss of calcium from their bones. So the first thing we need to do in building a city in space is to find something to take the place of gravity. (Strictly speaking, a satellite in orbit is not in a state of zero gravity. To someone in the satellite, it appears that the gravitational pull of the earth is canceled by the centrifugal force associated with the orbital motion. There is zero net force, a fact that is interpreted as producing "weightlessness." In what follows, I will use the terms "zero gravity" and "weightlessness" interchangeably, according to the common usage.)

You can get a clue to what that substitute for gravity might be by recalling the experience of being in a car and going around a curve at high speed. You probably remember being thrown to the outside, and you may even recall feeling your shoulder being pressed up against the car door. We usually attribute this experience to the effects of centrifugal force.

Centrifugal force is the name we give to a phenomenon associated with inertia. An object left to itself, Isaac Newton taught us, will always move in a straight line. To someone watching your car go around that curve, what is happening is this: Your body tries to continue moving in a straight line while the car turns underneath you. Eventually, the car door moves over and pulls you around the curve. To you, sitting in the car, the same sequence of events is experienced as a force tending to push you toward the outside of the curve, a force we call center-fleeing, or centrifugal.

In his space colonies, O'Neill envisioned centrifugal force as a substitute for gravity. A typical design for a colony resembles a hollow doughnut rotating around an axis perpendicular to the plane of the hole (see Figure 24), a shape mathematicians call a torus. If you were inside the "dough" of the doughnut, you would feel a centrifugal force tending to pull you through the side, just as you feel thrown against the car door when you go around a curve. If you were standing on a scale, as shown, you would be pushed down onto it and the scale would register a weight just as it would if it were on your bathroom floor at home. To all intents and purposes, centrifugal force would play the role in the colony that gravity plays on earth, provided that we think of the side of the doughnut as the "floor" of the living space.

The important point to realize is that to someone inside the colony, the action of centrifugal force would be indistinguishable from that of gravity. Let something go and centrifugal force

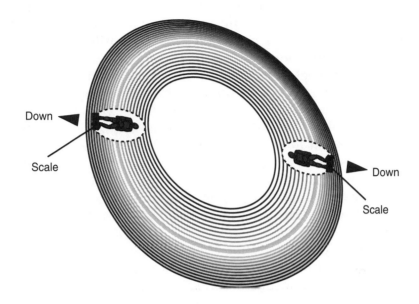

Figure 24. The O'Neill space colony

would make it "fall" toward the floor. Throw something up and the same force would slow it down, stop it, and make it come back down to you. To the casual observer, there would be no real difference between standing on the earth (where gravity pulls everything down) and standing in the colony (where centrifugal would do the same thing).

In principle, a doughnut of any size could be spun fast enough to produce earth-normal gravity. In practice, the inner ear, which controls our sense of balance, can deal with only a limited amount of spinning. And just as the design of the ear sets the limit on how fast elevators can go up in skyscrapers, it would set limits on how fast the O'Neill colony could rotate. Experiments seem to indicate that humans cannot detect a spin of one rotation per minute, so we can take that as the fastest rotation permissible.

The first engineering problem faced by builders of a space colony would be how to spin the doughnut fast enough to produce earth-normal gravity without upsetting the inner ear. This could be done by making the colony big—the larger the doughnut, the slower the rotation rate needed to produce the same level of centrifugal force. It turns out that you could meet both demands if the distance across the hole in the doughnut were about a mile. Any colony this size or bigger could produce earth-normal gravity while turning less than once a minute on its axis.

Another problem faced by these future builders would be how to provide things like air and water. The space colony would nearly resemble a closed ecosystem, one in which materials cycle through different forms but never leave. The earth is an example of a closed ecosystem, and some systems (nuclear submarines, for example) operate in this way for short periods of time. We don't know much about building long-term closed ecosystems, and we'll have to learn a lot more before we can design a space colony.

In 1991, a rather interesting experiment on closed ecosystems began in the Arizona desert. A group of people ("bionauts") entered a structure consisting of several connected glass domes and sealed themselves off from the outside world. The purpose of their operation: to collect data on how closed ecosystems work. They called the experiment Biosphere II because by their reckoning the earth itself is Biosphere I.

There was, unfortunately, a fair amount of media hype about Biosphere II, and many members of the scientific community criticized the bionauts over the way the experiment had been designed. To take just one example, consider the many plants within the domes. The original project statements left many people with the impression that the recycling of air in the biosphere would be accomplished as in nature—by having plants take in carbon dioxide and give off oxygen. It turned out, however, that there were a number of machines inside the domes to help extract carbon dioxide from the air—a discovery that caused one scientist to characterize the entire project as "a submarine with trees."

But the success of the bionauts (who were more or less unscathed in 1993) shows that human beings can live for substantial periods in an artificial ecosystem. I suspect that in the not too distant future we will be able to maintain truly closed ecosystems with people in them for really long periods of time. And this, in turn, means that we can begin to talk about generations of people being born and raised in space colonies.

The colonists' living space would probably look strange to anyone raised in one of today's terrestrial cities. Figure 25 shows a typical design for the interior of a space colony with a 1-mile diameter, for example. There are about 440 acres of living space on the outside ("downward") wall of the torus, with the ceiling being some 180 feet above the floor. Tightly clustered apartment complexes alternate with space given over to parks and agriculture.

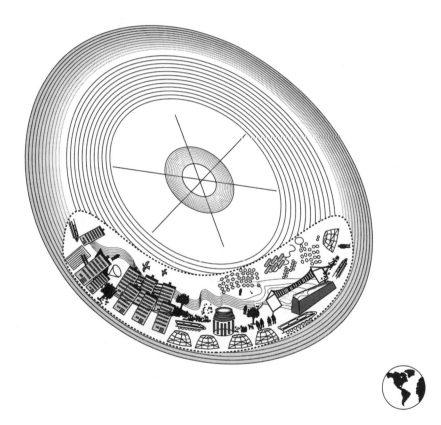

Figure 25. Interior of a space colony

Designers have talked about putting 10,000 people in such a structure, which would produce population density levels comparable to those in midtown Manhattan. Since, as we argue below, the main business of the colony would certainly be concentrated in space, most of the area inside the torus would be devoted to living quarters and food production. In one design, 20-story buildings housing apartments and hydroponic farms are clustered in a few places, leaving well over half the floor area for parks featuring greenery and trees. In fact, such a design could easily include enough green plants to keep the whole colony more or less self-sustaining.

If you stood in one of these parks, you would see a ceiling 200 feet above your head, curving away into the distance. There would probably be windows in the ceiling and mirrors outside to bring sunlight into the interior (you can even imagine engineers producing alternating night and day by moving them). It would be possible, in other words, to produce an ambience not too different (though in expanded form) from the sort of multistoried atria you now find in many large buildings, most noticeably hotels.

A space colony built like this wouldn't really be a city, however; it would be a small town. It would probably be some time before these "spacetowns" could be built in large enough versions to qualify as "space cities." If we kept population densities at the same level as in the sort of design I've been discussing, for example, the torus would have to be 5 miles in diameter to house a million people.

MOVING MATERIALS INTO SPACE

One thing we can say for certain about a future in which large communities exist in space is that they will require very large structures. This fact raises what is perhaps the most important technical question about O'Neill colonies: How are we going to get all these building materials into space? Even a minimum-sized colony would require hundreds of thousands of tons of such materials. The kinds of vehicles we have today, like the Shuttle with its 32-ton payload, simply couldn't do the job. Some other way will have to be developed.

Actually, the rocket—the traditional means humans have used to climb out of the gravitational well we live in—is an extraordinarily inefficient way to move things off the surface of the earth. The reason is simple: if you want to burn a ton of fuel when the rocket is 10 feet off the ground, you have to burn still more fuel to lift that ton of fuel 10 feet into the air. Almost all the energy generated by the engines of the Space Shuttle is used to lift its fuel (to be consumed later), and very little goes into the payload. The actual amount of energy needed to lift a 1-kilogram payload to the normal position of the Shuttle orbits, ignoring the energy needed to lift the fuel, is less than 10 kilowatt-hours. You could purchase this much energy for less than a dollar from any electric utility. It should not be surprising, then, that the same visionaries who talk about building space colonies also talk about developing new ways to move materials into space.

The most interesting solution to this problem, called the mass driver, was suggested by O'Neill in the early 1970s. Operating on the same principles as the magnetically levitated train, the mass driver (as sketched in Figure 26) would have a payload inserted into a large open-ended container (think of it as a high-tech garbage can), with superconducting magnets built into its fabric. This container, the analogue of the maglev car we discussed earlier, would be levitated above its track and accelerated by exactly the same sorts of magnetic forces.

The mass driver differs from the maglev in that the container would be accelerated up to escape velocity (7 miles per second for something on the surface of the earth). At this point, the accelerating magnets would be reversed and the body of the container slowed down. The payload, lying loose inside the "garbage can," would then fly out and sail off in space to the construction site, to be collected and added to the pile of building materials.

The energy needed to accelerate the container in the mass driver could be regained and fed back into the system when the container has stopped, with virtually all the energy consumed going into the payload. Thus, its energy requirements would be quite modest: a machine capable of launching 30,000 tons of material a year from the surface of the moon, for example, would require a solar collector only a few hundred feet on a side.

When the idea of the mass driver was first proposed, people thought of basing it on the moon because they felt that propelling a payload through the earth's atmosphere into space would be too costly, even if it were possible. But my student Ray Cheng and I did some calculations that indicate that this wouldn't be so: even in the worst-case scenario, with no attempt at streamlining the payload, the extra energy cost incurred in pushing the

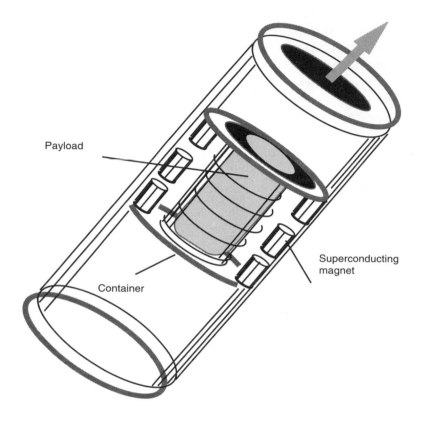

Payload

Superconducting
magnet

Container

Figure 26. Mass driver

payload through the earth's atmosphere would be only about a factor of three. In other words, even taking the atmosphere into account, the energy cost of putting a kilogram in near earth orbit would still be less than $3.00!

It is an interesting coincidence that both the space colonies and the future railroad suburbs may depend on the same technology: magnetic levitation. During the late 1970s and early 1980s, there was a small group of researchers who built and tested mass drivers. I got to know their names from reading the space colony literature. By the late 1980s, however, I had pretty much assumed that interest in (and funding for) the whole endeavor had died out. Imagine my surprise, then, when in 1992 I went to a daylong seminar on magnetically levitated trains and found the same cast of characters still pursuing their Holy Grail, this time under the aegis of the Department of Transportation. This is as good an illustration as I can imagine of a technology's ability to serve more than one end. Moving material into space or moving commuters to their jobs—it really makes very little difference to the magnets what job they are called upon to do.

Once the building materials have been placed in orbit, there are three features of the space environment that will make the construction process unlike anything seen on earth. Those features are (1) weightlessness, (2) the presence of abundant energy in the form of sunlight, and (3) an almost perfect vacuum. The weightless environment means that any structure that isn't rotating can be built in a very flimsy way; it needn't be strong enough to hold up its own terrestrial weight. A solar collector, for example, might be little more than a large sheet of tinfoil floating in space—no need for the kind of support structures a solar collector must have when located on the earth.

The energy in sunlight can be used in many ways. One example can be found in an unusual construction scheme for building a torus. It works like this: First, a balloon the size of the torus is inflated (it doesn't take much air to do this, since the balloon is in a near perfect vacuum). Then mirrors focus sunlight into a furnace where aluminum is first melted, then vaporized. The resulting gas is then squirted at the balloon. The spray is able to travel over long distances because there is no air to divert it. When the aluminum hits the balloon, it sticks, much like paint from a spray can. After several trips of the "spray can" around the torus, a solid metal shell will have accumulated. The balloon will then be deflated and removed (presumably to be used again), and workers can start fitting out the basic shell so that people can live there.

The economic raison d'être of space colonies near the earth will probably be related to the plentiful energy found in space. The same sorts of solar cells that produce electricity on earth can be used in space, with the advantage that the sun is always shining and there is no weather. People have actually drawn up plans for solar energy plants in space. A 1-billion-kilowatt plant, the equivalent of a large nuclear or coal-fired plant, would require about 5 square miles of collectors. In this scenario, the electric current generated in space would be beamed down to the ground in the form of microwaves.

There is another possible economic benefit to be derived from space colonies. We think of space, particularly near-earth space, as being empty; but in fact, it is full of asteroids, some of whose orbits bring them fairly close to the earth. These asteroids constitute the ultimate mineral resource in the solar system, for reasons that have to do with the earth's geological history.

When the earth first formed, it went through a period when it melted all the way through. At this time, most of the iron and other heavy metals in the planet sank toward the center under the influence of gravity. All that's left near the surface are a few veins of ore here and there, and this ore has been the basis of all human mining enterprise. The asteroids are materials left over from the formation of the solar system—materials that never got taken up into planets—and their heavy metals have not been removed. As a consequence, the asteroids are loaded with rare and expensive minerals. Astronomer Robert Rood and I once calculated that the market value of materials in a single asteroid 10 miles across exceeds the total national debt of the United States. If asteroids turn out to be an exploitable resource, then the first permanent residents in space may be miners, as were many of the first Europeans in the American West.

THE FUTURE IN SPACE

Living in a space colony would, I suppose, be like living in one of the superskyscrapers I described in Chapter 11: it would have predominantly man-made surroundings, rather high levels of population density, and a life-style very different from the urban sprawl that seems to be developing in American cities today.

I think that there are long-range forces that will drive the space-colony future—forces not yet as intense as those pushing us toward the superskyscraper. You need to take a very long range view to see them, but I think the case can be made.

There are two things that every technological civilization needs: materials and energy (or, more precisely, atoms and energy). We need atoms so that we can put them together to make the things we need to support life, and we need energy for transportation, manufacturing, and the like. Both atoms and energy can be obtained on the earth, of course, but at a cost. To give just one example, we have enough coal in the United States to supply our energy needs for centuries. To use it, however, we will have to strip-mine a large part of our arid high plains and dump large amounts of carbon dioxide into the atmosphere. As currently undeveloped nations start to build more industries, the added pollution will certainly put constraints on economic growth. In this sort of environment, it's not hard to see the attractiveness of a scheme in which materials and energy could be brought to the earth from outside. Whether the economic equation will ever favor the exploitation of space over the development of alternate resources on the earth is an open question. But if such is the case, then O'Neill colonies will, in all likelihood, become the cities of the future.

If they do, then there is another possible consequence that bears examination. The first generation of people living in space colonies will be like us. They will be used to moving around—going for long walks, doing all the things we associate with living in an extended ecosystem. They may well feel cramped in a city where the "sky" is only a few hundred feet above their heads, where they can walk only a few miles in a given direction until they come back to where they started. I know I would have a hard time living in the kind of urban beehive represented by either the space colony or the superskyscraper. But at least in the latter, there would be the consolation of mountains and beaches that I could get to if I wanted. In a space colony, that wouldn't be the case. I suspect that the first settlers there would miss the outdoors occasionally, although the romance of the move into space would undoubtedly help to console them.

Their children and grandchildren, however, wouldn't know any other kind of world. They would feel at home in their torus and wouldn't necessarily get nostalgic for the wide-open spaces. They wouldn't need to be near the earth, either, and over time you could expect the colonies to congregate in those regions of the solar system that best met their needs (just as settlements on the earth gravitated to harbors and other areas that facilitated economic activity). The prime real estate in our solar system isn't near the earth, but out in the asteroid belt. There the colonists would find virtually unlimited materials in an easily accessible form, as well as the same solar energy available near the earth (albeit in a somewhat diluted form).

And once a few generations of settlers lived out their lives in large man-made "cities" in the asteroid belt, there would be little left to tie them to the home planet. It would make little difference to them whether their torus was in the asteroid belt, the rings of Saturn, or—and here's the important point—halfway to Alpha Centauri.

The conventional wisdom has always been that interstellar travel is impossible because the distances are too large. It would require impossible amounts of energy to get a spaceship to a star and back within a single human lifetime. But what if it didn't matter how long the trip took? What if a space colony could be accelerated toward a nearby star at a leisurely rate, so that the trip took hundreds of years? In this case, only moderate amounts of energy would be needed.

Try to imagine the solar system as a kind of seedbed, sending containers of life out into the galaxy. If this happens, then O'Neill colonies will not only be the ultimate cities—they will be our calling cards as we venture out into the larger universe.

16

The Death of Cities

They say the lion and the lizard keep
The courts where Jamshyd gloried and drank deep.

  —*The Rubáiyat of Omar Khayyám*

Atlantis. Pompeii. Ur of the Chaldees. Angkor Wat. Machu Picchu. Thebes. Carthage.

This chapter is about doomsday—about the fact that cities can die as well as be born. This roll call of the vanished reminds us that people build cities for a reason, that every city meets an important human need. When it does not, or cannot, continue meeting that need, it is abandoned to the elements.

There is something irresistibly romantic about the ruins of ancient civilizations. The sight of vines growing around an old temple, of sands blowing across an ancient square, exerts a powerful force on the imagination. Consider Shelley's famous sonnet about a statue of Ramses II, one of the greatest pharaohs of Egypt:

> I met a traveller from an antique land
> Who said: Two vast and trunkless legs of stone
> Stand in the desert . . . Near them, on the sand,
> Half sunk, a shattered visage lies, whose frown,
> And wrinkled lip, and sneer of cold command,
> Tell that its sculptor well those passions read
> Which yet survive, stamped on these lifeless things,
> The hand that mocked them and the heart that fed:
> And on the pedestal these words appear:
> "My name is Ozymandias, king of kings:
> Look on my works, ye Mighty, and despair!"
> Nothing beside remains. Round the decay
> Of that colossal wreck, boundless and bare
> The lone and level sands stretch far away.

The problem with this romantic vision is that many of the ancient cities we assume to have joined Ozymandias in lonely obscurity are still around. Thebes, home to the drama of Oedipus Rex, is still a thriving provincial town a half hour's drive from Athens. Carthage was destroyed by the Romans at the end of the Punic Wars in 146 B.C. The victors razed the city, following the demand of Cato the Elder ("Carthage must be destroyed"), by plowing the earth with salt and decreeing that the place would never again be a human habitation. A hundred years later, however, there was a Roman colony on the site, and today it is a suburb of the city of Tunis. If there is a reason for a city to survive, it will do so regardless of the political and military vicissitudes that come its way. In real life, I'm afraid, those "vast and trunkless legs of stone" are as likely to be found in a supermarket parking lot as in the desert!

This is not to say that there are no ruins of cities in the world—there are. They tend to fall into two classes: cities that died because they no longer fulfilled the political or economic needs of their inhabitants, and cities that fell to a far more inexorable force—the earth's geology. And while it may be possible to imagine a particular city as immune from political or economic forces (Rome, after all, has done pretty well over the millennia), the same is not true of geological forces. Pick any city you like and you can find a geological force that, sooner or later, can destroy it.

There are many examples of cities that have died for economic or political reasons. The American West is dotted with ghost towns—towns that were filled with miners while the gold or silver or coal lasted and were abandoned when it gave out. They represent economic death. Angkor Wat and Machu Picchu, on the other hand, can be thought of as political ruins—places that were abandoned because they no longer fulfilled the specific political needs that caused them to be built in the first place.

Angkor Wat, that great temple complex in the Cambodian jungle, was begun in 1119 as a monument to the conquests of (and possibly as a tomb for) King Suryavarman II. It consisted of the stone temples that survive to this day (and, presumably, a large city of wooden residences for everyone from workers to the members of the court). By 1431, however, the political and military fortunes of the region had changed, and when Siamese armies sacked the city and marched the inhabitants off into slavery, there seemed little reason for people to move back. The vines invaded the magnificent temples, and the city disappeared beneath the jungle to slumber for centuries until it was rediscovered in 1860 by a French archaeologist.

Machu Picchu, that green-covered Inca ruin in the Peruvian Andes, probably has a similar story, although the details are less clear. At the peak of its existence, it covered over 5 square miles of the steep mountainside on which it was built. It was an administrative city in the Inca empire, but probably not a fortress (like most major Inca cities, it had no defensive walls). The city was abandoned sometime after the Spanish Conquest and the dissolution of Inca rule.

I suspect that during their prime these cities must have been something like Washington, D.C. Washington is the capital of a great nation, but logically speaking there is no reason why anything more than a small river port should stand at this particular spot on the Potomac. The designation of the site for the U.S. capital was, after all, a political compromise among eighteenth-century statesmen who could have had no notion of how important their choice would later become. Should some unimaginable catastrophe put an end to Western technology and our burgeoning information society, it's hard to see why a new Washington should rise from the ashes.

From a scientific point of view, a far more interesting class of cities are those that have disappeared because of changes in their physical environment. Sometimes these changes are violent, as with earthquakes or volcanic eruptions, and sometimes they are gradual, as with slow changes in climate or sea level. But slow or fast, their effect is the same: the city dies.

The disappearance of cities by this route is a consequence of one of the central truths about our planet. The earth, alone among its sisters in the solar system, is still in the process of being formed. Deep inside it, radioactive nuclei are still decaying and producing heat. This heat makes rocks in the earth's mantle plastic, and they move—in effect, the rocks are "boiling" underneath your feet. At the surface, this boiling motion manifests itself as the erratic movements of tectonic plates, and riding these plates, like passengers on a raft, are the relatively light rocks of the continents—the "solid earth." Earthquakes, volcanoes, and many long-term climate changes are due to this constant motion. Land is lifted up and put down, rivers flow and change course, glaciers form and melt. The earth is constantly changing, and a spot that may seem hospitable for a city today may not be hospitable tomorrow.

The geological city killers are the easiest for a scientist to discuss, but at the same time they are sometimes hard to visualize. Some of them, like sea level or climate changes, occur slowly, so that we don't see them operating on a day-to-day basis. Others, like volcanic eruptions or tidal waves, are dramatic but infrequent. But hard to visualize or not, they are present in the real world, and as we shall see, they have destroyed cities in the past and will undoubtedly do so again in the future.

WATER SUPPLY

One of the most common reasons for abandoning a city has been the loss of a previously dependable water supply. This was particularly true of an ancient desert city like Ur of the Chaldees, the home of the prophet Abraham and a major city in Biblical times. Located on the Euphrates River in what is now Iraq, it was both the site of religious shrines and the center of an irrigation system that supported a major agricultural enterprise. Geologically, Ur was in a location similar to the Mississippi delta today—a region of rich alluvial soil watered by a great river.

Like other cities in the Middle East, Ur had its political ups and downs and was destroyed and rebuilt many times. But while it may have needed rebuilding after each war, the essential reason for its existence—the irrigation system fed by the Euphrates—was put in danger by a totally unexpected turn of events. Sometime after the Persian conquest, the main channel of the Euphrates shifted about 10 miles to the east of where it had run throughout recorded history (we'll describe the process by which rivers change channels in a moment). With the source of irrigation gone, the plains around Ur reverted to desert and the city was abandoned. Today, it is nothing more than a series of mounds in an uninhabited wasteland, a location the Arabs call Tall al Muqaiyir (Mound of Pitch).

Places like Tucson and Phoenix are obviously desert cities. Their green lawns stand in stark contrast to the surrounding countryside, and everyone realizes that they could not exist without massive supplies of water brought in from reservoirs. It's a little harder for most Americans to realize that San Francisco and Los Angeles are desert cities in exactly the same sense. I was surprised to learn, for example, that until the beginning of Spanish settlement, there were no trees growing on the fabled hills of San Francisco. In fact, most of the southern two thirds of California has an extremely arid climate, complete with a classical dry season that lasts for months during the summer.

The great twentieth-century real estate boom in Southern California has been fueled by water brought from distant rivers, many of them in the lush mountains of the northern part of the state. Great aqueducts were driven across deserts and mountain ranges to rearrange the natural flow of water. Sometimes, indeed, the single-minded quest for water of those behind such massive changes seem strange to us today. For example, William Mulholland, an Irish immigrant and self-taught engineer who built the water system that started Los Angeles's explosive growth, once began talking about Yosemite National Park at a dinner party. He talked about how he would like to close the park for a year, bring in the world's best painters and photographers to record every detail of it, and make their work available to everyone. "And then," he said, "I'd build a dam from one side of that valley to the other *and stop the goddam waste!*"

In the eastern United States, we tend to lose sight of the importance of water because this region is blessed with abundant rainfall. In the western part of the country, however, the story is different, which explains why so much has been spent on water control there. I suspect that an archaeologist in the future, looking back at our time, may well be more impressed by the fact that we built a quarter of a million dams in the twentieth century than by our cities.

There's no question that the availability of water is going to be a major limitation on the growth of cities in the American West—particularly in Southern California. This fact has produced constant friction among communities on the West Coast, as Southern Californians cook up schemes to divert water from rivers like the Columbia to their desert. The most ambitious of these schemes, conceived in the early 1950s, was called NAWAPA (North American Water and Power Alliance). It involved damming most of the rivers of the Canadian West and running the water to Southern California and the Great Lakes by means of huge aqueducts. Needless to say, gigantic schemes like these have not made much headway in these environmentally conscious and litigious times.

Actually, the most likely solution to the water problem in California and the American Southwest is not massive diversion projects like NAWAPA but the development of new technologies to remove salt from seawater. We already know that this can be done on a large scale (much of Saudi Arabia's water supply comes from desalinization plants), and the main question seems to be whether it can be done cheaply enough to keep the building boom going.

But this is a chapter about doomsday—about the death of cities. If doomsday comes to America's desert cities, it will come in the same way that it did to so many ancient cities in the Middle East—the disappearance of water. Imagine, for example, a prolonged drought that, over a period of years, simply dried up the reservoirs in the Southwest. At first, people would meet the crisis as they have so often in the past, by rationing water, not watering lawns, and so on.

But what if the drought went on beyond that point? You can

imagine the responses: a moratorium on new building (or at least new water hookups), a flight of industry to wetter climes, a shutdown of the irrigated agricultural fields that produce so much of the nation's harvest. Eventually, the great American desert cities would follow Ur of the Chaldees and become another set of monuments to humanity's failed attempts to build a lasting civilization in the desert. And who knows—maybe someday they would be lucky enough to be immortalized by a poet like Shelley.

CHANGES IN RIVERBEDS

A city doesn't have to be in the desert to face a threat like the one that finished Ur of the Chaldees. A process similar to the one that changed the course of the Euphrates centuries ago is going on right now in southern Louisiana. Most of the land in the southern part of the state was formed by the rich sediment carried downstream by the Mississippi River. But the Mississippi, the lifeblood of this region, is about to change its channel.

As a river carries silt out into the ocean, it builds up a peninsula of land along its course. As time goes by, the river has to run farther and farther to sea over a channel that is becoming more and more level. The water slows down, dumping more sediment farther upstream and making the channel flatter and flatter. Eventually, perhaps during a large flood, the river finds a new channel that will provide it with a steeper and shorter path to the sea. In the language of geologists, the new channel "captures" the river and the whole process begins again.

Like a dealer fanning cards out on a table, a river will flow first through one channel, then through another, until it has built up the entire triangular piece of land we call a delta. For the Mississippi, the old channels have become long bayous. Bayou Teche, known to every aficionado of Cajun music, was the main channel of the river from about 800 B.C. until the second century A.D. Around A.D. 1000, the river assumed its present course; by the mid twentieth century, it was ready to change again.

The Mississippi is about to run to the Gulf of Mexico through a channel called the Atchafalaya (pronounced ah-CHA-fuh-LIE-yuh). The Atchafalaya is connected to the present Mississippi riverbed about 300 miles upstream from the mouth by a channel called the Old River. It's less than 150 miles from this point to the gulf via the Atchafalaya, and some water from the main channel already pours into the shorter route. In 1963, the Army Corps of Engineers built a huge dam and lock system in the Old River to prevent the Atchafalaya from capturing the Mississippi. So far, the system has worked, and it has withstood some pretty intense floods. For 30 years, the Mississippi has been controlled.

But, in the doomsday spirit of this chapter, it's not hard to see what fate could await New Orleans, Baton Rouge, and the huge petrochemical complex that lines the river between them. It would start with a few weeks of soaking rain in the Mississippi basin—rain so steady that the ground would turn into a sponge that simply couldn't absorb any more water. Farmers, squelching through their fields, would start to wonder if it would ever stop.

Slowly, as the rain fed its tributaries, the Mississippi would rise to flood stage, then rise some more. The waters would incessantly batter the huge concrete ramparts that keep the river from its new channel. At first they would hold, as they always had in the past, but then, suddenly, they would give way and the river, frustrated for so long by the works of Man, would surge into its new channel and find a new way to the Gulf of Mexico. The industries of southern Louisiana would find themselves on a tidal inlet without the continuously renewed supply of fresh water they have always had.

Could they survive by piping water in? Who knows?

VOLCANOES

Volcanoes are one of the most dramatic manifestations of the earth's restlessness, their most common image being an inexorable flow of molten rock that devours everything in its path. This is certainly the way volcanic eruptions behave in Hawaii and Iceland, two places where they attract the attention of North American audiences. But as a matter of fact, city doomsdays seldom result from lava flows. When cities have been destroyed by ordinary volcanic eruptions, the damage has almost always come from an effect that most scientists didn't even believe existed until the beginning of the nineteenth century.

A lot of things come out of a volcano's mouth besides lava. When conditions are such that molten materials are splashed up into the air, these materials can solidify quickly, producing all sorts of interesting stuff. In some cases, bubbles of gas in the solidifying magma grow so fast that the rock shatters into tiny shards, which then mix with the pulverized rock brought up from under the earth by the explosion.

At the beginning of an eruption, the rising hot air carries all these bits of rock and shards of lava up into the atmosphere. Soon, however, the heavier materials start to fall to earth, creating a powerful downdraft that hits the ground and spills out sideways.

Inside the cloud, the bits of rock give up their heat to the air, creating strong local air currents that constantly toss the bits of rock and lava up and down. The result of all this turmoil is a material that is neither a gas nor a solid, but something that behaves more like an extremely hot fluid. Once this hot cloud starts rolling down the mountainside, it moves quickly, sometimes reaching speeds in excess of 100 miles per hour. It twists and turns as it races along, destroying everything in its path until it cools off. Geologists call it a *nuée ardente* (hot cloud), and it is the natural equivalent of the material that flows from the base of the mushroom cloud in a nuclear explosion.

In the eruption of Mount Vesuvius in A.D. 79, a *nuée ardente* destroyed the cities of Pompeii and Herculaneum, which had been built at the base of the mountain. There is a letter from Pliny the Younger, who later became a noted Roman scientist, describing "a horrible black cloud, writhing snakelike and revealing sudden flashes larger than lightning . . . [that] began to descend and cover the sea." Recent excavations of the cities buried by that eruption have produced striking evidence of the destructive force of the cloud—one woman, for example, was thrown through the air so violently that when she hit a wall she suffered more than 200 broken bones!

Despite Pliny's vivid eyewitness account, scientists paid little attention to the possibility of a *nuée ardente* until 1902, when Mount Pelée erupted on the West Indian island of Martinique. There were only about ten survivors from the town of St-Pierre, but they all told the same story of a black cloud racing down the mountainside, knocking down stone walls, twisting metal beams into pretzels, and killing 30,000 people in a matter of minutes. The widespread destruction of the forests surrounding Washing-

ton State's Mount St. Helens in 1980—millions of trees felled—
was caused by the same sort of phenomenon.

Yet for all the devastation, the effects of such a cloud can be
surprisingly erratic. On Mount St. Helens, for example, some
campers experienced nothing worse than a few falling trees; a
few thousand feet away, other campers were burned to death. In
Herculaneum, while one house on a block was charred by gases
(over 700 degrees Fahrenheit), a few doors down the wax seals
on documents survived unmelted.

The destruction of Pompeii and the eruption of Mount St.
Helens loom large in our imagery of volcanoes, but they are
somewhat misleading from the point of view of doomsday. The
fact is that a volcanic eruption can destroy cities hundreds of
miles away from the volcano itself. According to some scientists,
such an event took place in the Mediterranean thousands of
years ago—an event whose existence is known to us only
through indirect scientific evidence and through the legend of
lost Atlantis, the city that sank beneath the sea.

Today, the Greek island of Thera (or Santorini, as it is sometimes called) has a strange shape. Nestled in the blue waters of
the Aegean Sea, it looks like a cone-shaped hill from which someone with an impossibly large ice cream scoop has removed the
center and one side. All that remains is a steep circular rim that
was once the lower slopes of a volcano.

If some scientists are right, the volcano that once existed on
Thera erupted in 1628 B.C., pulverizing most of the mountain
and putting 30 times more material into the air than Vesuvius
and St. Helens combined. The cloud from such a blast could
have spread over many of the islands in the eastern Mediterranean, and a killing fall of ash—along with a large *nuée ardente*—
could have blanketed the entire region. This is important, for as
the 1991 eruption of Mount Pinatubo in the Philippines shows,
deep layers of ash from a volcano can destroy a city even in the
absence of molten lava or a *nuée ardente*.

In addition, the eruption on Thera raised tidal waves that
swept over many other inhabited islands. On Crete, the back-
wash moved building stones and walls around like playthings.
On Cyprus, the wave crest deposited mats of floating pumice
(cooled rock mixed with air) on mountainsides 90 feet above sea
level. From the Turkish coast, the waves washed as much as 30

miles inland. In one day, the thriving civilization that existed on the rim of the eastern Mediterranean was simply wiped out.

Could something like this happen today? I don't see why not. Volcanic eruptions on such a scale are not all that uncommon. The most recent was in 1815, when Mount Tambora in the East Indies exploded.

How would a Thera-sized blast play out in today's Mediterranean? There would probably be a fair amount of warning—preliminary eruptions, lava flows, columns of smoke rising into the air. In fact, there would probably be enough material in the eruptions to form floating rafts of frothy pumice on the sea.

The explosion itself would send a killing cloud over the Mediterranean Basin—the original cloud probably extended well into Turkey. In addition, the fall of hot ash would be prodigious, perhaps reaching a depth of several feet in some areas. It's hard to see how anything, plant or animal, could survive that sort of smothering blanket. And then there would be tidal waves—waves a hundred feet high making landfall and moving buildings around as if they were toys. Today, hundreds of millions of people live in the region that was devastated by the original eruption of Thera.

Will cities die this way again? Unfortunately, we simply don't know enough about volcanoes to predict when or if such an event could happen. We can only wait for the next blast. And while we're waiting, we might reflect on the fact that a tremor on the flanks of Santorini in 1956 produced high waves at islands 50 miles distant!

SEA LEVEL CHANGES

Volcanic eruptions kill cities in a matter of hours. They are dramatic, they capture the imagination, but they are rare. A much more common, but less graphic cause of the death of cities is the slow, inexorable changes in climate that go on all the time. Climate change is seldom dramatic, but it has probably killed more cities than anything else. And when we talk about climate change today, there is likely to be one topic on people's minds: the greenhouse effect.

As we pointed out earlier, the expected outcome of burning more fossil fuels is a warming of the earth's climate. The expected warming is not huge—a matter of a few degrees Celsius by the late twenty-first century. Nevertheless, our ignorance of the workings of the world's water-ice system is sufficiently profound that it is worthwhile asking whether we are about to trigger a rapid rise in sea level.

It is worthwhile because historically the world's great cities have been built around the world's great harbors, and tidewater lowlands have always held the greatest fraction of the world's human population. In the United States, for example, well over two thirds of our citizens live within a hundred miles of the ocean.

This means that changes—even relatively small changes—in sea level could have a disproportionate effect on our cities. Even places that are far inland, like London and Washington, D.C., would be affected, since they are on tidal rivers. Add in all the beachfront vacation homes that now dot our coastlines and you have a situation in which people pay close attention to the level of the oceans.

The reason for the current concern has to do with a simple fact about our planet: the total amount of water on the earth does not change over geologic time. This means that when some of the world's water is taken up into polar ice caps, there is less available to fill the ocean basins. During the last glacial period, for example, the Atlantic coast of North America was 150 miles farther east than it is today. If global warming causes some melting of glaciers and ice caps, the runoff will enter the ocean basins and water levels will have to go up.

One point about sea level rise that doesn't get much notice: it is a *relative* concept. Sea level can rise because there is a greater volume of water, of course, but it can also "rise" if the ocean stays the same and the land subsides. On the East Coast of the United States, where sea levels are rising at the rate of about a foot per century, the movement of the land in response to the retreat of the glaciers 10,000 years ago has contributed significantly to the change.

At first it may seem strange that the removal of a weight like a glacier would cause land to subside rather than rebound, but you have to remember that the last glacier covered the middle part of the continent, not the coast. The effect of the glacier on North America, then, was similar to what you see when you step into some mud. The mud immediately under your feet is pushed down, but some mud always squirts up around the edges of your shoes. In the same way, when the last glacier moved south over North America, the land underneath it was pushed down while the land along the coast was lifted up. When the climate warmed and the glacier retreated, the land in the center of the continent rebounded by moving upward, but the land that had "squirted" up around the edges rebounded by moving down. The tail end of this subsidence allows the ocean to encroach on the East Coast today. The best guess (based on a rather incomplete data set) is that about half of observed sea level increase is due to land movement and has little to do with the oceans.

But it isn't these sorts of inch-by-inch changes that doomsday prophets want to talk about. After all, the Dutch long ago mastered the technique of keeping back higher seas than those on the east coast of North America. If you want doomsday, you have to look south, to Antarctica where 90 percent of the world's ice is locked up in the polar ice cap. If all this ice melted and ran into the ocean, the sea level would rise by about 200 feet, completely inundating all the world's coastal plains. It is this number that inspired a poster you may have seen—the one with the Statue of Liberty up to its neck in water.

I know of no reputable scientist who thinks that this scenario is likely to happen. In fact, because of the peculiar topology of the Antarctic continent, most of the stored ice (in what is called the East Antarctic Ice Sheet) is stacked up several miles deep over solid ground. This ice is unlikely to go anywhere, regardless of any foreseeable amount of global warming.

The West Antarctic Ice Sheet, however, is a different matter. It lies on low, sloping ground, and part of it actually floats on the ocean. It is crossed by rivers of flowing ice, and we are only now beginning to understand its complexities. The worry is that the sheet may be unstable and that a slight warming may cause it to break loose and slide into the sea. There is no evidence that this will happen, but no evidence that it won't, either.

Nevertheless, in the spirit of this chapter, we have to note that a complete melting of the West Antarctic Ice Sheet will raise sea level worldwide by up to 18 feet. The effects of this change won't be sudden—we won't wake up one morning to find Wall Street under several feet of water. Instead, the slow rise in sea level will start to affect cities like New York during big storms. One year, high waves will wash up on the roads bordering the harbor, forcing the police to close them for a day or two. As time passes, this will get to be a more common phenomenon, and the strength of the storm needed to trigger it will become less. Then, perhaps during one of those hurricanes that occasionally make their way up the East Coast, a big storm surge will send water into the streets of lower Manhattan. It will be a big news item, of course, but it will take some time before people realize that there's a problem to be dealt with. For cities like New York, Boston, Miami, and Los Angeles, there's no question about what the response will be. Large (and very expensive) dikes will be built to keep the rising waters away from the city. But what about smaller towns along the coast? Will we just allow them to be inundated? And what about harbors and shipping facilities? How will they be affected?

I don't know the answers to such questions, but they will have to be asked if the doomsday scenario for the West Antarctic Ice Sheet ever plays out.

A SUMMING UP

We could go on discussing city-killing disasters for a long time, but I think the message is clear: pick a city and you can find some geological phenomenon able to threaten its existence or destroy it outright.

I have argued that the birth of cities is a natural process, that it is nothing more than the replacement of one sort of ecosystem by another. The same is true when cities die. The man-made ecosystem is replaced (either suddenly or gradually) by another, and life goes on. The birth and death of a city are in no way fundamentally different from the movement of a sand dune or the change in course of a river flowing in the wild. Our cities, for all their complexity and technological virtuosity, are part of nature, and if other parts of nature live and die, it is only fitting that cities do the same.

Despite the generally gloomy tone of this chapter, I would like to point out that there is one way for cities to die which is beginning to seem more and more unlikely. Had I written this book anytime between 1950 and 1989, I would surely have included nuclear war on my list of potential city killers. Today, although that threat has not vanished, it has receded sufficiently for us to think about how our cities will live out all of their allotted time. The mere fact that we can contemplate the notion of London and New York lasting until rising sea levels drown them or falling sea levels force them to move is already a statement of hope in the future.

But the bottom line is simple: cities, like people, have a natural lifespan. We should look at them the way we look at any other system in nature. Like old friends, they should be enjoyed, even cherished, while they're here and mourned when they pass away. We should realize that they evolve with time, and that the death of cities, like the death of individuals, is a natural part of that evolution.

Afterword:
The City in 2050

The different futures I've discussed are all technically possible, but that doesn't mean that they are all equally likely to come about. I could, of course, refuse to speculate about which future (or mix of futures) I think will actually be present in the city of 2050. Such speculation, after all, requires that I go far outside my own area of expertise. But I think I owe it to readers who have come this far to be a bit more forthcoming about my own views. So, with the usual caveats and disclaimers, I've decided to use this afterword to talk about where I see the technological forces we've discussed taking us.

First and foremost, it seems to me that up to now the effects of new technologies on the modern city have been centrifugal. That is, new technologies tend to move people and businesses away from the old city centers. The railroad and the automobile played important roles in this trend in the past. A glance at today's city, though, shows that their effects have reached saturation. In the future, I think transportation systems will play less of a role in shaping growth. As the effects of these traditional technologies decline, however, a new and potentially more revolutionary player—information technology—is coming on the scene to continue the dispersal of the city.

I think the high-rise superskyscraper future outlined in Chapter 11 is pretty unlikely. We may have solved the technical problems encountered in putting up a 200-story skyscraper, but the reasons for creating such buildings seem to be vanishing. My sense is that while a few such structures may be built, more for reasons of vanity than anything else, the great wave of skyscraper building has pretty much passed.

This was brought home to me very forcefully while I was in the process of writing this book. One of the books I read for background was Karl Sabagh's *Skyscraper* (Penguin, 1989), which chronicles the construction of a 770-foot office building on 50th Street and Eighth Avenue in New York City. I took the book with me on a trip to New York, and spent a pleasant hour on a spring afternoon reading it in the courtyard of the newly completed building. After that, I took something of a proprietary interest in the building, and through the early 1990s I often adjusted my schedule while in New York so that I could walk by and see how things were going. As time went by, I began to wonder why the completed building, as attractive as it was, had so few tenants, why the ground floor windows remained empty. Part of the reason, I knew, was the business recession that was going on at the time. But I couldn't help wondering whether what I was seeing wasn't at least in part a result of businesses moving out of the city —of a drop in the importance of the central city in the modern metropolitan area.

One problem with highly centralized cities is dramatically illustrated by two recent events. In the spring of 1992, contractors drilling into the bed of the Chicago River as part of a bridge repair project penetrated into a forgotten tunnel. The subsequent flood as the river poured into the tunnel shut down most of the Chicago business district, causing a billion-dollar loss in property damage and lost business. In the spring of 1993, terrorists set off an explosion under the World Trade Center in New York, causing hundreds of millions of dollars in damage and shutting down the entire building complex for several weeks. Both of these incidents dramatize an important property of highly centralized systems—they are highly susceptible to accidental or intentional disruption. This fact isn't an absolute bar to superskyscrapers—we have, after all, learned to protect our airports from terrorists, and that's a much more difficult job than guarding a superskyscraper. It is, however, one more impediment to trends toward highly centralized systems in our cities.

Overall, I don't expect a dramatic change in central cities in the next half century. I expect the downtown business districts of most American cities to look pretty much the same in 2050 as they do now. There will be skyscrapers, stores, and all the other sorts of buildings we're used to. There will, of course, be new buildings that have been developed, and some peripheral land around those areas may get built up, but I don't expect to see anything like the radical change the last half century has brought.

I expect the real changes in metropolitan areas will be away from the city center, out in the neighborhoods, suburbs, and exurbs. Driven by forces already in operation, the current growth of networked edge cities will continue. I expect that the metropolitan area of the future will have many "downtowns," each equally important, each characterized by modest high-rise office buildings and surrounded by residential areas. I also expect that at least a few cities will have maglev train lines servicing them, producing a group of railroad suburbs as described in Chapter 12. In a sense, however, both the edge cities and the maglev suburbs represent the playing out of forces already well engaged in our society. Neither represents a fundamental surprise.

The most radical—certainly the most unpredictable—agent of change is the rise of information technology. This is in its infancy today, and as the discussion of virtual reality in Chapter 14 shows, it has within it the seeds of radical transformation not only of cities, but of our basic ways of life. How far will such technology have taken us by 2050? By the end of the 1990s, a large number of the homes in America will be hooked up to the fiber-optic information "superhighways" that are being built even as you read this. Although these superhighways will not be able to carry the information load required for an extreme virtual future, they certainly will enable Americans to carry out at home many of the functions that now require travel. More and more, we will work, shop, and be entertained at home.

Because of this fact, I suspect that many of the problems that we feel are completely intractable today (urban transportation, for example) will be greatly alleviated, if not completely solved. If, for example, half of the workforce stays home on any given day, roads and subways will be relatively empty, even at rush hour. If people can shop at home, they probably won't be crowding the malls on Saturday afternoon.

The city of 2050, then, may well be a quieter, more orderly place than it is today. Neighborhoods will become more important, and people who live out in the edge cities and the maglev suburbs will have fewer and fewer occasions to travel to distant parts of the metropolitan area. I suspect that this means that many of the amenities we associate with downtowns—fine restaurants and coffeehouses, for example—will join the dispersion and start appearing in distant locations.

My guess is that over the first half of the next century, this dispersal into edge cities and maglev suburbs will increase with the accelerating pace of information technology. Eventually, even the edge cities will start to empty as the need for central office space fades and every home acquires the capability of being its own node in the national (and international) network.

So what will be the glue that holds the city together? If we looked only at the technological forces at work, we would probably have to conclude that by 2050 the city as a human institution would be well on its way to oblivion. I doubt if this will happen. What will happen is that the reasons for people to congregate in cities will change. Instead of being held together for commercial or industrial reasons, the cities of the future will exist because many people just like living in them.

Small towns are safe places—places where individuals have a well-defined place in society, well-defined social roles. They represent safety, stability, predictability. Cities, on the other hand, are dangerous—you never know when turning the next corner will change your life forever. Cities represent change, freedom, possibility. People need both stability and change in their lives, and the mix can differ from one person to the next as well as from one period in an individual's life to another. There will always be people who value the freedom of the city more than the stability of the suburban neighborhood or small town. So long as this is true, regardless of the shifting technology of the future, there will be cities for people like me to write about.

Index

Coauthor of the bestselling book *The Dictionary of Cultural Literacy* and the highly acclaimed *Science Matters,* and author of *1001 Things Everyone Should Know About Science,* James Trefil has published more than ten books on science. A former Guggenheim fellow and a regular commentator for National Public Radio, he is the Robinson Professor of Physics at George Mason University, and a contributing editor of *Smithsonian* magazine. He lives in Annandale, Virginia.